Building the E-motive
industry

Building the E-motive Industry

Essays and Conversations
About Strategies for Creating
an Electric Vehicle Industry

Scott A. Cronk

Published by:
Society of Automotive Engineers, Inc.
400 Commonwealth Drive
Warrendale, PA 15096-0001
U.S.A.
Phone: (412) 776-4841
Fax: (412) 776-5760

Library of Congress Cataloging-in-Publication Data

Building the E-motive industry : essays and conversations about
  creating an electronic vehicle industry / (edited by) Scott A. Cronk.
      p. cm.
    Includes index.
    ISBN 1-56091-560-9 : $35.00
    1. Electric vehicle industry--United States. 2. Automobiles,
  Electric.   I. Cronk, Scott A., 1964-
  HD9710.U52B775 1995
  338.4'76292293'0973--dc20   94-48619
                                                             CIP

SAE Order No. R-148

To Dennis Cronk, my father and a man who helped to put the first EV on the moon, and Virginia Cronk, my mother who nurtured and supported a young man's dreams.

DISCLAIMER

The conclusions and opinions expressed in this book are those of the writer and acknowledged contributors and do not necessarily represent the position of the SAE, General Motors Corporation, U.S. Electricar, or their subsidiaries and affiliates, or their directors, officers, agents, or employees concerning the matters discussed.

Acknowledgments

Many people contributed their time, talent, experiences, and support to produce this book. This project would not have been possible without them. Specifically, I want to thank Dave Norton and Raleigh Grady from Delco Electronics, who allowed me to undertake this project in the first place. Derek Baker, whose time, patience, and skills as an editor helped an engineer to sound like a writer. Mark Mecklenborg at SAE, who believed in this project from the start and offered support and inspiration to the end. James Womack, whose love for ideas and learning brought us together and made it possible for me to befriend one of my heroes. Dr. Womack's editorial assistance also helped to focus the material in this book and make it a more meaningful piece for the reader. The Cronk family (Dennis, Ginnie, Mark, Brian, Jane, and Bobbie), who fill my life with love and inspiration. George and Mary Varcoe, my grandparents, who always taught me to try new things and be my own person. Joy and Arlene Cronk, my grandparents. Fritz and Wade Kiffmeyer (the "Trappist Monks"), who made my life whole over the years that this book took to complete. Maiqui Loyola from U.S. Electricar, who helped me get to where I am today. Annie Carson, whose patience was unwavering. Carolina Costa and Gina Jacupke, who pushed me to higher ground. Cindy Chupack, for setting an example and putting me in touch with a great editor. The Yolles family. The Broadripple crowd, Jeannie and Kevin. Nicolas Hayek at SMH/Swatch, who continues to inspire me. Wendy Makowski at Eisbrenner Public Relations, who made it possible to tell the GM side of the story.

I interviewed dozens of people while researching this project. Only a few made it to the final work. But each of these people helped to shape the story and make it better. I especially want to thank Don Chen, John Dabels, Frank Schweibold, Gary Starr, Bob Stempel, Dr. Paul MacCready, Bill Warf, Tom Hakel, Dan Rivers (who was the leader of the famous "Dolphin" system), Maryann Keller, Amory Lovins, Ted Morgan, and Harold Robinson III.

I also want to thank the other people I interviewed or met with during this project (in no particular order): Barbara Taylor; Geoffrey Harding; Bob McKee; Sir John Samuel of Clean Air Transport; E.J. Constantine of Clean Air

Transport; Victoria Nerenberg at Bay Area Rapid Transport and the Stationcar Association; John Wilson of the Southern Coalition for Advanced Transportation; Beatrice Howald at SMH Ltd.; William Taylor at FAST Magazine; Ellen Berman at the Consumer Energy Council of America; Mark Ahlheim at Chicago Regional Transit Authority; Bob Suggs at Florida Power and Light; the filmmaker extraordinaire Bob Andruszkiewicz (A-Z); Doug Cobb at Solarcar; Diego Jaggi at ESORO; Stan Bull at the National Renewable Energy Lab; Alan Cocconi; Tom Hawkes at Budget; Dr. Malcolm Curry; S. David Freeman (formerly at SMUD); Jim Hogarth at Boston Edison; Ron Skenes at EZ-GO; Ray Geddes at Unique Mobility; Tony Harris and Wayne Rechnitz at Pacific Gas and Electric; Malcolm Bricklin; Elmer Johnson at Kirkland and Ellis; John Barnett and Eric Toler at Rocky Mountain Institute; William Meurer at Green Motor Works; Dick Niel at Hawaii Pacific Technology and Trade; Steve McCrea; Noel Perrin; Joseph Pine; Burt Rutan at Scale Composites; Milton Sneller at Taylor and Dunn; Dr. Daniel Sperling and Carol Earl at the University of California-Davis; Bob Garzee at U.S. Electricar, Inc.; Dean Glen Urban at MIT; Phil Patterson at the Department of Energy; Jonathan Tennyson at Suntera; Barry Pearson at Pacific Electric Vehicles; James Worden and Arvind Rajan at Solectria; Dr. Lon Bell at Amerigon; Michael Peevey; Kevin Gunning at Amerigon; David Friedman; Roy Miller; Major Rick Cope at ARPA; Gary Dickinson at Delco Electronics; John Hambly at Europcar; David Andrea at the University of Michigan; Jean Mallebay-Vacqueur and Chris Preuss at Chrysler; Don Walkowicz and Larry Weise at USCAR; Fred Heiler at Mercedes-Benz; Michael Bradley at NESCAUM; Tom Cackette at CARB; Dr. Mary Good, the U.S. Undersecretary of Commerce; Virginia Miller at the Commerce office; Marla Romash at the White House; Henry Kelly at the White House; Dave Dilts at the Massachusetts Department of Energy Resources; California Assemblyman Bernie Richter; S. William Becker at STAPPA; Nancy Hazard at the N.E. Sustainable Energy Association; Curtis Moore; Tom Deen at the Transportation Research Board; Herb Hendrickson at the Hawaii Electric Vehicle Demonstration Project; Shiela Lynch at the Northeast Alternative Vehicle Consortium; Frank Jamerson; Matt Pape and Bill Fowler at Ryder; Reznor Orr at Powercell; Sam Smith at Electrosource.

Table of Contents

Foreword
by Maryann Keller

The automobile has an indispensable role in the lives of nearly all Americans. Our vehicle-dependent lifestyles are reflected in the steady growth in the number of vehicles and the miles traveled by each throughout its life. Even though most of us are aware that this has worsened air quality and traffic congestion in most large cities, we stubbornly cling to automobiles as our primary means of transportation.

During the past decade, the concerns of environmentalists and some legislators regarding the impact of vehicles powered by internal combustion engines on air quality and the interest risks from steadily rising crude oil imports have largely been ignored by the general public. Twenty years ago, consumers bought 12-miles-per-gallon cars until the energy crisis produced a temporary shift that favored smaller cars. Ironically, while U.S. automakers have successfully complied with government-mandated fuel economy targets, record numbers of consumers have switched from relatively efficient cars to 12-mile-per-gallon lightweight trucks. Personal vehicle choice has always been a function of purchase price, operating costs, and the perceived needs of the owner. Our cars, our cities, and our roads have ultimately been shaped by America's access to cheap energy, especially gasoline.

As much as promoters of radical change in vehicle technology see the problem in terms of technical advances, reality is more complex. Our cars are assets, too valuable to be discarded before their utility is fully exploited and too expensive to experiment with too much novelty that compromises perceptions of price and value. Because few of us can afford to scrap the automobile we are driving in favor of a radically different vehicle, technological change, from the consumer's standpoint, will be evolutionary unless and until it is perceived to offer advantages over what is known and predictable.

The motor vehicle industry is dominated by a few multinational giants. Both vehicle assemblers and component producers have tens of billions of dollars invested in fixed assets that produce salable, profitable vehicles with gasoline-burning engines. An equally industrial infrastructure exists to fuel and repair these vehicles. The magnitude of that investment logically dictates an evolutionary attitude on the part of managers toward unproven technologies that would both obsolete their current equipment and necessitate massive new investments.

Although a frustrating "go slow" mentality seems to pervade the automotive industry, there is also a recognition that the developer of an appealing, versatile vehicle that delivers safety, energy efficiency, and low emissions would have an enduring advantage in a highly competitive business. Hopefully, that search will spur the creation of small, entrepreneurial companies capable of acting quickly without the constraints imposed by in-place investments.

Although politicians see themselves as protectors of the environment through regulations they set for automobiles and trucks, the actions of government officials have played a fundamental role in promoting our car-oriented culture. They have encouraged residential and commercial development since the dawn of the motor-vehicle age, beyond the limits of cities and mass transit. Then they construct longer, wider highways and keep gasoline taxes low so we can commute back to the cities we escaped. They express surprise and anguish about the gray haze of air pollution and quickly retreat to the only politically acceptable solution: more regulation of new car emissions, even though faster progress would be made by discouraging driving and forcing heavily polluting old vehicles into retirement. It has always been easier to promise constituents that regulations will result in cleaner, safer cars that will not cost more or compromise the fun of driving.

In fairness to politicians, past regulations were technology forcing and fulfilled much of that promise. The motor vehicle industry has a history of fighting regulation, then rising to the challenge. The modern automobile is of higher quality, more reliable, safer, and cleaner than its predecessors, in no small part because of regulatory pressure brought to bear on vehicle assemblers.

But much of what has been accomplished resulted from modifications to existing technologies and the adoption of catalytic converters, airbags, or other devices that were essentially transparent to vehicle owners. Past success in this case may not be a predictor of future success when a technology

"Although politicians see themselves as protectors of the environment through regulations they set for automobiles and trucks, the actions of government officials have played a fundamental role in promoting our car-oriented culture."

such as electric power would necessitate a radical change in behavior from that associated with conventional vehicles.

Nevertheless, I am convinced that we are at the threshold of significant advances in automotive technology that will both improve gasoline-powered vehicles and give consumers attractive alternative energy choices. The magnitude of development initiatives around the world provides encouragement that technological breakthrough will be made in electrical power and toward the goal of creating a supercar.

The development risks of any new technology would be substantially reduced if all the interested parties saw the problem not merely in terms of the car alone, but also in terms of our car culture. Public education combined with appropriate incentives and disincentives can assist in the acceptance of new technologies and can speed achievement of the combined goals of clean air, reduced crude oil consumption, and personal mobility.

The debate about how fast a society can or should move toward alternative fuels for transportation, in particular electric power, demands a forum where opinions can be expressed and risks understood.

This important book brings together all the players who will shape our future vehicles and will be called upon to confront both problems of energy consumption and air pollution. Their opinions and beliefs are crucial to our understanding of the many facets of the debate.

— MARYANN N. KELLER

Preface

I have been interested in the electric vehicle industry since about the age of 10. At that time, the Arab oil embargo was infringing on the lives of most Americans. My interest in electric vehicles grew steadily throughout the last 20-odd years. As an engineer, I saw EVs as a technical challenge, certainly. But more interestingly still, as a businessman, I find EVs are a business challenge that, to be successful, requires pioneering efforts in organizational style and strategy. In short, EVs caught my imagination.

In 1990, I wrote a graduate-level thesis while attending the City University Business School (CUBS) in London, England. This thesis explored marketing issues surrounding electric vehicles. I was then working in London for Delco Electronics Corporation, part of the General Motors family of companies. As I worked, studied, and traveled around Europe, I saw tremendous opportunities for a new kind of transportation system based on electric vehicles.

In the year after my thesis was submitted, I wrote a business plan, based largely on the findings of my thesis and my experiences in Europe. There, I frequently experienced the inconveniences of air travel, automobiles, and mass transit systems. I also saw the Berlin Wall come down, capitalism flourish, and a global economy rise to the surface. At about this same time, the California Air Resources Board (CARB) passed the "2% in 1998" mandate, requiring zero-emission vehicles ("ZEV" or, more specifically, electric vehicles) to be offered for sale. The National Energy Policy Act of 1992 was also passed, which mandated the use of alternative fuels. These factors presented themselves as a great opportunity to me. I thought now was the time to turn my lifelong interest into a profitable business.

I wrote a private letter to Nicolas Hayek, CEO of SMH, Ltd. (a.k.a. "Swatch"). He was embarking on a new electric car program, based on what he described as a new form of personal transportation. I thought, perhaps, Mr. Hayek could use my business ideas.

To a young man's surprise, several weeks later, Mr. Hayek, one of the heroes of Switzerland and a fan of millions of watch wearers and marketing professionals around the world, called me at my home. But in the end, my business plan

"With due allowance for the influence of economic and geographic factors, Detroit became the capital of the auto industry because it happened to possess a unique group of individuals with both business and technical ability who became interested in the possibilities of the motor vehicle."
— John B. Rae, from *American Automobile Manufacturers: The First Forty Years,* 1959.

didn't go very far. Besides this conversation and one other I had with Nicolas Hayek, and a very brief encounter with a new start-up company in Massachusetts called Solectria, my attempts to grow a new business failed. I had discovered my naïveté, but pressed on.

Academics say the best way to get ideas out of your blood is to write a book. I took this advice and began to write a book, but not to get it "out of my blood." Rather, I thought that in the process of researching and writing the book, I would lose some of my naïveté and develop a network of contacts including, I hoped, some of the most influential people in the electric vehicle industry, the government, and the auto industry. It was for this primary reason that I decided to work through the interactive format of an interview. I was still focused on starting my very own, new transportation company.

I am a first-time writer. In hindsight, the interview format, which was originally designed as a selfish method of discovery, happens to be an excellent format for the subject of this book as well. The methodology I used presents a process of discovery and a telling story of the challenges faced by those involved in building the electric vehicle industry.

At this early point of the electric vehicle industry, it is difficult to use an in-depth business or technical analysis to describe how the industry is being built. Technology, government mandates, or regulations simply will not, by themselves, build this new industry. This lesson was learned through many failed attempts to commercialize electric vehicles in the past. Rather, it is through the actions of a few unique and powerful leaders across a diverse set of entities that this industry is being built. Therefore, understanding the emergence of this industry requires a glimpse into the minds of the people who are leading it. These leaders will help us to understand more easily the strategic styles or "business theories" being used to build the electric vehicle industry. This book handles the subject of the EV in much the same way that other very complex problems are dealt with by government, through a kind of forum or hearing format.

In the end, it is surprising to discover how small and tightly knit the leaders in the electric vehicle world are. Yet this small group of leaders are motivating changes in the larger auto industry. In researching this book, I interviewed close to

100 individuals. Perspectives from what I deemed to be the most interesting, powerful, or influential leaders follow.

These leaders have organized a group of excited, motivated employees who are working long, tiresome hours to build a new industry. Even in large organizations like General Motors and the U.S. government, the energy level is astounding from the perspective of my own 12 years at GM. These employees are not necessarily motivated for reasons typically associated with electric vehicles either—namely, "save the planet." Rather, these employees have seen a new, exciting, and satisfying way to earn a living and enjoy their days. This is something that has been absent from American corporate life in recent years.

A Process of Discovery

While exploring the electric vehicle industry, one of the first persons I called was Gary Starr (an interview that didn't make it through the editor's cutting process!). In June 1993, *Ward's Automotive News* published its list of the "top ten of the U.S. EV industry." In the *Ward's* list, Mr. Starr was described as "brash, hungry, and knows how to leverage publicity." At this time, he was the vice president of business development for U.S. Electricar. (In June 1994, Mr. Starr resigned from the company to spin-off his own EV company.)

From my first conversation with Mr. Starr, I was intrigued by his company's strategy for building its business. Later conversations with Ted Morgan, president and CEO, and Bob Garzee, another VP at Electricar, provided further evidence of a strong new company in the making. As I interviewed others—most notably Robert Stempel and Frank Schweibold of General Motors—I was convinced that this company was forging a new path in the industry and deserved to be highlighted in my work. The magnetism of U.S. Electricar drew me to them. Not since Apple Computer sprouted up in the 1980s had I seen a small start-up company with such vision and leading-edge activities.

While at General Motors, I had always felt that American companies could regain their strength in the automobile industry. I was convinced, however, that American innovation and the entrepreneurial spirit would prevail, rather than the Big Three's ability to change themselves incrementally. Having researched this book, my belief is stronger than ever

This book was actually written, for the most part, prior to my employment at U.S. Electricar. I joined the company because I was convinced that the time for an electric vehicle industry has arrived. As I researched the industry for this book, I became convinced that U.S. Electricar's strategy was the key to the successful birth of this new industry. And so I joined the company. This has provided me with a unique position where I am able to experience how a small company deals with the challenge of building new products and a new industry. Certainly, U.S. Electricar is not alone and I have attempted to bring in a wide range of examples and opinions from companies utilizing a strategy similar to U.S. Electricar's.

that American innovation and entrepreneurial skills will once again lead the world at the automobile game.

I spent hours trying to fit interviews into the schedules of the people we converse with in this book. The people building the electric vehicle industry are working 12-hour days, six days a week. The industry is being fueled by raw energy that we haven't witnessed in America since the dawning of the personal computer industry in Silicon Valley.

My process of discovery, depicted through this book, is presented here for the reader to enjoy. It is also my hope that I have produced a work from which the reader will develop a deeper understanding of the strategies being used to change behemoth industries like the auto industry.

— SCOTT A. CRONK

Introduction & Overview

*"From 1895 onward, America entered into an automobile craze, with the popular press celebrating every invention related to the automobile. Many prominent inventors, including Elmer Sperry and Elihu Thomson, were attracted to the excitement surrounding the automobile and developed their own vehicles. The potential for a self-propelled vehicle captivated Thomas Edison, too, and as early as 1896 he had a lab build a motorized tricycle. A little later, the Edison household acquired an electric carriage and in October 1899 Mrs. Edison requested that the lab build a garage for recharging this vehicle. Experiences with these vehicles apparently convinced Edison that the future belonged to the electric car and he began developing a battery for it. He was confident that a large and growing demand for his battery would offset the high R&D costs he might incur."**

*Carlson, W. Bernard, "Thomas Edison as a Manager of R&D: The Case of the Alkaline Storage Battery, 1895-1915," *IEEE Technology and Society Magazine*, December 1988.

Thomas Edison observed, "I don't think Nature would be so unkind as to withhold the secret of a good storage battery, if a real earnest hunt were made for it. I'm going to hunt."

Unfortunately for Edison, by 1910 electric vehicles began to lose out to gasoline-powered cars. In New Jersey for example, while 800 electrics had been licensed between 1899 and 1906, 98% had been abandoned by 1910. Edison was focused on the development of technology as a means to make EVs practical commercial products. (At the time Edison was developing a type of nickel alkaline battery, a similar technology to that in which General Motors invested in 1994, almost 100 years later.)

At the turn of the last century, other skilled businessmen and entrepreneurs attempted to commercialize electric vehicles in order to capitalize on the insatiable demand for automobiles in the United States.** In the end, every one of these companies failed to provide consumers a practical alternative to the internal combustion engine (ICE) vehicle for on-road use.

**Wakefield, Ernest H., *History of the Electric Automobile—Battery-Only Powered Cars*, Society of Automotive Engineers, Inc., Warrendale, PA, 1993.

The Product as Part of a Larger System

Now, as we turn the century, the world is once again challenged with efforts to commercialize electric vehicles, and we wonder why. And, what has changed that might make EVs succeed and find their place on the road this time around?

While Edison and others were good inventors and clear-thinking, pragmatic businessmen, they were not able to invent their way out of the serious disadvantages of the electric car, as compared to the ICE vehicle. Today we may not be able to *invent* our way into electric vehicles either. The auto industry today is composed of a group of large, powerful, deeply entrenched businesses operating globally in a fiercely competitive battlefield. Air quality in the Western world is rapidly improving, oil prices remain relatively low, and the automobile itself is a highly refined, reliable piece of machinery that serves consumers well. In this business environment, one wonders why the auto industry would, or should, innovate and embrace a shift to electric vehicles? Indeed, why would consumers? Yet government and consumers around the world have mandated a move toward more efficient, cleaner forms of personal transportation.

Cleaner automobiles are being called for because they are the last remaining heavy polluter in the Western world. Today, automobiles, trucks, and buses still contribute 33% to the overall U.S. air pollution (VOCs, volatile organic compounds, and NO_x, nitrous oxides).* Automobiles are more of an environmental nightmare in the emerging industrial countries around the world. Already countries such as Italy, Holland, Greece, Mexico, China, and Thailand have banned some vehicles in their large cities largely because of problems with pollution. The problems are here today and are continuing to worsen, especially in areas of rapid industrialization. We realize that improving the situation will take tens of years, since automobiles are durable goods with a long service life. This reality, when combined with the rapid increase in automobiles around the world leads environmentalists and transportation policymakers to the conclusion that we must start today to clean up our automobiles.

Pollution is now widely viewed as an external consequence of the automobile. We want less pollution, and therefore the automobile is being forced to change. But the "environmental" force is only one reason that cleaner automobiles are

*Dr. Mary Good, U.S. Undersecretary of Commerce, 1994.

being mandated. There are other equally important reasons. These reasons also serve to link the automobile to the larger system it affects.

The "E" in E-motive

Perhaps for the first time in modern history, we are witnessing the convergence of the four "E's": environment, energy, economy, and education. We have explained the environmental forces. We will now explain the other forces in more detail.

The energy force: The energy force is of central importance in the drive to cleaner and less oil-dependent vehicles. Motorists in the United States use about half of the imported oil and up to half the cost of maintaining a U.S. military presence in the Middle East—or $50 billion a year.* Ground transportation fuel makes up 43% of the U.S. petroleum-based energy supply. Petroleum imports represent three-quarters of the U.S. trade deficit.** The focus on the automobile's role in U.S. oil dependence is becoming clearer each day. Between 1973 and 1990, oil consumption declined 44% in buildings, 9% in industry, and 64% in power generation. Only in transportation has oil consumption increased: by 21% over this period. Transportation now accounts for almost two-thirds of U.S. oil consumption and, as was made clear by the Gulf War, oil imports threaten our national security.

There is a second, more subtle energy force: the energy producer industry itself, which is motivating the move away from oil-dependent automobiles. As our society becomes more and more dependent on electronic machinery and equipment (an "electric economy"), the quality of the electric power is challenged. To avoid brownouts and maintain the quality of the electricity supply, power producers now keep vast surpluses of generator power on hand to meet peak demands.

Excess capacity comes with a cost. The power utilities are working to find ways to eliminate waste and improve profits, or "become lean." The focus is on reducing surplus capacity by *leveling* the demand for electricity over the day. The electric power utility industry argues that electric vehicles can help the power industry become lean. The most common argument here is that EVs are charged at night when vast surpluses of electric generating capacity are idle and unpro-

*MacKenzie, James J., Roger C. Dower, Donald D.T. Chen, *The Going Rate: What it Really Costs to Drive,* World Resources Institute, June 1992.

**Dr. Mary Good, U.S. Undersecretary of Commerce, 1994.

ductive. It is believed the charging requirements for an EV load would utilize this capacity and thereby increase installed capacity usage and render the electric system more efficient. This is generally believed to be true, and if true, EVs will allow the electric utilities to reduce their cost per kilowatt because the utility's overhead will be spread over a larger production of energy.

As EV technologies mature, the power utilities are finding that the movement toward EVs helps utilities in other ways. Emerging EV technologies benefit utilities by providing alternatives to adding more capacity and allowing fuller use of otherwise dormant capacity. This is becoming more important for utilities whose industry is now becoming more competitive through changes in regulations that allow independent power producers to compete against the more established utility companies. Also, electric utilities, by law, are limited to a 12% profit margin. Therefore, with the advent of independent power producers, and the resultant greater competition within the industry, it will be efficient, low-cost providers that win market share.

Today, batteries and energy storage systems originally designed for EVs are now being used to level out the power demands in the utility's energy grid. In effect, large banks of batteries can become energy storage and delivery systems that charge when excess energy is available and discharge back into the power grid when energy demands a higher price. These battery systems can be built for a lower cost than the cost of new power generation stations. If not for the development of EVs, these technologies might not have otherwise become competitive ways for utilities to smooth their demand, thus lowering their cost and improving service quality.

The economic forces: Economic forces are also driving the shift to electric vehicles. As the Cold War thaws and defense spending lessens, defense industries find themselves saddled with excess capacity. At the same time, industry finds itself lacking the defense industry spin-off benefits that once emerged. Products such as Velcro, ceramic materials, and fuel cells can no longer be expected to emerge from the national labs and defense programs. EVs hold the promise of new jobs to fill the defense industry's capacity and of new technologies that will keep American industries vibrant and gainfully employed. Proponents of the e-motive industry recognize that while new industries create new jobs, new industries also obsolete old industries. This serves to rejuvenate the economy. Indeed, the successful birth of an e-motive industry may prevent America from losing the auto industry and other valuable industries.

The more powerful economic force driving the growth of an e-motive industry is the economies of the product itself. Electric motors are a fundamentally more efficient method for propelling vehicles. Electric motor drive systems currently propel vehicles with greater than 90% efficiency. They also allow for a greater proportion of the kinetic energy of a moving vehicle to be stored back into the vehicle upon braking through the use of regenerative braking systems. Modern EVs are also lightweight vehicles. Their lightness serves to make them efficient users of energy. Some researchers (refer to Amory Lovins' work printed in this book) suggest that lightweight vehicles are also lower in cost to design, manufacture, and market.

The education forces: Finally, the force of education is promoting the move toward EVs. Education has and will provide the glue that pulls the forces motivating an e-motive industry together. Through education, new technologies, practices and beliefs have become available that are making EVs practical and necessary. These have emerged to create a new technology base. Likewise, education has provided environmental understanding that compels a new transportation solution. Experiments at universities are now demonstrating solutions and educating government of their viability. The message is being multiplied, perceived by the public and creating pressure for change through monetary measures. Today we are seeing academics around the world converge on the idea that clean, efficient, less oil-dependent vehicles are a desired end. One only needs to monitor the growth in the number of academic papers and conferences to see that the academic movement concerning EVs has accelerated and blossomed in recent years. These academics are studying the role of EVs and suggesting ways to build an industry to support EVs.

E-motive Industry

Perhaps for the first time in modern history, these "E" forces are aligned in the direction of electric vehicles. The world seems to be at a crossroads and moving toward a new form of transportation and, it is interesting to note, a new form of transportation industry. For the purpose of simplicity, I call this new industry the "e-motive" industry. It is an industry that is emerging from the systematic influence of the four "E's," even while change in the auto industry is being initiated through the "E" forces. Yet, without a mechanism for creating change, the electric vehicle may be doomed, once again, to failure.

The Competitive Advantage of Enterprise Structures

There is a fifth "E" which is important to the topic of the e-motive industry for it helps create the mechanism for change. The fifth "E" relates to the structure of the organization that will enable the emergence of the e-motive industry. The structure is an *enterprise structure*, or simply *e-structure*. The e-structure strategy has the ability to combine and link the "E" forces into a competitive business enterprise. This structure represents a "theory of business" quite different from that being practiced by the larger, more established auto industry whose strategy is less multidimensional and focused more on the technological factor of their products.

One thing is for certain: when we speak of commercializing EVs, we must consider more than just vehicles and more than just batteries. This is why e-structures are important mechanisms for success. As Edison and hundreds of others have found, to simply develop an EV as a stand-alone product or technology does not necessarily make it a commercial reality. Rather, because systematic forces are renewing our attention on EVs, it will most likely be through systematic forces that EVs succeed as consumer products.

To be successful, EVs will require management of a multidimensional business environment. A new infrastructure and a new set of economic rules are needed to make EVs successful. Such changes, should they occur, will affect the manner in which we fuel and service vehicles, the way in which products are designed, manufactured, and marketed, and the manner in which governments subsidize and maintain transportation systems. To be successful, EVs will also require the rapid integration of new technologies and the quick exploitation of the evolving business environment. Dramatic changes such as these are not managed well by traditional "Fordian" organizations, or even by the more modern "lean production" organizations.

The demands of managing a commercial electric vehicle business may not be well matched to the more modern organizational structures witnessed in the computer industry, either—the so-called *virtual corporations*. Indeed, a new organizational model is called for. This model must continually be able to supply safety-critical products at the highest quality and lowest cost. To be successful, the new organization must also be able to operate effectively within a shifting business environment, propelled by a convergence of powerful external forces.

Certainly electronics, materials science, and technology in general are critical to the introduction of electric vehicles. These technologies are constantly emerging, creating new product and service possibilities. Government policies, economic conditions, consumer needs, and other competitive factors are also in seemingly constant motion. Therefore, the successful introduction of electric vehicles will require the efforts of a company or enterprise that can rapidly integrate the emerging technologies into its portfolio of products and services and effectively explain these new products to consumers. But just as importantly, a successful e-motive enterprise must effectively influence and respond to a complex business environment.

It is the continual state of change or emergence in a multidimensional business environment that creates the need for new organizational strategies if EVs are to succeed. One organizational structure called *e-structures* offers a solution.

On the Cusp of Enterprise Structures

A shift occurring in the automobile industry is important because of the immense size and power of the auto industry. Nearly one out of ten jobs in the United States is dependent on the auto industry. A shift in an industry this powerful dictates not only how we work, but what we buy, how we think, and the life we live.

Two times this century, the automobile industry has changed our most fundamental ideas of how we make things.* After World War I, Henry Ford and General Motors' Alfred Sloan moved world manufacturers away from craft production (which uses very skilled workers capable of multiple tasks) and into the age of mass production (which utilizes rigid tooling and is less reliant on worker skill). Then after

*Womack, James P., Daniel T. Jones, Daniel Roos, *The Machine That Changed the World*, HarperCollins, New York, NY, 1990, p. 10. (This book is the bible on lean production.)

*Womack, James P., Daniel T. Jones, Daniel Roos, *The Machine That Changed the World,* HarperCollins, New York, NY, 1990, p. 13.

World War II, Eiji Toyoda and Taiichi Ohno at the Toyota Motor Company in Japan pioneered the concept of *lean* production. Lean producers combine the advantages of flexibility from craft and high volume associated with mass production, while avoiding the high cost of the former and the rigidity of the latter.* Lean production is lean because it uses less of everything toward the goal of more production and variety by employing teams of multiskilled workers at all levels of the organization. Yet in the auto industry lean production is focused predominantly toward high volumes and on specific activities in specific companies. This condition combined with low margins does not handle a shifting, multidimensional business environment well.

Education is now taking us to a new paradigm—the next step is more flexibility. The auto industry appears to be on the cusp of a new production/consumption paradigm in which the external consequences of consumer products are rolled much more tightly into the core definition of the products and in which new organizational forms are pioneered to make these externality/internality products possible. This new organizational form is the *e-structure*.

How New Practices Emerge

When Henry Ford and Alfred Sloan adopted mass production techniques, they were not new. Rather, mass production techniques were adopted from other industries—such as the bicycle and textile industries—that had tested them previously. But it was not until the auto industry perfected these techniques that the full impact of mass production changed the world.

**For more information on virtual corporations, the reader should refer to: William H. Davidow, Michael S. Malone, *The Virtual Corporation,* HarperCollins, New York, NY, 1992.

Today's e-structure techniques being tested by the e-motive industry are not new. The term virtual corporation has been widely explained as it relates to industries from filmmaking to computer and electronics assembly. In virtual corporations, broad sets of companies, each with its own functional expertise, combine into enterprises to produce products, then disperse and move on to their next task.** Industry is now using some of the lessons from virtual corporations in making the transition from lean production to e-structures.

Another important industrial model which serves as a forebear to e-structures is the famous Japanese *keiretsu*. Each *keiretsu* consists of perhaps twenty major companies, one in each industrial sector.[†] These industrial structures arose after World War II as a form of industrial finance to help rebuild Japanese industry. In a *keiretsu* there is no central holding company at the top of the organization. Nor are the companies legally united. Rather, they are held together by cross-locking equity structures. This creates a sense of reciprocal obligation. Among the key companies in every group are a bank, an insurance company, and a trading company. Each of these has substantial cash resources that can be made available to the members of the group. In fact, their key purpose is to help each other raise investment funds.

The financing mechanisms exhibited in the *keiretsu* system are important for growing new business enterprises. It is the strength of this system that partially explains the rapid rise of Japanese industry after World War II. The *keiretsu* has proven to be a dynamic and efficient system of industrial finance. This system is also patient and extremely long-term in orientation. Another key feature of the *keiretsu* is that the members are well informed of each other's activities and strategies, and highly critical of inadequate performance. This creates considerable knowledge across the enterprise which reduces risks of failure.

The Japanese *keiretsu* system has never been replicated in America or Europe. The investment laws of the United States and a number of European countries do not allow such a system of private investment to take place. Therefore, outside Japan, e-structure companies cannot legally replicate the *keiretsu* but do mimic certain key features.

Also, the *keiretsu* system may be good at building and growing new industries, but has shortcomings in mature industries. These shortcomings were seen in the 1990s as cost and trade pressures in the world auto industry have forced Japanese automakers to find new sources of components outside their *keiretsu* to help lower their costs and increase the regional or local content of their products.

Virtual corporations and the Japanese *keiretsu* industrial systems are two models with important features that e-structure companies are adopting. For established organizations, adopting a new business theory is a challenge, for established organizational culture, practices, and structures are barriers to change. Building a new enterprise from scratch is another, equally difficult challenge. This book will compare and con-

[†]Womack, James P., Daniel T. Jones, Daniel Roos, *The Machine That Changed The World*, HarperCollins, New York, NY, 1990, pp. 194–196.

trast the response of the established auto industry—the so-called *auto purists*—with the new e-motive-industry companies that are attempting to build an industry through e-structures.

Defining EVs in a Broader Sense

Many mistakes have been made in past attempts to commercialize electric vehicles. One basic mistake may have been the simple way that EVs were defined. In the past, EVs have been defined as battery-powered vehicles. The definition stopped there. Today when we speak of EVs, we are not limited to vehicles with conventional batteries for energy storage. Rather, EVs refer to any vehicle which is focused on efficient use of energy predominantly through the use of lightweight structural materials and electric motors that drive the vehicle's wheels. It is important to define EVs in this way because at this time it is far from clear which type of energy-storage device will win out in the end. In fact, it may not be a single energy-storage device, but rather a mixture of devices, across different vehicles or within any particular vehicle. For example, electric buses may utilize fuel cells, passenger vehicles may utilize gas turbine generators with supercapacitors, and neighborhood electric vehicles may utilize batteries only. At any given time, the energy storage and supply system in vehicles may be any of a multitude of possible combinations. It is widely believed, however, that the wheels of most automobiles in the future will be driven by electric motors.

We should go further still in defining EVs. The world economy has consistently forced us to be more efficient—to do otherwise is to lose because your costs become too high. Already cars are lighter and becoming more so due to economic pressures. Therefore, the auto industry is being forced to seek lighter materials. Educators in the material sciences have shown the way, the economic forces will drive the result. So, rather than focus exclusively on the energy storage and delivery system of EVs, it is important to also acknowledge the other large component in the vehicle system, namely the body/chassis. Along with the drivetrain, the vehicle's body/chassis is a great user of material and a critical component in the vehicle's dynamic performance. Energy is required to move mass, and mass equates to cost. The efficient utilization of energy and mass is therefore of central importance in the engineering of an EV. This means that great attention needs to be paid to creating strong, light-weight vehicle structures. Therefore, unlike the traditional steel automobile, EVs will most likely be built of composite materials that have the strength of steel, but at a fraction of the weight. The use of new materials in EVs is important to this discussion because new materials mean that new vehicle design, manufacturing, and product support methods will also be required.

New electric energy storage and delivery systems and new structural materials: this is what EVs are about. Defining the product "EV" in this way is important, for it moves the dis-cussion away from "the battery" and allows us to focus on a larger, more multidimensional set of challenges.

This book will concentrate on the types of organizations which will be needed to bring EVs to market. To be success-ful, these organizations are challenged to embrace new tech-nologies and new organizational practices. In the following pages, we'll examine how organizations face the continual challenge to introduce radically new products that meet strict world-class standards in competitive global markets, which now see the product as a significant part of a larger economic and environmental system.

The Structure of This Book

The story of the building of the e-motive industry is impor-tant because it demonstrates how companies and industries will be built in the future. Part I, called "On a Clear Day You Can See the E-Motive Industry," sets the vision. Here I explain the challenge to reshape our transportation system, and what EVs are, how they can be designed, built, and brought to market.

Part II serves as a contrast to the enterprise structure, or "e-structure." Here we will hear several perspectives from the mainstream auto industry. These perspectives will serve to define the strategy being utilized by the auto industry to meet or beat the challenge. This strategy, called the "superstruc-ture" strategy, is not necessarily new. For all practical purpos-es, it is the same strategy the auto industry has used for the past century whenever EVs raised their heads only to fall back on their face. It is a strategy based on incremental changes to the auto industry's system of product development, production, and marketing.

In contrast to Part II, Part III will explain how e-structure companies are working to bring EVs to market. As we will hear, e-structure companies are based on a new theory of business that is quite different from the incremental change process practiced by the auto industry's superstructure strategy.

Cast of Characters

Here is the list of characters in *Building the E-motive Industry*, in order of their appearance. Their biographies appear at the end of the book.

- Amory Lovins, Director of Research, Rocky Mountain Institute
- Dr. Paul MacCready, Chairman, AeroVironment Inc.
- Tom Cackette, Chief Deputy Executive Officer, California Air Resources Board
- John Dabels, former Director of Market Development, GM Electric Vehicles, General Motors Corporation; Vice President of Sales and Marketing, U.S. Electricar
- Dr. Mary Good, U.S. Undersecretary of Commerce
- Henry Kelly, Assistant Director for Technology, White House Office of Science and Technology Policy (OSTP)
- Don Walkowicz, Executive Director, USCAR
- Jean Mallebay-Vacqueur, General Manager, Special Products Engineering, Chrysler Corporation
- Gary Dickinson, President and CEO, Delco Electronics Corporation
- Frank Schweibold, Director, Finance and Strategic Planning, General Motors Corporation
- James Womack, partner, Transitions Group; Principal researcher at the MIT Japan Program; Co-author, *The Machine That Changed the World*
- Robert Stempel, former CEO, General Motors Corporation
- Major Richard Cope USMC, Program Manager, Advanced Research Projects Agency, U.S. Department of Defense
- Dr. Lon Bell, President, Amerigon; Member, CAL-START Board
- Arvind Rajan, Vice President, Planning and Business Development, Solectria Corp.
- Bob Garzee, President, Synergy Electric Vehicle Group, U.S. Electricar
- Ted Morgan, President and CEO, U.S. Electricar

Part I
ON A CLEAR DAY YOU CAN SEE THE E-MOTIVE INDUSTRY

In 1976, Amory Lovins redefined the energy problem in the United States. In a *Foreign Affairs* article he wrote*, Mr. Lovins demonstrated how energy conservation was actually a better investment for the power utilities than investment in new power generation plants. This thinking, which Mr. Lovins calls "negawatts" has created a multimillion-dollar, energy-conservation industry, led by the power utilities.

Mr. Lovins is now using a similar philosophy to show the world how energy conservation in automobiles can lead to wide-reaching benefits for the auto industry as well as the wider population. This time, Mr. Lovins' landmark paper is called "Supercars: The Coming Light-Vehicle Revolution" and was presented June 4, 1993, in Rungstedgard, Denmark, at the Summer Study of the European Council for Energy-Efficient Economy. This paper has gone on to spur activity in governments, academia, and industries around the world who are now focusing their attention on "supercars." Perhaps the most obvious impact of Mr. Lovins' work happened in September 1993 when President Clinton's administration announced a new government-industry program now known as the "Supercars Program" (formally titled "Partnership for A New Generation of Vehicles"). We will consider this program in more detail in Part II. First, however, we will hear from Mr. Lovins and his wife, Hunter. They will set the stage for the discussion of EVs that follows.

*Lovins, Amory B., "Energy Strategy: The Road Not Taken?" *Foreign Affairs,* October 1976, vol. 55, no. 1, pp. 65–96.

AMORY LOVINS AND L. HUNTER LOVINS
Reinventing the Wheels

Hunter and Amory Lovins direct Rocky Mountain Institute, the nonprofit resource policy center they cofounded in 1982, and collaborated with transportation researchers Dr. John Barnett and Eric Toler, who with Don Chen contributed to this article. This research at RMI's Supercar Center was supported by The Nathan Cummings Foundation and The Surdna Foundation, and is documented in RMI's technical reports, one of which won the Nissan Prize at ISATA, a major 1993 European car-technology conference. This article is reprinted in part here with permission of Hunter and Amory Lovins.

New ways to design, make, and sell cars can save 80% to 90+% of their fuel, yet make them safer, sportier, more beautiful and comfortable, far more durable, and probably cheaper. Here comes the biggest change in industrial structure since the microchip.

● ● ● ● ●

On September 29, 1993, the unthinkable happened. After decades of adversarial posturing, the heads of the Big Three automakers accepted President Clinton's challenge to collaborate. With the help of government technologies and funding, they committed their best efforts to develop a tripled-efficiency "clean car" within a decade. Like President Kennedy's goal of putting people on the moon, the Clean Car Initiative aims to create a leapfrog mentality in Detroit. However, its goal is both easier and more important than the Apollo Program's. It could even become the core of a green industrial renaissance—a profound change not only in what we drive but in how our whole economy works.

Cars' fuel efficiency has been stagnant for the past decade. Yet the seemingly ambitious goal of tripling it in the next decade can be far surpassed. Well before 2003, competition, not government mandates, may well bring to market cars efficient enough to carry your family coast-to-coast on one tank of fuel, more safely and comfortably than now, and more cleanly than electric cars plus the power plants needed to recharge them.

To understand what a profound shift of thinking this represents, imagine that one-seventh of America's GNP was derived from the Big Three typewriter-makers. Over decades they've progressed from manual to electric to typeball designs. Now they're developing tiny refinements for the forthcoming Selectric XVII. They profitably sell over ten million excellent typewriters a year. There's just one problem: the competition is developing wireless subnotebook computers.

That's the Big Three automakers today. With more skill than vision, they've been painstakingly pursuing incremental refinements on the way to an America where foreign cars fueled with foreign oil cross crumbling bridges. Modern cars are an extraordinarily sophisticated engineering achievement, but are fundamentally obsolete—the highest expression of the Iron Age. The time for incrementalism is over. Striking innovations have occurred in advanced materials, software, motors, power electronics, microelectronics, electric storage devices, small engines, fuel cells, and computer-aided design and manufacturing. Artfully integrated, they can yield safe, affordable, and otherwise superior family cars getting hundreds of miles per gallon—roughly ten times the 30 miles per gallon of new cars today, and several times the 80-odd miles per gallon sought by the Clean Car Initiative.

Achieving this will require a leapfrog to a completely new car design—the ultralight hybrid. Its key technologies are already available. Many firms around the world are starting to build prototypes. The race for the global car market has already begun. America is best positioned to bring the concept to market—and had better do so, before others do it to us. Supercars*, not Toyota's next luxury sedan, are the biggest threat to Detroit. But they are also its hope of salvation.

The Ultralight Strategy

Decades of dedicated effort to improve engines and power trains have reduced the portion of cars' fuel energy that is lost before it gets to the wheels to only about 80-85%. (About 92% of the resulting wheel power hauls the car itself, so less than 2% of the fuel energy actually ends up hauling the driver.)

This appalling waste has a simple main cause: cars are made of steel, steel is heavy, so powerful engines are required to accelerate them. Only about 16% of the average engine's power is typically needed for highway driving, 4% for city driving. That gross oversizing halves the engine's average efficiency and enormously complicates efforts to cut pollution. And it's getting worse: half the efficiency gains since 1985 have been lost by making engines powerful enough to drive at twice the speed limit.

Every year automakers add more gadgets to sweat out a bit more of the huge driveline losses inherent in propelling steel behemoths. But a really efficient car can't be made of steel, for the same reason that a successful airplane can't be made of cast iron. We need to design cars less like tanks and more like

Amory & Hunter Lovins

"Modern cars are an extraordinarily sophisticated engineering achievement, but are fundamentally obsolete—the highest expression of the Iron Age. The time for incrementalism is over."

* The term "hypercar" is now preferred to the earlier term "supercar," because "hypercar" also refers to ultra-powerful cars that get a couple of hundred miles per hour rather than per gallon.

airplanes. When we do, magical things start to happen, thanks to cars' basic physics.

Because about 5 to 7 units of fuel are needed to deliver one unit of energy to the wheels, saving energy at the wheels offers immense leverage for efficiency. Wheel power is lost in three ways. In city driving on level roads, about a third of the wheel power is used to accelerate the car, and hence ends up heating its brakes when it stops. Another third (rising to 60-70% at highway speeds) heats the air it pushes aside. The last third heats the tires and road.

The key to a super-efficient car is to cut all three losses by making it very light and aerodynamically slippery, then recovering most of its braking energy. Such a design can:

- cut weight (hence the force required for acceleration) by three- to fourfold by using advanced materials, chiefly synthetic composites, while improving safety through greater strength and sophisticated design;
- cut aerodynamic drag by two-and-a-half- to sixfold through sleeker streamlining; and
- cut tire and road losses by three- to fivefold through the combination of better tires and lighter weight.

Once this "ultralight strategy" has largely eliminated the losses of energy that can't be recovered, the only other place the wheel power can go is into braking. And if the wheels were driven by special electric motors that can be reversed, those motors could act as electronic brakes that convert motion back into electricity.

However, a "supercar" isn't an ordinary electric car run by batteries that you recharge by plugging it into utility power. Despite impressive recent progress, such cars still can't be very big or go very far without needing heavy batteries that suffer from relatively high cost and short life. Since gasoline and other liquid fuels store a hundred times as much useful energy per pound as batteries do, a long driving range is best achieved by carrying energy in the form of fuel, not batteries, and then burning that fuel as needed in a tiny onboard engine to make the electricity to run the wheel-motors. A few batteries (or, soon, a carbon-fiber "superflywheel") can temporarily store the braking energy recovered from those wheel-motors and reuse at least 70% of it for hill climbing and acceleration.

With its power so boosted, the engine needs to handle only the average load, not the peak load, so it can shrink to about a tenth the normal size. It would run very near its optimal point, doubling its efficiency, and turn off whenever it's not needed.

This arrangement is called a "hybrid-electric drive," because it uses electric wheel-motors but makes the electricity onboard from fuel. Such a propulsion system weighs only about one-fourth as much as that of a battery-electric car, which must haul a half-ton of batteries down to the store to buy a six-pack.

One Plus Two Equals Ten

Both automakers and private designers have already built experimental cars that are ultralight or hybrid-electric, but generally not both. Yet combining these approaches yields extraordinary, and until now little-appreciated, synergies. Adding hybrid-electric drive to an ordinary production car increases its efficiency by about one-third to one-half. Making an ordinary car ultralight, but not hybrid, approximately doubles its efficiency. But doing both together can boost a car's efficiency by about tenfold.

This surprise has two main causes. First, as already explained, the ultralight loses very little energy irrecoverably (to air and road friction), and the hybrid-electric drive recovers most of the rest (the braking energy). Second, saved weight compounds. When you make a heavy car one pound lighter, you really make it about a pound and a half lighter, because it needs lighter structure and suspension, a smaller engine, less fuel, etc., to haul that weight around. But in an ultralight, saving a pound may save more like five pounds. Indirect weight savings snowball faster in ultralights than in heavy cars, faster in hybrids than in nonhybrids, and fastest of all with both.

All the ingredients needed to capture these synergies are already demonstrated and need only to be combined. As far back as 1921, automakers demonstrated cars about twice as aerodynamically slippery as today's production cars, with most of the drag reduction coming from such simple means as making the car's underside as smooth as the top. Today's best experimental family cars are one-fourth more slippery still. At the same time, ultrastrong new materials make the

Amory & Hunter Lovins

"All the ingredients needed to capture these synergies are already demonstrated and need only to be combined."

car's shell lighter. A lighter car needs a smaller engine, and stronger walls can be thin; both changes can make the car bigger inside but smaller outside. That smaller frontal area combines with the sleeker profile to cut through the air with about three times less resistance than today's cars. Advanced aerodynamic techniques may be able to redouble this saving.

Modern radial tires, too, waste only half as much energy as 1970s bias-ply models, and the best 1990 radials about halve the remaining loss. Rolling resistance drops further in proportion to weight. Result: 65-80% lower losses to "rolling resistance."

Suitable small gasoline engines found in outboard motors and scooters can already be more than 30% efficient, diesels 40-50% (56% in lab experiments). Other emerging technologies also look promising, including miniature gas turbines and fuel cells—solid-state, no-moving-parts devices that silently and very efficiently turn fuel into electricity, carbon dioxide, and water.

In today's cars, accessories—power steering, heating, air conditioning, ventilation, lights, and entertainment systems—use about a tenth of engine power. But a supercar would use about that much energy for all purposes by saving most of the wheel power and most of the accessory loads. Ultralights can handle nimbly without power steering, and their special wheel-motors even provide all-wheel antilock braking and antiskid traction. New kinds of head- and taillights shine brighter on a third the energy, and can save even more weight by distributing a single pea-sized lamp's light throughout the car by fiber optics. Air conditioning would need perhaps a tenth the energy used by today's car air conditioners, which are big enough for an Atlanta house. Special paints, vented double-skinned roofs, visually clear but heat-reflecting windows, solar-powered vent fans, etc., can first exclude unwanted heat; then innovative cooling systems can handle the rest, run not directly by the engine but by its waste heat.

Perhaps the most striking and important savings would come in weight. In the mid-1980s, many automakers demonstrated "concept cars" carrying four to five passengers but weighing as little as 1000 pounds (versus today's average of about 3200). Conventionally powered, they were two to four times as efficient as today's average new car. Those concept cars, however, did it the hard way: they used mainly light metals like aluminum and magnesium. Today, the same thing can be done better with composites made by embedding fiberglass, carbon fiber, Kevlar, and other ultrastrong fibers in special moldable plastics.

In Switzerland, where 2000 lightweight, battery-electric cars are already on the road (a third of the world's total), the latest roomy two-seaters weigh as little as 575 pounds without their batteries. Equivalent four-seaters would weigh under 650 pounds, or under 850 including their whole hybrid propulsion system. Yet crash tests prove that such ultralights can be at least as safe as today's heavy steel cars, even when both kinds collide head-on at high speeds. That's because the composites are so extraordinarily strong and bouncy that they can absorb far more energy per pound than metal. Materials and design are much more important for safety than mere mass, and the special structures needed to protect people don't weigh much. (For example, just a few pounds of hollow, crushable carbon-fiber-and-plastic cones can absorb the entire crash energy of a 1200-pound car hitting a wall at 50 miles per hour.) Millions have watched on TV as Indy 500 race cars crash into walls at 230+ miles per hour: parts of the car buckle or break away in a controlled, energy-absorbing fashion, but despite crash energies five times those of 100-combined-miles-per-hour head-on collisions, the car's structure and driver's protective devices prevent serious injury. Those are carbon-fiber cars.

In 1991, 50 General Motors experts built an encouraging U.S. example of ultralight composite construction, the sleek and sporty four-seat, four-airbag "Ultralite." Packing the interior space of a Chevrolet Corsica into the exterior size of a Mazda Miata, the Ultralite should be both safer and far cleaner than today's production cars. With only a 111-horsepower engine, smaller than a Honda Civic's, its light weight (1400 pounds) and low air drag, both less than half normal, give it a 135-miles-per-hour top speed and 7.8-second, 0-to-60 acceleration, comparable to a BMW 750iL with a huge V-12 engine. But it's over four times as efficient as the BMW, averaging 62 miles per gallon—twice today's norm. At 50 miles per hour, it cruises at 100 miles per gallon on only 4.3 horsepower, a mere fifth of the power normally needed.

If equipped with hybrid drive, this first-cut 1991 prototype, built in only 100 days, would be three to six times as efficient

Amory & Hunter Lovins

"In Switzerland, where 3000 lightweight, battery-electric cars are already on the road (a third of the world's total), the latest roomy two-seaters weigh as little as 575 pounds without their batteries. Equivalent four-seaters would weigh under 650 pounds, or under 850 including their whole hybrid propulsion system. Yet crash tests prove that such ultralights can be at least as safe as today's heavy steel cars, even when both kinds collide head-on at high speeds."

Amory & Hunter
Lovins

as today's cars, easily beating the Clean Car Initiative's target for 2003. We've simulated 300 to 400-miles-per-gallon four-seaters with "state-of-the-shelf" technology, and over 600 miles per gallon with the best ideas now in the lab.

Similar opportunities apply to larger vehicles, from pickup trucks to 18-wheelers. A small Florida firm has tested composite delivery vans that weigh less loaded than normal steel vans weigh empty, and has designed a halved-weight bus. Others are experimenting with streamlined composite designs for big trucks. All these achieve roughly twice normal efficiency with conventional drivelines, nearly redoubleable with hybrids.

Supercars also favor alternative, ultraclean fuels. Even a small, light, cheap fuel tank could store enough compressed natural gas or hydrogen for long range, and the high cost of hydrogen would become less important if only a tenth as much of it were needed. Liquid fuels converted from sustainable grown farm and forestry wastes, too, would become ample to run such an efficient U.S. transportation system without needing special crops or fossil hydrocarbons. Alternatively, solar cells on a supercar's body could recharge its onboard energy storage about enough to power a standard Southern California commuting cycle without even turning on the engine. But even with conventional fuel and no solar boost, the tailpipe of a supercar would emit far less pollution than would the power plants needed to recharge a battery-electric car. Being therefore cleaner, even in the Los Angeles air shed, than those so-called "zero-emission" vehicles (actually elsewhere-emission, mainly from dirty, coal-fired power plants out in the desert), ultralight hybrids should qualify as ZEVs, and probably will.

Beyond the Iron Age

The moldable synthetic materials in the GM and Swiss prototypes have fundamental advantages over the metals that now dominate automaking. The modern steel car satisfies often conflicting demands with remarkable skill: steel is ubiquitous and familiar, and its fabrication is exquisitely evolved. Yet superior synthetic alternatives could quickly displace it. It's happened before. U.S. car bodies switched from 85% wood in 1920 to over 70% steel only six years later, making possible the modern assembly line. Today, synthetics domi-

"The modern steel car satisfies often conflicting demands with remarkable skill: steel is ubiquitous and familiar, and its fabrication is exquisitely evolved. Yet superior synthetic alternatives could quickly displace it. It's happened before. U.S. car bodies switched from 85% wood in 1920 to over 70% steel only six years later, making possible the modern assembly line. Today, synthetics dominate boat building and are rapidly taking over aerospace. Logically, cars are next."

nate boat building and are rapidly taking over aerospace. Logically, cars are next.

Driving this transition are the huge capital costs for design, tooling, manufacturing, and finishing steel cars. For a new model, a thousand engineers spend a year designing and a year making more than a billion dollars' worth of car-sized steel dies whose cost takes decades to recover. This inflexible, costly tooling in turn demands huge production runs, maroons company-busting investments if products flop, and magnifies financial risks by making product cycles far longer than markets can be forecast. That this gargantuan process works is an astonishing accomplishment, but it's technically baroque and economically perilous.

Moldable composites aren't "black steel," and must be designed in utterly novel shapes. Their fibers can be aligned to match stress and interwoven to distribute it, just as a cabinetmaker works with wood grain. Two or three times fewer pounds of carbon fiber can achieve the same strength as steel, and for many uses, other fibers such as glass and Kevlar are as good or better and are two to six times cheaper. But composites' biggest advantages emerge in manufacturing.

Only 15% of the cost of a typical steel car part is for steel; the other 85% is to pound, weld, and smooth it. But composites and other molded synthetics emerge from the mold already in virtually the required "net shape" and final finish. Large, complex units can also be molded in one piece, cutting the parts count by about 100-fold and the assembly labor and space by tenfold. The lightweight, easy-to-handle parts fit precisely together without rework. Painting—the costliest, hardest, and most polluting step in automaking, accounting for nearly half the cost of painted steel body parts—can be eliminated by lay-in-the-mold color. If not recycled, composites last virtually forever: they don't dent, rust, or chip. They also permit advantageous car designs, including frameless monocoque bodies (like an egg, the body is the structure) whose extreme stiffness improves handling and safety.

Composites are formed to the desired "net shape" not by multiple strikes with tool-steel stamping dies but in single molding dies made of coated epoxy. Those dies wear out much faster than tool-steel dies, but they're cheap enough that it doesn't matter. Total tooling cost is about two to ten times less per copy than with steel, because there are far

Amory & Hunter Lovins

fewer parts, one die set per part rather than three to seven for successive hits, and much cheaper die materials and fabrication. Stereolithography—a three-dimensional process that molds the designer's computer images directly into complex solid objects overnight—can dramatically shrink retooling time. Indeed, epoxy tools' shorter life is a fundamental strategic advantage, because it permits the rapid model changes that continuous improvement, product differentiation, and market nimbleness demand—a strategy of tiny design teams, small production runs, weeks' or months' time-to-market, rapid experimentation, maximum flexibility, and minimum financial risk.

Together, these advantages cancel or reverse composites' apparent cost disadvantage. Carbon fiber recently cost around 40 times as much per pound as sheet steel, though better processes are shrinking this gap. Yet the mass-produced cost of a composite car is probably comparable to or less than steel's at both low production volumes (like Porsches) and high ones (like Fords). What matters is not cost per pound but cost per car.

Shifting Gears in Competitive Strategy

Ultralight hybrids are not just another kind of car. They will probably be made and sold in completely new ways. Their industrial and market structure will be as different as computers are from typewriters, fax machines from telexes, and satellite pagers from the Pony Express.

"Ultralight hybrids are not just another kind of car. They will probably be made and sold in completely new ways."

Many people and firms in several countries are starting to realize what supercars mean; at least a dozen capable entities, including automakers, want to sell them. This implies rapid change on an unprecedented scale. If ignored or treated as a threat rather than grasped as an opportunity, the supercar revolution could cost America millions of jobs and thousands of companies. Automaking and associated businesses employ one-seventh of U.S. workers (approaching two-fifths in some European countries). They represent one-tenth of America's consumer spending, and use nearly 70% of the nation's lead, about 60% of its rubber, carpeting, and malleable iron, 40% of the machine tools, 13% of the steel, and about 15% of the aluminum, glass, and semiconductors. David Morris, cofounder of the Institute for Local Self-Reliance, observes: "The production of automobiles is the world's number one industry. The number two industry supplies their fuel. Six of America's ten largest industrial corporations are either oil or auto companies.... A recent British estimate concludes that half of the world's earnings may be auto or truck related." Whether the prospect of supercars is terrifying or exhilarating thus depends on how well we grasp and exploit their implications.

Distributing supercars could change as profoundly as manufacturing them. Today's cars are marked up about 50% from production cost (which includes profit, plant cost, and warranted repairs). But cheap tooling might make supercars' optimal production scale as small as a regional soft-drink bottling plant. Cars could be ordered directly from the local factory, made to order, and delivered to your door in a day or two. (Toyota now takes only a few days longer with steel cars.) Being radically simplified and ultrareliable, they could be maintained by on-site visits (as Ford does in Britain today), aided by plug-into-the-phone remote diagnostics. If all this makes sense today for a $1500 mail-order personal computer, why not for a $15,000 car?

Such just-in-time manufacturing would eliminate inventory, its carrying and selling costs, and the discounts and rebates needed to move premade stock that's mismatched to current demand. The present markup would largely vanish, so supercars should be profitably deliverable at or below today's prices even if they cost considerably more to make, which they probably wouldn't.

America leads—for now—both in startup-business dynamism and in all the required technical capabilities. After all, supercars are much more like computers with wheels than they are like cars with chips: they are more a software than a hardware problem, and competition will favor the innovative, not the big. Comparative advantage lies not with the most efficient steel-stampers but with the fastest-learning systems integrators—with manufacturers like Hewlett-Packard and Compaq and strategic-element makers like Microsoft and Intel more than with Chrysler or Matsushita. But even big and able firms may be in for a rough ride: the barriers to market entry (and exit) should be far lower for supercars than for steel cars. As with microcomputers, the winners might be some smart, hungry, unknown aerospace engineers tinkering in a garage right now—the next Apple or Xerox.

Amory & Hunter Lovins

"Distributing supercars could change as profoundly as manufacturing them."

"America leads—for now—both in startup-business dynamism and in all the required technical capabilities."

All this is alien to the consciousness of most (though not all) automakers today. Theirs is not a composite-molding/electronics/software culture but a die-making/steel-stamping/mechanical culture. Their fealty is to heavy metal, not light synthetics; to mass, not information. Their organizations are dedicated, extremely capable, and often socially aware, but have become prisoners of their sunk costs. They treat those historic investments as unamortized assets, substituting accounting for economic principles and continuing to throw good money after bad. They have tens of billions of dollars, and untold psychological investments, sunk in stamping steel. They know steel, think steel, and have a presumption in favor of steel. They design cars as abstract art, then figure out the least unsatisfactory way to make them, rather than seeking the best ways to manufacture with strategically advantageous materials and then designing cars to exploit those manufacturing methods. Their institutional form, style, and speed of learning have become as ponderous as those steel-based production technologies. Most of them appear to want to write off their obsolete capabilities later when they don't have a company, rather than now when they do.

"**The wreckage of the mainframe computer industry should have taught us that you have to kill your products with better new products before someone else does.**"

The wreckage of the mainframe computer industry should have taught us that you have to kill your products with better new products before someone else does. (As 3M puts it, "We'd rather eat our own lunch, thank you.") Until 1993, few automakers appreciated the starkness of that threat. Their strategy seemed to be to milk old tools and skills for decades, watch costs creep up and market share down, postpone any basic innovation until after they've all retired—and hope none of their competitors is faster. That's the bet-your-company strategy, because it only takes one competitor to put you out of business, and you may not even know who that competitor is until too late. The Clean Car Initiative will stimulate instead a winning, risk-managed strategy: leapfrogging to ultralight hybrids. Then you can feel sorry for your former competitors—if and only if you reach the goal first.

Encouragingly, some automakers now show signs of understanding this. In the past few months, the intellectual mold-breaking of the Initiative has sparked new thinking in Detroit. The automakers' more imaginative engineers are discovering that the next gains in car efficiency should be easier than the last ones were, because they will come not from sweating off fat ounce by ounce but from escaping an evolutionary trap. Although good ultralight hybrids need elegantly simple engineering, which is difficult, it's actually easier to boost efficiency tenfold with supercars than threefold with today's cars.

Little of this ferment is visible from the outside, because automakers have learned reticence the hard way. A long and unhappy history of being mandated to do (or exceed) whatever they admit they can do has left them understandably bashful about revealing capabilities, especially to Congress. Any firms that harbor leapfrog ambitions, too, will hardly be eager to telegraph them to competitors. There is a natural desire to extract any available business and political concessions, and to hold back from extending to traditional adversaries (such as media, politicians, and environmentalists) any trust that could prove costly if abused or not reciprocated. For all these reasons, public pronouncements from Detroit are more likely to understate than trumpet progress. The Big Three are also progressing unevenly, both internally and comparatively: their opacity conceals a rapidly changing mixture of exciting advances and inertia. Some managers appreciate, but many do not yet, that supercars fit the compelling strategic logic of changing how they do business, especially by radically reducing cycle times, capital costs, and financial risks. It is difficult but vital for harried managers to focus on these goals through the distracting fog of fixing flaws in their short-term operations.

The Cost of Inaction

Supercars' potential public benefits are enormous—in oil displacement, energy security, international stability, avoided military costs, balance of trade, climatic protection, clean air, health and safety, noise, and quality of urban life. Promptly and skillfully exploited, supercars could also propel an industrial renewal. They're good news for such industries—many now demilitarizing—as electronics, systems integration, aerospace, software, petrochemicals, and even textiles (which offer automated fiber-weaving techniques). However, if ignored, the opportunity could be botched, retarded, or ceded to others, with disastrous effects on U.S. jobs and competitiveness. There's abundant talent in American labor, management, government, and independent centers to guide the transition,

Amory & Hunter Lovins

"Little of this ferment is visible from the outside, because automakers have learned reticence the hard way."

"Promptly and skillfully exploited, supercars could also propel an industrial renewal."

but it's not yet seriously mobilized. The costs of that complacency are high.

Cars and light trucks, their efficiency stagnant since 1982, use 37% of the nation's oil, 43% of which is imported at a cost around $50 billion a year. We Americans recently put our kids in 0.56-mile-per-gallon tanks and 17-feet-per-gallon aircraft carriers because we didn't put them in 32-mile-per-gallon cars—enough, even if we'd done nothing else, to eliminate the need for American oil imports from the Persian Gulf. Of course there was more at stake in the Gulf War than just oil, but it's hard to imagine we'd have sent half-a-million troops there if Kuwait just grew broccoli. Even in peacetime, Persian Gulf oil's direct cost to the nation—roughly half at the pump, half in taxes for some $50 billion a year in military readiness to intervene in the Gulf—totals around $100 per barrel of crude, surely the costliest oil in the world.

Had we simply kept on saving oil as quickly after 1985 as we did for the previous nine years, then ever since 1985 we wouldn't have needed a drop of oil from the Persian Gulf. But we didn't. Gulf imports were cut by over 90% during 1977 to 1985 (chiefly by Federal standards that largely or wholly caused new cars' efficiency to double during 1973 to 1986). They are now reapproaching historic highs—the direct result of twelve years' national oil policy consisting mainly of weakened efficiency standards, lavish subsidies, and the Seventh Fleet.

The national stakes therefore remain large. And even though the Clean Car Initiative is starting to recreate Detroit's sense of adventure, supercars still face formidable obstacles, both culturally within the auto industry and institutionally in the marketplace....

Fasten Your Seat Belts

...New policies, whether imaginative or mundane, often diffuse more sluggishly than new technologies. Americans are reinventing the car faster than they can rethink it. We'll probably have great cars before we've figured out when not to drive them. The recent history of computers, telecommunications, and other technological fusions suggests that the switch to supercars could come far faster than basic shifts in where people live, work, shop, and recreate or in how people

> "The national stakes therefore remain large. And even though the Clean Car Initiative is starting to recreate Detroit's sense of adventure, supercars still face formidable obstacles, both culturally within the auto industry and institutionally in the marketplace."

choose among means of mobility. Supercars can buy time to address these issues, but cannot resolve them.

The speed and size of all these changes could be deeply disruptive as well as beneficial; but perhaps we can choose whether to make them help or hurt us. If so, we had better start thinking about how best to do them, with the least pain and the most benefit, before others do them first or to us. If the technical and market logic sketched here is anywhere near right, we are all about to embark on one of the greatest adventures in industrial history. 🚗

Amory & Hunter Lovins

AMORY LOVINS
Moving Toward a New System

"The energy problem is conceptually solved, but 50 years of details remain."
— Amory B. Lovins

Amory Lovins is the director of research at Rocky Mountain Institute. His paper "Supercars: The Coming Light Vehicle Revolution" focused on ultra-light hybrid-electric vehicles and spurred on a flurry of research and product development activities around the world. This transcript is from an interview held on March 24, 1994, and corrected September 2, 1994.

We are currently working with approximately 20 capable entities eager to bring Supercars to market, and there are more entities joining the list almost weekly. Several are automakers. The rest are non-automakers with impressive capabilities that they wish to apply to becoming automakers—in a new and different sense, obviously. They are chiefly manufacturing firms in other areas; some small, some very large. We're working with all of them on a non-exclusive, compartmentalized basis in order to maximize competition among them; *pour encourager les autres.*

The U.S. government has adopted many of your teachings in bringing about its Partnership for a New Generation of Vehicles program, also called the Clean Car Initiative. You speak of "maximizing competition," but one of the criticisms of the government's Partnership for a New Generation of Vehicles Program is that it isn't based on free-market, competitive forces.

Anything the federal government does is funded by Congress and therefore subject to a very unfortunate degree of direction by influential legislators who wish money to go to their own districts and who may allocate all of the money available, or more, to projects that may or may not merit them. That's a sort of central planning by several hundred people—well, actually the group involved is smaller—but by a small number of people who probably don't have any way of comparing the merits of their pet projects with other projects. That ends up making the program a lot less coherent than it ought to be.

The proposals that the Big Three put into the Clean Car Initiative were far short of what they can, and I think will, do. They will end up with a much more ambitious set of achievements than is currently on the table. But they will do so because of competitive forces, not government mandates or encouragement.

The Pump is Primed

It seems to me the Clean Car Initiative has already had several very important and successful functions. The most important is to create a leapfrog mentality that brings the more imaginative engineers in Detroit out of the woodwork and validates their interest in going far beyond incrementalism. There is, additionally, some helpful technology transfer. The National Labs really do have useful things. There is a new opportunity for conversations that have never occurred before where, for example, aerospace composites experts who are used to making onesies and twosies, with cost no object, meet steel guys who want 100,000 a year at four dollars a pound. The most interesting discussions are now in the advanced materials manufacturing technique arena, where these two kinds of people have, apparently, never before talked to each other and are learning a lot from each other, even in this short time.

That said, I think in the Clean Car Initiative, as in the Advanced Battery Consortium or any of the other joint efforts underway, the most interesting things cannot be discussed in such an inter-company forum because they're already too proprietary. I think the proprietary efforts are already moving far ahead of what is visible from the outside.

The automakers have compelling strategic reasons to go in the direction of Supercars even if such cars did not save fuel or pollution. These reasons have to do with radical shortening of production cycles, reduction in tooling costs, and hence reduction in financial risk. These competitive forces are, I think, even more powerful than presidential encouragement or regulatory mandate and will lead to the same result, only more so. The strategic logic of cheap, frequently renewed tooling, net-shape materials, and enormously simplified, highly integrated design has already occurred to all of the Big Three at high levels and is starting to receive the management attention it deserves.

What is the role of Rocky Mountain Institute in this?

Historically, we've had three main skills to contribute to creating new efforts like, say, the "negawatts"* industry, which is now a $5-billion-a-year electric efficiency effort nationwide. First, we reconceive an old problem by looking at it in a new way. In the case of cars, rather than focusing on

Amory Lovins

"The most interesting things cannot be discussed in such an inter-company forum because they're already too proprietary."

*"Negawatts" is a term Amory Lovins uses to describe how societies can meet their energy needs not by building new 1000-megawatt power plants, but by producing "negawatts" of saved energy. This concept is now being practiced by utilities that teach their customers how to adopt smarter technologies that wring more work from each kilowatt-hour.

Amory Lovins

***Published by
RMI's subsidiary
E- Source
(Boulder, CO
80302-5114)**

the incremental efficiency of the driveline, we started with the basic physics of the platform in order to achieve the huge leverage of saving power at the wheels, and then found this unexpectedly powerful synergy between ultralight construction and hybrid-electric drive; the 1-plus-2-equals-10 equation.

Second, we tend to be synthesists from a wide range of information in different disciplines. For example, one of the five *Technology Atlases* I've written on advanced electric efficiency* is on space cooling and air handling and how, in that application, one can save 80% or 90% of the energy in most buildings and make them cheaper and more comfortable. Exactly the same approach applies to cars and involves roughly two dozen technologies of which perhaps half are known in the car industry, but the rest are not. The notion of synergistically integrating them is quite novel.

We're trying to do the same thing not just with cooling, so as to reduce accessory loads by up to an order of magnitude, but also with the design of the whole platform. This is, I think, the most important area of our collaboration with the entities we're working with. We can help them think in a more integrated fashion about how to put the pieces together, as well as help them find the people who have the best pieces, because of our international network from such a wide range of technical areas.

Third, we are in a peculiar and, I think, advantageous position of having been nonadversarial and transideological for so long that we can work with everybody. That is, we can have the trust and respect of a wide range of stakeholders and therefore may be better able to help them align their interests than somebody who is not so clearly a disinterested "honest broker." There are, of course, a lot of political as well as technical dimensions to introducing the Supercar, so this is an important area to which we are devoting a lot of attention. We're getting involved in issues like the California ZEV mandate, financing, and a lot of other things.

Grounded in Reality

I don't think we want, ourselves, to get into the car-building business, although we have people on staff who could do that. But I think we will be increasingly involved at a hands-on, prototype-building level with other entities and their shops and not simply talking about design.

I'm originally an experimental physicist, accustomed to building things and making them work. The car guys we have on staff are, too. One is 26 and has been doing cars for 20 years. Another, at 29, had designed two good cars in a small team, two more by himself, and built one of these single-handedly from scratch, then sold, before he entered college. These innovators have what hackers would call the "hands-on imperative." I think we will stay grounded in the reality of car practice only to the extent that we have that degree of involvement. We can't be purely theoretical.

Is there international activity going on with Supercars?

Yes. There is a great deal of activity in Europe and some in Asia. We're involved in all of that.

I think it's all going to move much faster than we expect. Think about it this way, just by way of illustration using public information. It took about 50 people at General Motors about 100 days to build two copies of the Ultralite concept car in 1991. It took approximately a year, starting at a similar stage of concept car development, to productionize the Impact battery car. Both of those processes largely used the traditional model-building techniques with clay and other media, rather than, like a Stealth bomber, going straight from CAD screen to digital tooling instructions or, indeed, straight to stereolithography. It's always seemed to me that the logical development path for an ultralight hybrid starts with ultralights, both in order to achieve at the beginning the short cycle times and cheap tooling inherent in the net-shape materials, and because ultralight cars by themselves have roughly double the efficiency and are potentially a very attractive market product. One should then add the hybrid drive line that meanwhile would be developed in a parallel process drawing on experience from battery car development. There's a great deal of hardware and software work required to do a really good hybrid.

The alternative, which many hybrid developers are pursuing, is to start with a heavy production platform and then hybridize it. We call those "tank conversions." They yield, typically, a 30-50% efficiency gain, but I don't think its advantages are compelling enough to make it that interesting a market product, and you're still in the Iron Age, dealing with all the ponderous nature of the steel technology.

Amory Lovins

"I think it's all going to move much faster than we expect."

Amory Lovins

So given the choice between hybridizing an ultralight and lightening a heavy hybrid, I think the choice is quite clear. Its consequence is, of course, that the development and production time could be very much shorter than we've been accustomed to in the car business. My own guess, from public information, is that we will see prototypes dribbling out from a variety of established and new market actors just over the next few years and significant production volumes starting around 1998 or 1999. By roughly 2000, I think it will be clear that the era of the steel car is about to add its right parenthesis. Dr. Paul MacCready has said that by 2005 he thinks most, if not all, of the cars in the showroom will be electrically propelled. Probably most of those in turn will be hybrids. I think he's right.

The analogy to personal computers and how Apple bit into the mainframe business is often used when speaking of Supercars.

Well, it's a powerful analogy and indeed some of the entities we're working with have a great deal of experience in that field. The analogy is not exact, however. You don't, for example, put your family in a computer and wrap it around a tree at 60 miles per hour. But I think in terms of market development, the analogy is as good as any and better than most. It's easier culturally for, say, a computer-based company to become a Supercar maker than for an established car maker to do so. To change the existing car companies means you're going from steel to synthetics, stamping to molding, welding to adhesives or simply parts integration, actual to virtual prototyping, mechanicals to electricals, hydraulics to electronics, hardware to software, and mass to information. It's a profoundly different kind of product. For that matter, in particular skills as well, there's a similar transformation—for example, from die making to stereolith. It's such a big set of leapfrogs in so many areas that it's hard to imagine its being successful for most automakers unless they are thoroughly committed to a cultural transformation of such unprecedented dimensions that it's painful for them to think about it.

"It's easier culturally for, say, a computer-based company to become a Supercar maker than for an established car maker to do so. To change the existing car companies means you're going from steel to synthetics, stamping to molding, welding to adhesives or simply parts integration, actual to virtual prototyping, mechanicals to electricals, hydraulics to electronics, hardware to software, and mass to information. It's a profoundly different kind of product."

A New Kind of Industry

Amory Lovins

We're trying to bring this about with several automakers, and I think with some of them there is a good shot at it. But it takes an unconventional style and structure of project management to bring it about. I think it will only happen in the companies that pursue it not simply as a fringe activity or as an insurance policy, but as a whole-hearted commitment to the most fundamental kind of reinvention of what a car is, how you make it, how you sell it, and what business the company's in.

The pace of cultural change in some automakers is certainly impressive and gives me some hope that it may be possible to pull this off, but it's not guaranteed. I therefore suspect that the advantage, to an extent that's hitherto inconceivable in this field, may go to companies, both big and small, that learn as fast as computer companies do, that are not afraid of new stuff, and that are accustomed to very market-driven products, most of whose money is made in the first six months and where there are one or two new product generations in a year with extraordinary short cycle times.

We're talking about rapidly speeding up the time to market. At the same time, we're talking about using materials that can be expected to last at least twice as long as steel lasts.

They can be an heirloom.

How does that affect the market?

I think the consequence of that, and also from a material flow management and recycling perspective, is that it may be highly desirable not to sell Supercars but to lease them. You wouldn't want them lasting so long that they clogged up the market 10 generations later like the DC-3 did in keeping out jets. Leasing would be like the new policy under which the German automakers own the car forever, because they have to take it back. This gives them a strong incentive for designing in what to do with the material afterwards. I think we can already recycle composites with methanolysis. It's brute force, but it works. We can develop much better methods, like resins that unlock with a chemical key. It's just that there hasn't been a demand for that until now.

> "The advantage... may go to companies, both big and small, that learn as fast as computer companies do, that are not afraid of new stuff, and that are accustomed to very market-driven products, most of whose money is made in the first six months and where there are one or two new product generations in a year with extraordinary short cycle times."

Amory Lovins

> **"Fast learning and being unafraid of profound change tends to favor small companies. The obvious comeback is that small companies don't have the production capability."**

Back to the smaller companies' role: What I said a minute ago about fast learning and being unafraid of profound change tends to favor small companies. The obvious comeback is that small companies don't have the production capability.

Or the capital?

The capital is not necessarily a problem, because the amount required is an order of magnitude less than we're used to thinking about for cars, and you could start even much smaller than that. You can imagine something analogous to the Honda CRX, where they surged rapidly from bench scale to full production when they found there was a market there. The capital doesn't worry me so much. I think with the products and the kinds of capabilities behind them that we're now seeing enter the field, we'll find capital all right.

It's more a combination of capital, management, and other capabilities needed to produce large volumes of anything this big. I think a logical consequence could be an unusual degree of partnership between large and small companies, somewhat analogous to the joint ventures and strategic alliances we see all the time in the computer business. There will be important differences, but I think the similarities will be even more important.

Are the entities you are working with able to find win-win relationships with other entities?

A lot of that is already emerging. There's been an astonishing flurry of licensing and other partnering arrangements just in the last few months with many of the key enabling technologies. 🚗

PAUL B. MACCREADY
Views on Transportation Policy

The broad picture of how you really get electric vehicles developed starts with getting the people who are interested in this area of transportation to write down clearly what their goal is. It's absurd to hustle and get right to technology and regulations.

Draw back. What are we trying to do? What is the goal? Pick some year. Pick what you're trying to do with transportation then, and set that goal and figure out the best of various strategies. There's not just one. When you do this, you'll find that electric vehicles are a very attractive way but are not the only way. Most of the electric vehicle stuff starts with people wanting to do electric vehicles. They don't care about real goals or competitive technologies or other ways of solving these problems. So this business of setting goals is something that is very neglected.

The Goal

I've concocted various versions of what I call "the goal." Basically, any goal in the transportation/energy/environment area involves improving our personal mobilities while decreasing cost, pollution, and foreign oil consumption. That is really it. You can put numbers on those various items. How much do you want to accomplish by which years? It goes without saying that you want industries to be healthy, and you need global markets for what we're doing. Electric cars can help with achieving this goal, but they're not the only solution to the problem. In fact, what solutions you have will depend on the time scale at which you set your goals. If you're trying to have decreased traffic, electric vehicles don't necessarily help. Subcars* do, and as you get to subcars you find that electric is attractive. When it comes to saving fuel and decreasing pollution, even with gasoline cars you can make giant improvements in efficiency, if there is a culture to treat efficiency seriously. Really, nobody cares.

One number that is interesting is that, by Herculean effort and a tie-breaking vote by the vice president, we actually got a 4.3-cent gas tax increase—a 4% increase in our gasoline cost as opposed to the $3.00-per-gallon tax that's in Europe.

Dr. Paul MacCready is chairman of AeroVironment, Inc., a company partially owned by General Motors Corporation that is actively involved in GM's efforts to design electric and hybrid-electric vehicles. This transcript is from an interview held on August 26, 1993.

*"Subcar" is a term Dr. MacCready coined to refer to vehicles which are smaller in size and power than the automobile. This includes vehicles ranging from bicycles to golf carts to small "neighborhood" electric vehicles.

Paul MacCready

That adds 4% to gasoline cost, equivalent to a little over 0.5% of your total car cost for the year. With inflation being a little over 4% a year, the country has gone ballistic over the fact that they're going to be paying 0.5% more for their cars per year. Gasoline, in California, is the cheapest liquid you can buy except tap water. They give it away, then tell you to save it. It doesn't compute. If you priced gasoline at what it should be, at what it's really costing the country, then people would start looking at various solutions. Our political circumstances mean it's politically impossible. Subsidize, regulate, and look at other solutions instead, and electric cars are probably good for you.

How to Make EVs Work

So how do we make them work? Number one is making vehicles so they just don't use as much energy per mile. This can be done. In fact, one good thing about the California mandate on zero-emission vehicles is that it got this whole feeding frenzy going on electric cars, which immediately stumbles over the fact that a battery doesn't hold much energy and these vehicles aren't going to work well unless we make all sorts of compromises, one being to pay attention to efficiency. That stimulated the culture of efficiency attention to all cars. You can make lightweight, aerodynamic cars, more efficient air conditioners, and so on. There's great potential in this item number one, which incidentally helps with regular cars. The joker in it is that people don't want to buy efficient cars. In many cases, they want to buy a four-wheel-drive pick-up, get the suspension raised, and put on bigger tires, even if they're never going to go off-road. So the customer doesn't really care. Maybe customers forced to pay $4.50 a gallon for gasoline might, but now they don't.

There are many things that can provide increased efficiency in cars. Amory Lovins, in the "Supercars" paper, goes a little bit far in accepting some numbers and puts all the numbers people tell him together and comes up with great conclusions—a vision to head toward, even if a bit beyond reach. I feel he does not pay enough attention to the pragmatic side of what you need to do for vehicles you're going to warrant and market. Yet the overall gist of what he's doing is correct. Much of what he talks about is stuff I had talked to him about in prior years during a great sharing of ideas. The point is, if

> **"One good thing about the California mandate on zero-emission vehicles is that it got this whole feeding frenzy going on electric cars"**

you really wanted, you could make very efficient cars, and a lot of that reasoning applies to gasoline power. The vehicle does not have to be electric, but electric does look especially appealing for some realistic goals in realistic time. Incidentally, the technologies in all aspects of electrics—the batteries, power electronics, or hybrid-power devices—are rapidly moving ahead to the point where I don't think there are any basic technological barriers to achieving amazing results.

Including battery technology?

I think if you say you must have a battery that substitutes for a gas tank, you can be accommodated, but the battery will dominate the car. If you say we want cars that are very efficient and cheap and good and so on, of all sizes, you find electric drive has some attractive features. For the bigger cars, electric drive will be part of a hybrid system. For the hybrid, what you care about is not the energy in the battery, but the power from what we call the surge unit, the part of the car that takes care of accelerations and stores regenerative braking. Flywheels, super capacitors, or high-power batteries seem to be the logical approaches. Nobody yet has a good, cheap, high-power battery, but I believe as more attention is focused on that, there will be some successes. Actually, some lead acid approaches look very appealing.

Several people I talk to consider EVs computers on wheels. What's the reality of such an analogy?

Modern cars are getting to be rolling computers anyhow as the amount of electronics in them is rapidly increasing. There will have to be a lot of that in the electric cars. As you get into mass production on any electronic thing, the price goes way, way down. I don't think electric vehicle complexity is going to be substantially different from that of gasoline-powered cars in the future. The differences will not be enough to worry about.

Does Detroit have the skills and knowledge to work with the new composite materials or does this skill reside else-where?

You'd be amazed how much talent resides in the giant auto industries, how many things they've been experimenting on

Paul MacCready

> "I think if you say you must have a battery that substitutes for a gas tank, you can be accommodated, but the battery will dominate the car. If you say we want cars that are very efficient and cheap and good and so on, of all sizes, you find electric drive has some attractive features."

but don't tell you about. In fact, for proprietary reasons, they really are worried about exposing their new things and what they're working on. The concern is that if some things look very good and legislators hear about it, they'll legislate in a very undiscerning fashion. So there is much more going on in the auto industry than you are aware of. The small dogs that are nipping around the heels of the industry do not have any muzzles on what they're saying. They're bragging about what highly visible little groups are doing and criticizing the industry. If you draw way back and look at the car industry, you will find that it is still a big boys' game and the big boys are GM, Ford, and Chrysler. Just as if you're making and selling jumbo jets, you'd better be Boeing or McDonnell Douglas. You can't be a garage shop and hope to get into that business. Anybody can quickly come up with a nice looking car for a showroom or convention, but when you get to the point where a prototype of your production version looks right, you're still only about 1% of the way to having a true production car which can be mass produced, warranted and sold to the public. Just because you make a lot of noise during that first 1% doesn't mean that you can do the other 99%; that takes a giant investment in time and dollars.

In the "Supercars" paper, Amory Lovins talks about how computers are assembled in a simple, modular fashion. He goes on to ask if we can do it with a $1500 computer, why not a $15,000 car? Do you buy that thinking?

Well, it's just one version of the just-in-time business: you have a production line and you don't have any storage of parts, but somehow they just all come in, magically, at the right moment. If everything works perfectly, then great—you don't have any inventory. Inventory just goes out as a completed car that day. It turns out that when you do that, all your suppliers have to be storing their products as inventory so they can give it to you just when you want. So it's not a change for society, it's just a change of where the inventory is.

Cars seem so modular that for a new model, you just get a power system from an existing car and a chassis from another one and a steering wheel from another, prior design. But what you find is that when you change one part, the ripples go all through the whole vehicle. Change some configuration one place and it changes where you position some other com-

> "What you find is that when you change one part, the ripples go all through the whole vehicle. Change some configuration one place and it changes where you position some other components, which changes the center of gravity and changes the suspension dynamics, and so on. It is a demanding systems job to get the vehicle just the way you want it."

Paul MacCready

ponents, which changes the center of gravity and changes the suspension dynamics, and so on. It is a demanding systems job to get the vehicle just the way you want it. You'd like to be able to sell the same sort of vehicle year after year, just slowly improving it. Airliners take a long time, as do cars, to go from concept to production, but once you get into production you can go for quite a few years with the same plane. Competition requires styling change all the time in the car industry, unfortunately.

Everyone wants an inexpensive Testerossa that runs on cold fusion. But if you had it, it wouldn't help traffic, parking, your lifestyle in the city, or how many hours you spend commuting, because you'd be addressing a symptom or technological detail more than the big issue of transportation, mobility, and accessibility.

"Everyone wants an inexpensive Testerossa that runs on cold fusion. But if you had it, it wouldn't help traffic, parking, your lifestyle in the city, or how many hours you spend commuting, because you'd be addressing a symptom or technological detail more than the big issue of transportation, mobility, and accessibility."

When you make products in large quantity, you automate the process. When you have to adapt to a rapidly changing field, some production techniques will lend themselves better to that than others. I suspect that some of the composites will be very helpful there. A problem I find with judging the potential for composites is that, while they make some large exterior things simpler and cheaper, they are not of fundamental help on the many little details. If you want a door that opens with the proper hinges and latches, you find the dies for shaping the exterior shape of the metal is not the big cost. It's the fact that there are so many details that go into the finished door. There are so many operations that you have to do, whether in steel or plastic, before the final part emerges. If there are breakthroughs in manufacturing, you will see them being used by large car companies. Sure, big companies have their inertia problems, but those are rapidly lessening. The special problem is economic. If the car company is in, or recently had, some tough years it is going to concentrate on making and selling cars efficiently and profitably. Wild new technology is annoying to digest, especially when there is just no way you are going to have any economic benefit from it for 10 years or so. It's awkward having regulations forcing you into an area that's a loser, where all you can make, at least in the short run, is something that does less for the customer and costs more. That's a hard sell.

Paul MacCready

"The fundamental trouble is that we do not have institutions of government organization that are really capable of doing a good job of fast-changing, complex things like transportation. Nevertheless, if you look around ten years from now, you'll find that very useful things were done.... It's a wonderful time to be onboard."

Do you have any comment about how we should set about this task of setting goals?

Compared to two years ago, I think there is huge attention being paid to transportation issues, as opposed to just car issues. I'm really much encouraged compared even to a year ago. There are a lot of good voices out there. The problem is not that the subject isn't even recognized, which was the case a few years ago. The problem is not that there aren't a lot of good people with good will and brains trying to help solve it. The fundamental problem is that the field is so complex and many different entities are associated with it. We need methods of management that don't exist. There is no one group or entity, anyplace, that is truly in charge of this. You look at professional societies and the Department of Transportation, the Department of Energy, the Air Resources Board, the American Automobile Association, the American Society of Mechanical Engineers, people like Amory Lovins and Elmer Johnson. There are conferences, exhibitions, and widely varying media treatments. The subject is so complex that it takes a Solomon to try to get on top of it. You want to manage it, but you don't want to micromanage and stifle it. The fundamental trouble is that we do not have institutions of government organization that are really capable of doing a good job of fast-changing, complex things like transportation. Nevertheless, if you look around ten years from now, you'll find that very useful things were done. Perhaps a huge amount was wasted, and you should have done things in four years that took twelve years, but the field changes in the right direction. It's a wonderful time to be onboard. 🚗

PAUL B. MACCREADY
Perspectives on Vehicle Energy Efficiency and
Electric Vehicles

Fifteen years ago, the staff of AeroVironment, primarily an environment and energy services and products company, began working with vehicles that operated on the tiny power of human muscles, photovoltaic cells, or small batteries, vehicles created for sport, prizes, or records. With power in the 0.1 to 2 horsepower range they were "impractical" compared to ordinary gasoline-powered cars, boats, or airplanes. However, the use of tiny power to move people forces technology, and attitudes, toward efficiency, toward doing more with less. Such technology now becomes valuable for new vehicles that save energy and decrease pollution.

Five years ago, when General Motors decided to enter the solar car race across Australia, it became aware of AeroVironment's unusual background in all the required technologies, and established a unique GM/AV team relationship that resulted in the winning Sunraycer. This was the start of what has become a long-term partnership. The next vehicle project of the GM/AV team was development of the Impact battery-powered car, shown to the public early in 1990. A few months later, GM announced that a derivative of the Impact would be mass produced, to reach the public in the mid 1990s—a practical vehicle, with roots in those impractical AV devices from a decade earlier and in prior GM forays into electric vehicles.

Now a great deal of development and media attention is taking place worldwide concerning electric vehicles—ones operating solely on batteries (BEVs), and hybrids (HEVs) that incorporate some electricity generated on board from burning chemical fuel. There are many kinds of batteries, many types of onboard generators, many systems engineering approaches, and many challenges in technology, economics, regulation, and public perception. The EV field deserves continued high priority, and continued examination from a broad perspective.

Overview: Electric Vehicles, Emissions, and Efficiency

The modern gasoline-fueled car is a very satisfactory solution to our need for personal mobility, balancing safety, com-

This essay original-ly appeared in the November 1992 issue of *ESD Technology*.

Paul MacCready

> "At the moment, the dominant feature of a BEV is its zero emission of local pollutants. However, the BEV has a basic technological disadvantage: short range."

fort, performance, reliability, style, and low cost with good fuel economy and low emissions. The direct descendants in 2005 will be even better in all respects. If the electric vehicle is to emerge as significant against this successful existing and evolving car technology, the electric must offer some unique positives. At the moment, the dominant feature of a BEV is its zero emission of local pollutants: hydrocarbons, oxides of nitrogen, and carbon monoxide. Where control of these emissions has high priority, as in Southern California, regulatory pressures can give BEVs an initial advantage. However, the BEV has a basic technological disadvantage: short range. Per kilogram of lead acid battery, the mechanical energy derived to propel a battery-powered vehicle is only some 1% as much as per kilogram of gasoline. Only by extreme emphasis on vehicle efficiency can the BEV overcome this factor of 100-to-1 technological penalty to where the vehicle can be considered a real substitute for the conventional car.

U.S. Transportation Energy/Environment Goals for 2005

- Substantially decrease U.S. reliance on oil imports, especially from the Mideast. (Decrease to 25-50% of 1989-1990 value. Exact goal to be clarified in 1993 on basis of study considering technology, environment, security, and economics.)
- Substantially decrease release of greenhouse gases in the U.S. and globally. (Decrease to less than 1990 values. From intensified studies of pollutant effects on climate, reassess urgency in 1995 and adjust target. Note that all fossil fuels are implicated, not just automobile fuel.)
- Substantially decrease release of local pollutants (by a factor of 5 from 1990 vehicles).

Key Conditions for 2005 Goals

- That the transportation energy/environmental goals be met, while permitting the increasing number of U.S. consumers to continue to have adequate and affordable personal mobility.
- That the viability of the automotive and energy industries be maintained.

Figure 1

The BEV does open three significant new doors in the efficiency arena:

1. The need for getting by on the small energy per kilogram of a battery forces a high priority on vehicle efficiency. For the General Motors Impact, for example, efficiency of aerodynamics, tires, bearings, accessories, etc., received much more than the usual attention. This efficiency permitted a reasonable, although limited, range. The vehicle requires only about one-third of the energy per mile of a conventional car, saving fuel and CO_2 emissions, even if electricity comes from a fossil-fueled power plant. These lessons in efficiency can eventually be applied to gasoline-powered cars.

2. The battery permits regenerative braking, recovering kinetic energy by recharging the battery during deceleration rather than wasting that energy in heating the brakes. In the urban driving cycle, almost half of the mechanical energy for propelling a car is otherwise squandered in this kinetic energy loss. The battery system (or flywheel or supercapacitor equivalent) gets rid of most of this loss.

3. With a hybrid electric vehicle, a battery or battery equivalent provides this regenerative braking and also handles transient acceleration loads, while an onboard electric generator burning chemical fuel charges the battery as needed (and may also power the electric drive motor directly, or even provide mechanical drive to the wheels). The chemical fuel overcomes the range problem. In addition, the onboard generator is operated over a more benign power-rpm regime than the internal combustion engine of a conventional car, and thus becomes much more efficient (and with lesser emissions). The battery can be much lighter than in a BEV since its energy storage is no longer of concern, but it (perhaps with some simultaneous assist from the generator) must have enough power to give the vehicle the desired performance in hill climbing or accelerating. Incidentally, the battery weight saved improves vehicle weight, acceleration, and rolling friction, and thus overall efficiency.

It is interesting to note that the HEV is somewhat analogous to the power systems in humans and most advanced animals. Humans draw on stored glycogen to produce high power for a few seconds, but burn fuel with oxygen from the air for long, continuous aerobic energy that is delivered at an average rate of power five to ten times smaller. Nature's evo-

Paul MacCready

"It is interesting to note that the HEV is somewhat analogous to the power systems in humans and most advanced animals."

lutionary development, by selection for what succeeds, tends to yield creatures that "cost" the least in terms of energy consumption, maintenance, and weight (and there are also often some psychological considerations of style).

The HEV looks especially appealing from the standpoint of greatly increased miles per gallon while also being valuable for its lessened emissions. Might it eventually offer cost advantages in spite of the fact that two power systems are involved? With such considerations, we enter the complex realm of efficiency versus consumer cost versus societal cost. In this realm, regulators, trying to represent society's best interests but being inhibited by political realities and the unpredictability of future technologies, need Solomon-like wisdom. To oversimplify, local pollution emission limits can be mandated on all cars, for society's benefit, and the consumer has no choice but to pay the cost. However, the consumer can choose what priority to put on efficiency, and costs can put the consumer's decision criteria out of step with society's best interests.

"Local pollution emission limits can be mandated on all cars, for society's benefit, and the consumer has no choice but to pay the cost. However, the consumer can choose what priority to put on efficiency, and costs can put the consumer's decision criteria out of step with society's best interests."

Where the Energy Goes: Efficiency Now and In the Future

A present-day car can be thought of as a device that converts the stored energy of sunlight from some tens of millions of years ago into heat, pollution, and transportation. We need the transportation, we are steadily decreasing the pollution, and the heat is a measure of inefficiency.

If an average car employs 100 units of energy from gasoline to go a particular distance, the following generalizations emerge from taking a crude average of urban and highway driving cycles and ignoring accessory loads. Of those 100 units, 82 go into heat lost in the engine system. Of the remaining 18 units that become mechanical energy:

- 1/3, or six units, overcomes aerodynamic drag (the energy ending up heating the air).
- 1/3, or six units, overcomes rolling friction (the energy ending up heating the tires).
- 1/3, or six units, powers acceleration (the energy ending up heating the brakes).

The improved gasoline-powered car of the future, say the year 2005, can perhaps lower the 18=6+6+6 to 13=4+4+5 (4 from greatly improved aerodynamics, 4 from a bit lighter weight and lower drag tires, 5 from lighter weight). Because of improved engine efficiency, the 13 units of mechanical energy might require only about 55 units of energy from gasoline.

The 2005 HEV, if drawing on gasoline, might reduce the numbers to 10=4+4+2 (reducing the 5 to 2 by regenerative braking). Because of gentler operating conditions for the engine powering the generator instead of the transmission, the 10 net units of mechanical energy might require only about 30 units of energy from gasoline.

These numbers should be considered only as qualitative, presented to help clarify the issues. As customer demands for fast acceleration and accessory convenience grow, by 2005 fuel efficiency will be poorer than implied here. A main point is that the gasoline car in the future could be very efficient compared to the present, and the hybrid even more so—to where fuel cost even with increasing prices will be a small part of car ownership. The CO_2 emissions would decrease in proportion to fuel used. The local emissions will do even better, as heated catalysts get into use and other emission controls improve—with the gentler use of the generator engine for the HEV providing further help that might make local emissions insignificant although finite. The use of other fuels and conversion technology for the HEV can both reduce emissions still further and help wean us from dependence on foreign and domestic oil.

A direct comparison of BEVs with the standard gasoline-fueled vehicles involves too many variables to treat here, except to note that local emissions of BEVs would be zero—of very high desirability in some urban areas.

Two major concerns in this 2005 scenario may be vehicle cost to the customer, discussed in the next section, and the huge investment required if HEVs and BEVs are to be developed and mass produced; but the exciting potentials of EVs are clear.

Cost To The User

We now want society, overall, to buy high-miles-per-gallon cars. But society is the sum of individuals, ourselves, who

Paul MacCready

"The gasoline car in the future could be very efficient compared to the present, and the hybrid even more so—to where fuel cost even with increasing prices will be a small part of car ownership."

have a sense of how little we pay for gasoline and hence tend to select preferentially the more powerful, larger, lower-miles-per-gallon vehicles. In this instance, the motives of the individual are not in concert with those of society.

Total annual costs for a typical car one to three years old divide approximately as shown in Figure 2.

These figures will vary widely with the type of car, and where and how much it is operated, but the main point still emerges: gas is only a small part of total car cost (here 13.3%). The capital-related costs—depreciation, interest, and a portion of insurance—are all larger and total some 67%! Cars are selected more for style and function than fuel economy. When cars become still more efficient, the fuel cost will be even less significant and will represent little reason to alter vehicle selection or driving habits.

If the car used zero fuel (had infinite miles per gallon) and thereby saved 13.3%, but cost 20% more to purchase, the owner would not gain economically. If the reference is a more expensive modern car, a more efficient one, and if the annual driving is less than average, the result is more dramatic: if the car purchase price were only 5% more to get an efficient vehicle of twice the miles per gallon, the owner would save more by sticking with the less-efficient reference vehicle.

This economic problem hangs over all car efficiency improvements and all alternative fuel and electric vehicle options. With gasoline in the U.S. at about $1.25 a gallon, cheaper than bottled water, the incentives for the purchaser of a car to vote for economy are not strong. Fuel cost per mile, considering gasoline price, inflation, and improved car efficiency, is about as low as it has ever been, and only a third of what it was 40 years ago. Considering externalities associated with pollution, with the limits on U.S. resources and the

	Cost	Percentage
Gasoline	$600	13.3
Depreciation	$1300	28.9
Interest on capital	$1000	22.2
Insurance	$900	20.0
Maintenance, service, misc.	$400	8.9
License, registration	$300	6.7
	$4500	100.0

Figure 2

military and political consequences of our dependence on foreign sources, gasoline may be costing the U.S. more than the gas station price, but this only affects the car owner as a voter, not as a purchaser of vehicles or fuel.

Cars must be mass produced to permit low cost, and styling has a large effect on sales, while fuel efficiency has a smaller effect. Over the last decade, pressures to control local pollutants have stimulated efficiency improvements (which also help with the global pollutant CO_2), and regulatory pressures have played a role. But all in all, the marketplace, which "designs" cars by selection, has been saying to manufacturers that it is better to put efficiency at as low a priority as regulations permit in order to save a bit in initial cost. A look at the unstreamlined underside of any car shows that the manufacturers have responded rationally to these "instructions."

Cars can be designed and built with the airplane philosophy, i.e., with wonderful energy efficiency, but they will be so expensive that few will be purchased and used. Thus, these elegant cars will have negligible societal value.

Electric vehicles will serve to help us meet our goals only if they become so widely used that they cause the retirement of large numbers of older conventional vehicles. Adding an efficient, zero pollution vehicle to the fleet does not by itself decrease oil consumption and pollution; getting rid of a polluting, low-miles-per-gallon car does. Regulatory pressures can help stimulate BEV and HEV use and the retirement of obsolete vehicles, but major adoption of electrics requires that they compete well in the minds of users when judged by cost, safety, performance, convenience, comfort, and style.

EVs have a good chance of being the cost winners in the future as new technologies receive high priority and as the vehicles increasingly move toward large-scale production. Electronic systems continually go down in price, and reliability can be high and maintenance low. Such a revolution in car design will take a major investment that would pay for itself over and over in dollars and in energy and emission goals.

Some Tentative Conclusions

My cloudy crystal ball gives the following picture:

• In the short run, BEVs fit certain limited market niches based on emissions considerations.

Paul MacCready

- In the intermediate run, the fuel efficiency obtainable with HEVs is likely to stimulate their development and use in most market niches, the amount of penetration depending on the evolution of the technology (especially emissions and performance), costs, and regulations. Gasoline will certainly be the primary chemical fuel, but the high efficiency of the vehicles will stimulate the use of alternatives which yield less CO_2, are not imported, or are renewable.

- In the long run, if (as I suspect) the above pressures on HEV development produce really inexpensive and extremely low emissions vehicles, HEVs could dominate the car and van market—and probably that of light trucks and city buses. With the improved batteries that are anticipated, there will also be wide application of BEVs (cars and low-speed subcars) for certain local travel purposes.

The success of HEVs in the intermediate and long runs depends strongly on one new technology: a low-cost, high-power "surge" unit—battery, supercapacitor, flywheel, or equivalent. Improved energy capacity of batteries (the primary goal of the Advanced Battery Consortium) will be helpful in the intermediate and long runs for BEVs, but will always fall so short of the energy available from chemical fuel used in regular ICE cars or HEVs that I feel surge unit technology should be getting more R&D emphasis than it has in the past. For BEVs, development will continue on rapid battery exchange and quick replacement chemicals that generate electricity.

The development of the intermediate and long term vehicles should be the responsibility of everyone: manufacturers, energy industry, customers individually, and customers in concert via government sponsorship support, regulation, and incentives. Dramatic changes to meet aggressive goals for societally desirable personal transportation will only be achieved if we realize we are all in this together.

When in 1991 I forced myself to set a goal for our transportation energy situation for 2005, I came up with Figure 1. Reaching this goal will require the development and wide application of revolutionary technology; it will not be reached by cautious, evolutionary steps. Other people would

> **"The development of the intermediate and long term vehicles should be the responsibility of everyone. ...Dramatic changes to meet aggressive goals for societally desirable personal transportation will only be achieved if we realize we are all in this together."**

choose the timing and the quantities differently, but would have to cover the same items. Almost any reasonable choice of details would also define a goal that dictates strong emphasis on new technology.

All in all, technology that now exists or can be reasonably predicted can provide us with increasingly wonderful and economical cars. More fundamental challenges arise from traffic and parking, associated with population growth (now 250,000 more people on earth every day) and the growth of cities and wealth. New car technology must be integrated with substitutes for our conventional use of cars: telecommuting, mass transit, car pools, alternative work habits and home/office relationships, bicycle lanes, etc. But in 2005 there will certainly be more cars than in 1992. If enough of them are electric, we may achieve the 2005 goal. 🚗

Paul MacCready

"Reaching this goal will require the development and wide application of revolutionary technology; it will not be reached by cautious, evolutionary steps. Other people would choose the timing and the quantities differently, but would have to cover the same items."

Tom Cackette is the chief deputy executive director of the California Air Resources Board, the powerful environmental agency in California that enacted the mandates for zero-emission vehicles. This transcript is from an interview held on September 23, 1993, seven months before CARB ruled to keep the mandates intact.

TOM CACKETTE
Explaining California's Continuum

Our strategy has been to reduce, to the maximum extent feasible, both stationary- and mobile-source emissions of hydrocarbons (HC) and oxides of nitrogen (NO_x), because these pollutants in the atmosphere form ozone and fine particles called "PM-10." These air pollutants cause the greatest health damage to people that live in the urban areas of California.

This strategy has been quite successful, especially over the past ten years. For example, the highest ozone concentrations in Los Angeles have been reduced by 25%, and overall population exposure has decreased by 50%. In the late 1970s, the San Francisco Bay area experienced ozone pollution nearly twice the allowable federal limits. This year we have applied to USEPA (United States Environmental Protection Agency) for a designation of "attainment" of the ozone-ambient-air-quality standard. Our strategy of reducing emissions of both HC and NO_x has been the reason for these successes, and we are continuing to pursue this strategy for the future.

Despite these successes, the future holds a great challenge. Emissions of HC and NO_x need to be reduced by another 70-80% in Los Angeles in order to meet clean air standards for ozone and PM-10. To do this will require the use of new emission control technologies for all of the major sources of emissions. It will also require efforts to accelerate the turnover of the vehicle fleet to use these new technologies. But even this is not enough to bring Los Angeles into compliance with federal clean air laws. A significant number of vehicles with zero emissions are needed to reduce air pollution to the low levels needed to protect public health.

Why EVs are Attractive to California

With these facts in mind, our board adopted the low-emission vehicle (LEV) and zero-emission vehicle (ZEV) standards in 1990. ZEVs were particularly attractive to us for a number of reasons. First, they have no tailpipe emissions nor fuel-evaporative emissions. Unlike conventional cars whose emissions increase with age, malmaintenance, and tampering with control devices, ZEVs will never emit pollutants.

The second reason ZEVs were attractive relates to California's electricity generating system, which is one of the cleanest in the world. The state has successfully diversified its power generation system to rely heavily on nonpolluting sources such as hydro, wind, nuclear, and geothermal. For those fossil-fueled generating plants located within our urban areas, they all use natural gas and low-emission technology, and by the turn of the century most will have installed emission aftertreatment to further control NO_x by another 70%. The result is the urban emissions which result from charging an electric vehicle will be 50 to 100 times less than the tailpipe and evaporative emissions from the cleanest internal combustion engine vehicle, the ultralow-emission ULEV.

Finally, while ZEVs alone are not sufficient for attaining clean air standards in California (further emission reductions from stationary sources and consumer products are also needed), they are a necessary technology in our clean air formula. And ironically, the severity of the air pollution problem in Los Angeles, with its solution at least 15 years away, means we have the time to develop new technologies such as ZEVs and see them commercialized and contributing to the cleanup of our air. This may not be true for some other areas of the country that are striving to meet clean air standards by the turn of the century.

Today there is a lot of talk about how EVs will help us convert defense industries to commercial enterprises and help improve the California economy. Were these issues considered when the mandates were debated?

In 1990, when the LEV/ZEV regulations were adopted by our Board, California's economy was much stronger and the impact of the defense phase-down had not been felt to the degree it has today. Our focus was almost exclusively on achieving cleaner, healthier air for our citizens. We knew we needed to get started on a transition to a cleaner, more efficient electric transportation system, and we recognized that Californians had the experience and technologies to contribute to this goal. After all, the first truly advanced electric vehicle, the GM Impact, was designed by a California firm, and used a motor designed and built in California. But the opportunities for developing a new EV-technology-based industry in California was not foremost in our mind or the

Tom Cackette

"Our focus was almost exclusively on achieving cleaner, healthier air for our citizens. We knew we needed to get started on a transition to a cleaner, more efficient electric transportation system, and we recognized that Californians had the experience and technologies to contribute to this goal."

Tom Cackette

"It appears there was a pent-up demand to start developing electric vehicles and advanced batteries that was unleashed by the ZEV requirement."

minds of our board when the regulations were adopted in 1990.

That has changed today. California firms are on the cutting edge of advanced transportation technologies. CALSTART and Project California, two groups that are coordinating California's efforts to develop an advanced transportation technology industry, project tens of thousands of new jobs for our state resulting from the ZEV requirement.

We see similar activity worldwide, and it started soon after the ZEV requirement was adopted. It appears there was a pent-up demand to start developing electric vehicles and advanced batteries that was unleashed by the ZEV requirement. We saw formation of the U.S. Advanced Battery Consortium and its commitment to spend hundreds of millions of dollars to develop a better battery to support the California program. We immediately saw prototypes being put out for trials, even by companies who were not subject to our program until 2003. Interest in improving the efficiency of vehicles began to grow, including use of advanced manufacturing and material technologies, and our country began talking of becoming a world leader in these important, job-creating areas. I refer again to the GM Impact as an example. It's extremely aerodynamic and uses efficient components, including an aluminum structure. With an internal combustion engine, it would get upwards of 100 miles per gallon. With an electric drive, it is even more efficient.

The biggest remaining technological challenge is development of a better battery for the electric vehicle. Advancements in the lead acid battery are continuing, and longer-life, more efficient batteries are starting to roll off prototype production lines for evaluation in the latest-generation vehicles. We are also excited about several advanced-technology batteries, such as the nickel metal hydride technology of Ovonics Battery, and the sodium nickel chloride battery from AEG, which we believe will be ready by 1998 or soon thereafter. These batteries promise a range for a small four-passenger car of at least 150 miles, and lifetimes approaching ten years. Operating costs will be no more than a comparable gasoline vehicle, once production volumes increase to allow economies of scale to be realized. Other, even-more-efficient and cost-effective batteries are being developed for early in the next century.

Are you considering refinements in the regulation that will give hybrid EVs some partial emission credit?

Tom Cackette

Our regulations already allow hybrids EVs partial credit. For example, if you build a hybrid which has a 60-mile range on batteries, it will count as though two ULEVs were produced. However, it does not count toward the requirement that 2% of new vehicles produced have zero emissions, since hybrids do have emissions.

At our biennial review of implementation of the LEV/ZEV program, our board heard testimony that hybrids should be allowed at least partial credit toward the ZEV requirement. Proponents of hybrids argued that HEVs would be used for more trips because of a lack of range constraints and because most of the travel would still be on battery power. Of course, on the flip side, with a hybrid you can choose not to charge the batteries from the electricity grid, instead relying on the vehicle's internal combustion engine to generate the electricity. Unless this internal combustion engine is very clean, as clean as the power plant emissions from electricity generation, using a hybrid in this manner will have higher emissions than a ZEV. Our board has asked us to provide a better assessment of the factors that influence the emissions from a HEV, and return to them with recommendations in the near future.

The Hybrid and Electric Vehicle Act of 1976 largely failed in its efforts to commercialize EVs. What makes you think EVs have a better chance of succeeding today?

I'm not familiar with that legislation, but there are several things different today, compared to 1976, that favor a successful introduction of EVs. The first is the battery developments I discussed previously. The second is the developments in vehicle efficiency. Together these developments led to the ability to produce a high-performance vehicle with a range that far exceeds the needs of 90% of the public, at least as regards a second car.

But you must have looked at more than technology. What about consumer lifestyles and other important factors?

There is tremendous public interest in EVs. Research shows that range is the biggest concern of the potential purchaser, and a range of 100 to 125 miles is desired. With the

Tom Cackette

new battery and vehicle technologies we discussed earlier, this range requirement can be met. The research also shows most people do not need this much range in a commuting or second car, which is the niche we think the initial EVs will fill. Data show most commutes are less than 40 miles round trip and that the vast majority of commuters' needs would be met with an 80-mile range. Our research shows that when car buyers better understand their actual driving needs, demand for EVs increases sharply. You have to recognize that much of the current consumer understanding of electric vehicles relates to golf cars and some the EV "boxes" produced in the 1970s. That is not what we are talking about for 1998. We are convinced the vehicle manufacturers will produce desirable EVs, and the public will want to buy them.

JOHN DABELS
The Consumer's Viewpoint

People are frustrated with gasoline stations. They're the dirty parts of maintaining ICE cars, but probably the most important reason is that people are beginning to feel guilty about the emissions of an internal combustion engine vehicle. I'm not saying they're willing to change behavior yet. They're just beginning to feel guilty. As that becomes much more prevalent, and as children begin to talk about it more, as they are, then this guilt starts to spread. I suppose you could equate that to recycling a few years ago, when not many people were doing it, they were talking about it, but not much action was taken. Then with peer pressure, and really through children, they began to change. In our neighborhood, we sort of look outside and see who's put out their recycling bin. It went from virtually no one two years ago to everyone now.

It's persisting. I don't think EVs are going to be a fad this time if product comes along at the same rate that I think it will. You've got the atmosphere where people are willing to become aware of it. But I don't know that buyers are ready to pay a big premium because of that.

A System in Need of Change

You know they do an annual fraud survey. This week, auto dealerships were number one again. Have you ever run across anybody that's said, "Wow, I want to go out and buy a new car"? The buying process and service issues are the pain. The car itself is fun. So most of the pain is eliminated with electric vehicles. I'm not sure that people fully appreciate that concept, but we mail-order everything else. I used to get custom-made shirts. I'd call Lands' End. It's a lot easier. You call them on a Monday, go on a trip and they're here when you get back. They last and they're reasonably inexpensive. I think we can begin to order cars in the future by telephone. The home shopping networks just got consolidated, so they are either going to take off or fall flat. EVs are also evolving. Not every segment will adopt them, but as people become much more used to technology, use will increase. The EV is more akin to a giant personal computer on wheels than it is to a regular automobile.

John Dabels is the former director of marketing for Buick and later director of market development for electric vehicles at General Motors. He is now vice president of sales, marketing and government affairs at U.S. Electricar. This transcript is from an interview held on July 24, 1993, nine months before Mr. Dabels joined U.S. Electricar.

"I don't think EVs are going to be a fad this time if product comes along at the same rate that I think it will."

John Dabels

Sensible Markets for EVs

I think for short trips, EVs make more sense than ICE vehicles. Sun City, Florida, is a good example. That's a real confined area. But if you look at the absolute emissions, most occur within the first three or four miles. Once you get an ICE car warmed-up, it's a very efficient way to propel somebody. But in those three- to four-mile trips, you're spewing out emissions. So a small electric car, a stationcar for in town, makes a lot of sense.

The other market here is for kids. Most of their running around is between friends and downtown. The trips are short distances. Besides, with an EV they can only go so far.

I think there is a huge potential with fleets. Probably bigger, initially, than the retail customer. Fleets are defined as rental companies, the local florist. R.L. Polk defines it as ten vehicles or more, but I'd group together business uses. A lot of those have regular-duty cycles and predictable range. It's the perfect application for an EV. I'm just looking out my den window. A Sears truck went by. Chances are, that Sears truck doesn't travel more than 10 to 15 miles between stops and then goes back to Sears.

Will fleets want to use EVs because they're cheaper?

That's one reason. They're easier to maintain. There are also some government mandates and incentives. I deal a lot with fleet managers of the utilities. Maintenance is a big issue. So if there's a way to get reduced maintenance and downtime, then they're all for it. With the right kind of design, the maintenance will be minimal for EVs.

If you look at electric vehicles versus an ICE vehicle, we've been building engine blocks for 90 years now and we've got them refined just about as far as we're going to get them. If you look at computer technology, and how that's dropped in price, I think the price of the electronic components can only go down, and down dramatically. Again, this is looking at EVs as giant computers on wheels.

If EVs are giant computers on wheels, is the traditional auto industry ready to market a product like this? If EVs are this technical, how will the auto industry deal with an even-faster-changing product line and the problems with residual value and standards this might create?

"We've been building engine blocks for 90 years now and we've got them refined just about as far as we're going to get them. If you look at computer technology, and how that's dropped in price, I think the price of the electronic components can only go down, and down dramatically."

Was IBM good at personal computers? Were the Swiss good at electronic watches? Even though they invented it, did they end up marketing it? It took them ten years before they figured out how to market it. So, my guess is no. Honda, of all the auto companies, probably has the best chance. They've been renegades for a long time. I think General Motors, Ford, and to a lesser extent Chrysler, because they've been through a lot, are pretty nimble these days, but traditional thinking has a way of creeping in on Detroit. I think there will be some guys wildly successful before the Big Three figure out what to do.

One of the things I did before I left Buick to go to the electric vehicle program at GM was to write a paper and present it to our general manager. I said our future was electric. It's consistent with everything Buick stands for, even though Buick is big and all that other stuff. I said it's American, it's comfortable, quiet, and the only thing different is the propulsion system. The argument was rejected.

You said EVs are American. Does America have a competitive advantage in EVs from a marketing perspective?

People want America to win. It is amazing how tolerant companies are of the ineptness of the American auto industry. A number of people that I run into on both coasts and in the heartland say they want to buy American. Detroit has stonewalled these utilities in terms of EVs. Chrysler is charging $120,000 for a car that doesn't even work. Yet these guys say, "Yep, we want to buy American." So there is that true desire to see America succeed.

America also has a worldwide lead in software and pretty much the same in computer hardware. So if you say we're good at new technologies, and I think we are, then there's a great chance there to win.

You don't seem skeptical at all.

I'm new to the EV game, but everyone is. I guess, relative to everyone else, I'm old at it. I've been involved almost three years now. The Ray Geddeses [Ray Geddes is president of Unique Mobility, a Colorado electric-drivetrain company] of the world have been around a long time. But there aren't many of those guys. Unfortunately, many of those guys take an engineering approach, rather than a consumer approach.

John Dabels

"Was IBM good at personal computers? Were the Swiss good at electronic watches? Even though they invented it, did they end up marketing it? It took them ten years before they figured out how to market it."

John Dabels

Today, if you're not a car guy you don't qualify in the auto industry. You've got to be a car engineer. Those guys aren't even good innovators, in the marketing terms of innovators, early adopters, and so forth. These guys hit such a small, narrow market that they literally forget about the consumer. They'll come out with engineering ideas that are not well executed. They have a great disdain for marketing people.

You mentioned that an outsider may be wildly successful before the Big Three are.

Yes, like a Daihatsu or a Honda. It will probably still be a car-related company or a tie-in. Some of these little guys that can move quickly and whose lives are totally reliant on ICEs have a great advantage here.

Can someone completely outside the auto industry, like a Swatch, make an impact?

As a tie-in. This may be my automotive background coming out, but it is very, very difficult to produce a high-quality car. There are certain things you need to understand about that. A lot of people have tried and found it more difficult than they realized. Swatch, maybe in conjunction with a VW, a Honda, a Daihatsu, or someone like that who understands the base technology and uses the Swatch marketing technique and positioning, would be a great formula.

Do you think the Swatch formula, where a watch is a fashion statement first and a watch second, is applicable to vehicles?

When I first got on the EV program, I designed my concept of the car. Because it is a space-frame assembly, you can literally change the style of the car in your garage. The rest you can order and ship by Federal Express or UPS. From the front edge of the windshield to the beginning of the trunk, you can't change that. But you can have a very rakish hood because you have no engine. What you have is a box to drive motors and you have small motors driving the wheels. If you decided you wanted a sedan-style vehicle for some reason or you got tired of this car, you could order new fenders and screw them on yourself. If you bang a fender, you can order another and screw it on. With certain kinds of materials and paints, you can apply electric current and change color. This will be more advanced in about ten years' time.

You asked about a fashion statement. Those are the kinds of things that this technology allows you to do. The size of the engine in ICE cars inhibits the amount of rake in front, so you can only get so low in terms of making a swoopy-looking front. You don't have that problem at all with an EV. You could build an ICE car on a space frame. The Fiero was there. So that's not totally new technology. There's a lot of things you can't do with an ICE car that a personal computer-type of car allows you to do.

I've heard you talk about how utilities used to hand out light bulbs in their early days and how something similar could be done with EVs. You've talked about constituency building. What role might traditionally noncore auto companies play in the marketing of EVs?

Utilities are trying to build awareness and consideration for the product. They don't want to get into the sale or service of EVs. I'm working with 13 utilities now that have formed a network across the country. They're working together to build EV showrooms. They're going to have material and a car in it. They have information panels and video tapes in the showroom. They're building awareness about EVs, having people begin to ask the question, "Is the EV for me?" and demonstrating that EVs are real, maybe by doing ride-drive programs. They might run contests so people can figure out the number of miles they actually travel. So utilities are very involved with a lot of promoting, buying cars, and helping the automakers.

Rental car companies are a fantastic way to test a product. For the past six of seven years, the auto companies have been taking new production vehicles to rental companies. It's a good way to get early market feedback and give you a higher profile right away. You get the most demanding people renting cars. A lot of businesspeople rent cars. I know a lot of people who go out and rent cars before they buy them. Rental companies are willing to help here, also. It's good advertising for them.

Component suppliers are coming forward with product ideas—motors, controllers, things like that—and doing some engineering that the auto industry has traditionally done. So

John Dabels

"There's a partnership here. Not all the expertise resides in the automakers."

there's a partnership here. Not all the expertise resides in the automakers. Once they get up and running and innovation gets a lot more standard, that relationship may change.

People I'm talking to are breaking off into two camps. The one camp says that EVs can't compete with ICE vehicles, that the technology isn't ready. The other side says that given the fact the EVs can't compete directly with ICE vehicles, don't pretend they can: find a market where they are competitive in their own right.

I agree with the latter. Very much so. We're talking about a new form of transportation, this personal computer on wheels. That is how I view it. My reference points are not the internal combustion engine. I say: What do I need to do and does this vehicle do what I want? For this new form of transportation, the answer is yes. I want low maintenance. I want to be able to charge at home. I don't want any emissions and I want to have fun. It does all those things. In fact, it does them better. Not necessarily better than my Miata, but it does them better than a lot of ICE cars. That was my view at GM and it was not a popular one. 🚗

Part II
SUPERSTRUCTURES:
The Strategy of Incremental Change

The U.S. auto industry is at a crossroads and must decide on a superstructure strategy—one of incremental, go-it-alone change—or a leapfrog strategy—one of dramatic, strategic-alliance-driven change. Each approach involves high-stakes poker as evidenced by a few case studies depicted in this part.

The Call for Change

There is a clear call from academics, consumers, and business and government leaders for fundamental, dramatic change in our transportation systems. Their hope is that these changes will minimize the many serious problems of motor vehicle use: traffic congestion, air pollution, disposal of automotive parts, traffic deaths and injuries, the hostile environment for pedestrians and bicyclists, urban stratification, the immobility of the disadvantaged, energy dependence, and global warming. In response to these goals, one leader, Elmer Johnson, in his report *Avoiding the Collision of Cities and Cars*, proposes three broad strategies:* near-term, social and people habit-changing strategies; mid-term strategies for changing the vehicle, its fuels, and infrastructure, which are markets that emerge from education; and long-term strategies for changing mobility structures and land-use patterns, which are made possible by new products. The remainder of this book will concentrate on industry's response** to what Mr. Johnson identifies as mid-term strategies: marketlike incentives to encourage the development and introduction of alternative-fuel vehicles. Specifically, we will concentrate on how the established auto industry's organizational structure responds to incentives and mandates calling for EVs, widely considered the toughest of alternative-fuel vehicles to commercialize.

One iconoclastic energy expert, Amory Lovins, described in Part I how enabling a fundamental shift away from oil-based transportation to electric-based transportation means facing up to "formidable obstacles, both culturally within the auto industry and institutionally in the marketplace." Mr. Lovins suggests that "the time for incrementalism is over" because a

*Johnson, Elmer W., *Avoiding the Collision of Cities and Cars: Urban Transportation Policy for the Twenty-first Century.* American Academy of Arts and Sciences, Chicago, IL, 1993.

**Executives from General Motors Corporation and Chrysler Corporation are represented in this book. Ford Motor Company was contacted on numerous occasions but refused to cooperate. Japanese and European automakers were researched and contacted; however, this book focuses on the situation for American companies and therefore does not make specific reference to foreign automakers. The reader should note, though, that the superstructures strategy seems to be practiced, to varying extents, by all of the world's large automakers.

large set of leapfrog achievements are required to successfully design, build, and market electric-drivetrain automobiles.

While the auto industry recognizes the need for innovative, "leapfrog" changes, the industry also knows that such action comes with problems. Therefore, when fundamental changes in the automobile are deemed necessary, automakers naturally react by attempting to buffer change. This is because their product, the automobile, is a complex mixture of technology, capital, market acceptance, and legal obligations, which are outside the automakers' sphere of control. Automakers have learned to approach change carefully to limit risk. In fact, as we will hear, the automakers' organizations are fundamentally designed to resist change. The rise and fall of diesel cars in the United States serves as a good case in point, helping us to understand the automakers' position.

Detroit's Diesel Car Lesson: A Quick Change Hurts

In the United States, sales of diesel vehicles increased from less than 1% of new motor vehicle sales in 1976 to approximately 6% nationwide and 9% in California in 1981. Sales then collapsed to less than 1% by 1985.* Kenneth Kurani and Daniel Sperling, in their analysis *Rise and Fall of Diesel Cars: A Consumer Choice Analysis*, conclude that government and fuel industry shortcomings, combined with poorly performing products, led to the fall of the diesel car. Poor regulation on the part of government and fuel suppliers resulted in a series of fluctuations in diesel fuel prices relative to gasoline prices. As a result, the diesel vehicle demonstrated "little or no economic advantage" compared to gasoline vehicles, and this resulted in a "failure of the market to move beyond a core of buyers."

Negative publicity about diesel cars also stymied their growth. Since the vehicle market is heavily dependent on repeat purchases, poor publicity, whether factual or not, dramatically affects vehicle sales. Although many automakers offered high-quality, reliable diesel products, negative publicity was focused on General Motors and its trouble-plagued, 5.7-liter engine. This publicity, while perhaps not representative of the diesel products market as a whole, served to dissuade the larger car-owning public from purchasing diesel vehicles.

*Kurani, Kenneth S., Daniel Sperling, *Rise and Fall of Diesel Cars: A Consumer Choice Analysis*, University of California-Davis, Davis, CA, 1988.

There were also user problems with diesels. As a new product in the hands of consumers accustomed to gasoline vehicles, diesel cars had "user friendliness problems, such as start procedure peculiarities." It is this hypersensitivity to problems with new products that leads automakers to look for a buffer, something that will buy them time to beta test the technical qualifications and market acceptability of their products and support structures before risking a consumer-level effort, ready for scrutiny by the wider public.

The development and failings of diesel auto in the U.S. is a good example of how auto companies fail to exploit new product opportunities because of their one-sided, technology-based approach to product launch. Detroit automakers invested large amounts of time and capital developing diesel products, but little economic gain resulted.

This case study also demonstrates the large liability exposure automakers face when bringing a new product to market.* This liability may steer automakers away from methods of launch that do not give them an adequate amount of control over the launch process and may also lead to a "not invented here" syndrome.

*In 1994, General Motors recalled thousands of natural gas pick-up trucks, due to safety-related problems, which added to the large automakers' sensitivity to product liability.

Detroit's Japanese Invasion Lessons: A Leapfrog Saves

In the 1980s, American automakers called for import restrictions on Japanese automakers. The U.S. government gave the industry some protection. This protectionism allowed the American automakers time to change their business systems and practices to lean systems so they could compete with Japanese automakers. But protecting markets didn't necessarily work. Rather than continue to fight the enemy, General Motors decided to join the enemy: Toyota.

At the third United States–Japan Automotive Industry Conference at the University of Michigan in March 1989, General Motors' then-director of worldwide planning, Jack Smith, said in support of a new manufacturing arrangement with Toyota: "We could wait until we develop additional new small cars of our own, of course—American cars. Built in an American way. By American workers. To American standards. To appeal to American tastes and preferences. But in today's competitive marketplace, such a car would have to be more than just a new car. It would have to be built in a new way. A way that makes use of new product technology and manufac-

*Keller, Maryann, *Rude Awakening: The Rise, Fall, and Struggle for Recovery of General Motors,* William Morrow and Company, Inc., New York, NY, 1989, pp. 92-93.

**Flink, James J., *The Automobile Age,* MIT Press, Cambridge, MA, 1988

turing efficiency to help narrow our current cost disadvantages. And, as you know, that takes time."* Further, then-chairman of General Motors, Roger Smith, suggested that, while it was true that GM was relying on the Japanese, this was only a temporary measure until GM could cut costs, boost efficiency, and develop the necessary quality to *go it alone.* GM's partnership with Toyota was a survival tactic that kept U.S. jobs and preserved U.S. technology. For Toyota, an alliance with GM provided access to a protected market.

The Basis of a Superstructure Strategy

The world has gone through an Automobile Age where the automobile and its powerful industry were a prime shaper of lifestyles and economies.** The auto industry has been a world economic leader and, indeed, a world shaper. Historically then, the auto industry has been a basis for change in our world. It is from this viewpoint that the auto industry has developed its approach to business.

A "superstructure" is a structure that rests upon another, usually larger structure (the foundation or base). We can apply the definition of a superstructure to the auto industry's strategy for introducing change in their products and business. In the auto industry, new products emerge from existing, usually in-house or understood capabilities and partnerships. This is a "build from the base" approach to business that is fundamentally focused on technological solutions, rather than market and business solutions. In a mature market, the supplier (i.e., automaker) drives the market. Technology is predominantly used to get market share. (In a new market, the marketplace drives the market and the fastest supplier wins more market share.)

Developing new products in the auto industry usually requires the leadership of the largest player in the organizational structure, the automaker, to manage a new product program. Smaller players, while they may bring new technology to the product development process, are basically considered suppliers or contractors to the process. Other, equally large and powerful "partners" are generally considered only short-term participants as automakers attempt to bring the partner's skills in-house over time (as GM attempted with Toyota).

The Auto Industry's Struggling Partnerships

The auto industry's superstructure strategy assumes that success requires a product-change process based on incremental change to existing products, rather than a reliance on a steady stream of fundamental innovations, as is more characteristic of the computer industry. The industry holds this assumption because its experience has shown that successful introduction of new vehicle technologies and fuels is highly vulnerable to changing economic conditions and public perceptions. However, auto industry leaders also acknowledge that sustained success in today's technology-based economies and consumer-driven markets calls for the regular introduction of innovative products and practices.

Based on their superstructures approach to business, the automakers aim to bring the new products and practices in-house and adapt them to their in-house structures, in effect to aim to "go it alone." This process of "naturalization" nurtures an incremental approach to business. With this business theory presumably in mind, Roger Smith was able to bring into GM new technologies and initiate dramatic new business programs including: the manufacturing joint venture with Toyota, known as New United Motor Manufacturing, Inc., or "NUMMI"; the acquisition of Hughes and Electronic Data Systems (EDS); the Saturn car project; and, of prime importance for this book, the Impact electric vehicle production program. By these bold, drastic technical innovation programs, Roger Smith intended to reestablish GM as the worldwide industry leader.

The naturalization of each of these programs has grown into a qualified success. The Hughes and EDS businesses are good examples of the type of success a superstructures strategy nurtures. At the time of GM's acquisition of both of these companies, analysts generally considered the companies to be mature and chided GM for grossly overpaying for them. Yet, within a few short years, GM had more than tripled the revenues and profits of the allegedly mature EDS. And ten years later, in 1994, EDS had a market value six times the amount that GM paid for it and ten times its original revenues and profits. Similarly, GM bought Hughes just before the defense industry collapsed. Under GM management, Hughes has actually increased its defense profits and has become the only

*Drucker, Peter F., "The Theory of the Business," *Harvard Business Review*, September-October 1994.

big defense contractor to move successfully into large-scale nondefense work.*

Despite these successes, the parent, GM, has not exhibited similar success in its core business—automobiles. Why is this? The answer may lie in the theory or strategy of business that is applied. A superstructure strategy seems to work in businesses whose success is based on the proliferation of established technology (such as EDS's expansion of computer services), or in a business being rationalized and fine-tuned (such as Hughes).

However, in recent history the auto industry has been in a constant state of fundamental change, be it in technology, practices, or customer desires. It is in this kind of business environment that a superstructure performs poorly. We see this result in the Saturn Corporation, a separate, wholly owned subsidiary of General Motors that was designed to leapfrog (or at least catch up to) the Japanese automakers in small car production.

Saturn was launched in 1982 after a GM internal study revealed that the Japanese could build a small car for $2000 under GM's cost. Saturn, a $4.5 billion project, was the largest commitment of resources of any GM experimental project.** To attain its ambitious goals, Saturn focused mainly on in-house practices and supplier/customer relations.

**Flink, James J., *The Automobile Age*, MIT Press, Cambridge, MA, 1988, p. 402.

Today Saturn produces a good car, provides a good service, and offers a competitive price. The project also brought General Motors many benefits. Saturn gave GM a halo during troubled times and brought new practices that competitors now copy: a nationwide "no dicker, no hassle" sales network; close dealer-factory relations to keep retailers peaceful during rocky roll-outs; a new standard for product recalls. In addition, Saturn proved that GM could engineer cars with fewer parts, using fewer suppliers while demanding more from them.

Yet overall, a Saturn is not seen as an innovative car. It remains just one among several, equally good, small cars offered by a host of auto companies, including other divisions of GM. For a high price, Saturn brought GM another incremental step, but not a "leapfrog."

†Peters, Tom, *Thriving on Chaos*, Alfred A. Knopf, New York, NY, 1988.

In the end, GM was trapped by its own inertia. Tom Peters, in his book *Thriving on Chaos*, suggested four root causes for this almost inevitable loss of innovativeness in bigger firms:†

(1) slowness to move to test new ideas; (2) a bias toward the conceptual rather than application; (3) a concomitant overdependence on ponderous planning systems; and (4) "Big Projects." The Saturn project fits the bill; worse yet is the U.S. Government's "Supercars" program, which we will discuss later. The future is simply too unknowable for this approach, and, frankly, the auto industry does not lead the economy or lifestyles of people any longer. Therefore, the auto industry's reliance on the success of big programs that take years to complete is fundamentally flawed.

GM is recognized as one of the world's premier performers when it comes to successful acquisitions. EDS and Hughes offer two good examples of GM's skills. However, GM's base—its automobile business—remains sluggish and only incrementally changed. Had EDS or Hughes bought GM, the story may have been altogether different, for this would have changed the power base of GM's business.

While a superstructure strategy may not work well in the current auto industry, it is even less likely to succeed when the industry change is even more radical, as is the case with EVs. To be successful, EVs call for the growth of brand-new products and practices. In essence, this means building a new business. This calls for a strategy based on growth and change, rather than a strategy based on incremental improvements to an established system.

To hear firsthand how the superstructure style reacts to the opportunities to commercialize electric vehicles, we now turn to several leaders in government and the auto industry. We'll start with the leaders of the "Partnership for a New Generation of Vehicles" program, also called the "Supercars" program or the "Clean Cars Initiative."

The Supercars Program

It is said that government in the United States is representative of the people. Today the government, after analyzing the problems of the American transportation system, economy, and environment, has stepped in and said that cleaner, less-oil-reliant modes of transportation are a desired end. This has resulted in mandates and regulations designed to reshape the auto industry. But as we'll hear, most of these government programs are actually designed to buffer the auto industry from the process of change; in the following case of Supercars, the government program may have been designed to help sideline EV mandates.

In September 1993, the Clinton administration, and more specifically Vice President Al Gore, initiated a new program called "Partnership for A New Generation of Vehicles" (a.k.a. "Supercars"). This program is billed as a "historic partnership forged with automakers" that "aims for threefold increase in fuel efficiency in as soon as ten years." (It is commonly assumed that these goals will be met through the incorporation of electric drivetrains and lightweight material, i.e., EVs.) The program will be managed for the Detroit automakers by USCAR, the lobbying and technical research consortium of the Big Three.

This massive partnership combines the Big Three Detroit automakers (GM, Ford, and Chrysler) with the U.S. Government's resources, including the Departments of Commerce, Defense, Energy, and Transportation, and with the Environmental Protection Agency and NASA. The research goals are scheduled to be met before 2005 and include:

(1) Manufacturing: Pursue advances in manufacturing techniques that can reduce production costs and product development times for all car and truck production.

(2) Near-term advances: Pursue advances in vehicles that can lead to increases in the efficiency of standard vehicle designs, reduce emissions, and improve safety.

(3) Long-term, next-generation vehicle: Develop a revolutionary new class of efficient, environmentally friendly vehicles to meet consumers' needs for safety, quality, performance, utility, and affordability and achieve up to three times the fuel efficiency of today's comparable vehicles.

Speaking at the White House during the announcement of this program, Jack Smith, president and CEO of General Motors, described this program as a "revolution" where government "partnership and cooperation, rather than the old command-and-control adversarial approach of the past," represents a "fresh, new, and very welcome way of coordinating and focusing our national efforts to achieve the technological breakthroughs that can make regulatory interventions irrelevant and make our industry even more competitive internationally."

In the area of electric and alternative-fuel vehicles, it is clear that the auto industry thinks large, cooperative efforts with the government "offer the best chance of achieving the necessary breakthroughs," as Harold Poling, CEO of Ford Motor Company, said. Yet, throughout all of the celebration at the announcement of this program, the auto industry executives exhibited loyalty to their paradigm of incremental change and offered no real assurances of achieving revolutionary results. Robert Eaton, CEO of Chrysler Corporation, summarized this line of thinking best when he said: "Our progress will be measured in inches, not in miles." Also, the reader should recognize that the Supercars program is focused on technology, not a reinventing of the industry or its practices.

We now turn to conversations with three leaders in the Supercars program: Dr. Mary Good, undersecretary of commerce; Henry Kelly, Assistant Director for Technology for President Clinton; and Don Walkowicz, executive director of USCAR.

MARY GOOD
Supergoals

Dr. Mary Good is the U.S. undersecretary of commerce and the program manager for the Supercars program. This transcript is from an interview held on November 29, 1993.

In government programs in the past, there have been initiatives to provide improved battery systems. There have been some initiatives to build electric prototypes. There have been some initiatives to build hybrid prototypes. But there has not been a program with a goal set for a vehicle that actually has three times the fuel efficiency and appropriate pollution control, and in which we're asking people not to pre-judge what that vehicle will be. The issue is performance. This program gives you an opportunity to look at the technology that will move the vehicle to that performance. Other initiatives, like the California regulations, provide performance specifications that apply to a pure electric vehicle only.

There are two things that have changed. First, you have an agreement that says these are really the goals, that the goal really is three times the fuel efficiency. That's a real number. Second, you have a goal that the pollution issue will meet all the standards at that point, and you also have an agreement that it will be met, not by a prototype vehicle, but by a vehicle that is manufacturable and has all of the safety features, all of the performance features, and so forth, that the current automobile has.

The Partnership for New Generation Vehicle (PNGV) is an interagency program, which means we will have access to technology across the government, and across companies. Those companies bring with them their suppliers. So it's going to have that group of people that has the resources to actually accomplish those goals. In addition, the program will be designed so that we end up with a project orientation, which means that the pieces we bring together are all focused on this same goal, rather than the pieces focusing on each piece. The goal is to end up with a system that works. The automobile is the system.

"The goal is to end up with a system that works. The automobile is the system."

We're trying not to pre-judge the technology up front, because we want to push it to the limit that we can. In other words, we don't want to build a hybrid vehicle that has the technology that exists at this moment. We want to push the technology to the extent that it will be possible in ten years. In the meantime, we will obviously have some prototypes available, because you learn from them. That's where you learn where the weaknesses are.

The Keys To Success

We need all of the agencies to work together toward a common goal, rather than working toward an agency goal. We need the car companies all working toward this ten-year goal and not spending all of their energies on incremental improvements to the systems they have. It's going to require a lot of coordination and a lot of dedication.

How is this program helping to promote change in the auto industry?

In the sense that we are researching and developing a vehicle that will replace the internal combustion engine vehicle. That's change.

The goal is to build a vehicle in essentially the same price range as you have today, with inflation thrown in. With many of the components that will go into what we want to do, the technology has made a lot of strides in the last 10 or 15 years. So the issue is whether, with those technologies, you can get there and whether you can improve those that need improving. For example, take fuel cells: an enormous amount of improvement has been made on those in the last ten years. There are still some technical hurdles, and the question, both in terms of technical issues and system applications, will be whether fuel cells will be the winners when this thing is all done. 🚗

Mary Good

"We need the car companies all working toward this ten-year goal and not spending all of their energies on incremental improvements to the systems they have."

HENRY KELLY
Put Your Supershoulder into It—Right Now!

Henry Kelly is Assistant Director for Technology in the Office of Science and Technology Policy (OSTP) for President Clinton's administration, the office that helped initiate the Supercars program. The transcript is from an interview held on October 19, 1993.

The vice president and the president talked to the auto industry, even before the inauguration, about working together in a variety of different areas. The issue of technology was one of the things mentioned early on, so in its technology plan, the administration laid out a series of new initiatives for making science technology a key part of their economic program. Particularly, focusing on civilian technology development. One of the initiatives laid out was a program in advanced automobile technology. We have been working on it ever since.

The whole idea was to try to find a way of using government resources to help the U.S. automobile industry restore its technological leadership. From the very beginning, that has been a goal talked about by both the heads of the Big Three and the administration. So it's really a joint idea and has been pursued by both the high management in the industry and by the administration in parallel. And, of course, the announcement was a parallel announcement.

Our office is a coordinating organization in technology and science policy, so we helped the vice president put together an interagency team to negotiate the agreement with the industry.

It's publicized as an agreement with the Big Three and the government. Is there any opportunity for smaller companies to get involved in this also?

"We want to get good ideas from all over the place, including smaller companies."

We want to get good ideas from all over the place, including smaller companies. Particularly, a lot of the good ideas for vehicle technology have come from suppliers and the auto companies recognize that. We're just trying to have the most efficient way of doing that.

It's a program to decrease the time between concept and product on the road. First, we have a lot of work that we are trying to focus on in that area: everything from advanced design tools to better sensors and control systems where the actual production tooling takes place. Second is a series of incremental changes to the existing system that will be consistent with the long-term goal: things like lightweight mate-

Henry Kelly

rials, better air dynamics, better tires, better crash-test modeling, things like this. And the third is the moon shot, which is a long-term, ambitious goal to get up to a factor-three increase in fuel economy while meeting all the other objectives of tailpipe emissions, safety, affordability, and marketability. The technical capability of doing that has never been at question. But can you achieve the goal with an affordable, practical vehicle? It's a tough challenge.

No one would have said we would go forward with it unless we thought it was at least possible to do it. And, plainly, the three industry leaders have looked to do it. We have a good—at least a reasonable—chance of accomplishment.

It's basically the same problem we have had with electric cars all along. The technology is there, but the economics don't play out quite right. At the end of the day you have to come up with a product that people want to buy. That's not something the government knows how to do. It's something the people in the business of marketing vehicles to real markets have got to find: what a marketable vehicle will look like. And the government can bring a lot of technology and a lot of sophisticated people and design tools to the table. But the government doesn't sell mass-produced products.

This is truly a technical agreement. There's nothing in this agreement about regulations, one way or the other. The hope is that we get an attractive technology—that's both affordable and inherently clean—that we can put on the table, making it possible to meet the extremely ambitious environmental and other objectives—without the need for conventional regulation. That's not to say that any regulatory authority we have had has been given up in this agreement, but we hope we can, at least, make sure the regulations are not standing in the way of where we want to go.

> "The government can bring a lot of technology and a lot of sophisticated people and design tools to the table. But the government doesn't sell mass-produced products."

Just One Part of the Puzzle: Technical Innovation

Personal vehicles are overwhelmingly and intricately associated with American business and lifestyle. It's very difficult to see how their share of overall transportation is going to be shrinking significantly in the foreseeable future. In fact, just keeping mass transit at a competent share of personal movement is going to be a major challenge here. The Department of Transportation is trying to put together a new, broad vision of transportation. But clearly, you want to push things

Henry Kelly

that will reduce travel by personal vehicles by trying to make other options more attractive. You want to pursue alternative fuels and you want to pursue better vehicles, which is what this is all about. So it's one part of the puzzle.

The CAFE battle has been going on for years and years. And the air pollution problem we are facing is a huge one. If you look into the future, you have a 3% growth in the VMT (vehicle miles traveled) per year. It's actually been higher in the past few years. Plus, you have greater population. Plus, you have a greater shift to light trucks and vans. So you are moving sharply in the direction of increased fuel consumption. And you have to have a 3% per year improvement—that's average vehicle on the street, not just new vehicles—just to break even, let alone try to reduce anything. That's a huge problem. You really need something beyond just incremental.

> "That's not to say incremental changes aren't worthwhile. But you really need some kind of new paradigm to get you off this curve. And that's not something you do through regulations. Not to say that no regulatory activity is ever going to be relevant, but if you are going after the kind of improvement that we are contemplating here, you really do need a technical change here."

Now, that's not to say incremental changes aren't worthwhile. But you really need some kind of new paradigm to get you off this curve. And that's not something you do through regulations. Not to say that no regulatory activity is ever going to be relevant, but if you are going after the kind of improvement that we are contemplating here, you really do need a technical change here.

Moving a Supertanker

Suppose we had this Supercar in our hands right now. It would take three or four years to get it into production. Realistically, you would have to retool a plant. It takes more than three years to get a new standard automobile in production. That's your first production car. Now, it might take as much as ten years to make it the average production car, to have it dominate all new production. And then cars last 13 years. So it takes at least another decade. You are talking 20-25 years to get a radically new technology to be the dominant vehicle on the road, even if you had it in hand right now. You are really securing a supertanker here. Even if you have your rudder full-left, it will take a long time to turn this thing. If you are going to make a serious assault on a problem that's 20 or 30 years away, you've got to start really putting your shoulder to this thing, right now. 🚗

Don Walkowicz
Agreeing to Work Together

Our CEO, Jack Smith, says if the Apollo program was a moon shot, this program is like going to the stars, only because in the Apollo program, cost was not an object. Affordability is a big objective in creating a vehicle that will meet all of these requirements and yet still meet the needs of the consumer, including emissions, safety, performance, utility, reliability, and so forth. We're not only going to produce just a couple of them—like going to the moon; we're going to produce millions of them. We have to know how to produce them in vast quantities. They have to be highly reliable.

We're going beyond the Apollo program. The Apollo program, while there were some technical challenges, was done primarily with known technologies. We have a lot of challenges that go beyond that. There are things—get lower emissions, triple fuel economy, or whatever—that we don't know how to do. It's going to take some technology breakthroughs.

In the Apollo program, the government took all the resources together to work on this immense task. That's the comparison. We're taking the national labs and other federal labs and, instead of having them off in separate corners working on different technologies, we're going to define the needs of the program.

Understanding the Task at Hand

Bob Frosh, a retired vice president of General Motors Research, used to tell a story about when he was director of NASA and he tried to enlist the spirit of the task at hand—"to get to the moon." He'd walk into the vehicle assembly building down in Florida. He asked some people what their job was. A janitor might say, "My job is to sweep the floor," lacking understanding of what the task was. But after a while, that janitor would say, "My job is to help us get to the moon." At this point, Bob said he thought he had it done.

So if we can get all the national labs and all the people that are going to get assigned to automotive technology to understand what the vehicle performance requirements are and to say that our task is to produce a vehicle that gets up to three

Don Walkowicz is the Executive Director of USCAR, the Detroit Big Three automakers' research and development consortium. This transcript is from an interview held on October 20, 1993.

Don Walkowicz

times the fuel economy—as opposed to saying our task is to develop a material that is twice as light and stronger than today's material—then I think we'll have achieved it. To me, that's what the comparison to the Apollo program is: a shared goal and objective.

USCAR's Limited Role in EVs

Until this point, the only thing USCAR has been involved in on EVs is—number one—USABC, the United States Advanced Battery Consortium, to create a better battery. And then, under the USCAR umbrella, we announced our intention to have the three companies get together to do something beyond batteries on the electric vehicle, including research, development, systems, and components, and perhaps even some joint production—all the way through the possibility of joint production of a vehicle.

Chrysler pulled out of these talks. Are they falling apart?

Well, that's what the press says. Chrysler hasn't pulled out of anything, yet. They are up to their ears in the USABC, and that's still going strong. The talks continue on electric vehicles, but no agreement has been reached and it's very possible that Chrysler will not participate to the full extent that GM and Ford will. We really don't know where that's going to go. And in the middle of all of this, I guess everybody's worried: "Hey, by the way, is anybody going to buy these things?"

Government-Industry Cooperation

I think there has been a shift in the attitude in working together with the government to solve problems of mutual need. The government wants us to clean up the environment, and so do we. And instead of passing a new regulation that we don't have the foggiest idea how we can meet, the government now recognizes that it's got some technology resources that it can contribute to the solution. They also recognize, as the result of the number of meetings that we had with them, that the auto industry's resources are not unlimited.

A key point somebody brought up recently is that, in the last five years, the industry has invested, in capital, $73 billion. Industry profits over those five years are $125 billion. Something is missing in that equation. You finance your capi-

> "A key point somebody brought up recently is that, in the last five years, the industry has invested, in capital, $73 billion. Industry profits over those five years are $125 billion. Something is missing in that equation."

Don Walkowicz

tal expansion, or your plant modernization, or whatever, out of your profits. We ain't making them, so where's that money coming from? It's coming out of cash on the end, borrowing money, and everything else that you can do to leverage the business.

Are you more active in the Supercars program than you are with, say, electric vehicle collaborations?
Yes. But understand that electric vehicles, in terms of where we go from here in technology development, are going to be very much a part of the Supercars program as well. When you start talking technologies, to do a hybrid electric you have to develop an electric vehicle. The hybrid electric depends on all the electric car components, it's just that you don't need quite so many batteries because you have an auxiliary power supply.

Supercars is a partnership between USCAR, which is the industry umbrella organization, and the government. Everything the industry does on Supercars will be in the name of USCAR. So we're now setting up a new group within the USCAR to be the primary motivators, doers, contacts, whatever, on the Supercars program.

There are 12 consortia under USCAR. There are only seven of us on the staff at USCAR. Our job here is to facilitate, monitor, and promote—these are the terms we use. We keep the things running. We're like a planning department for USCAR. The Big Three's folks go away, without any technical guidance from us, and do their job. We help them out, perhaps, administratively and with some strategic direction, but technically, they get the job done. For the most part, I would say there are no central research and development facilities. Everything happens back at GM, Ford, and Chrysler.

How does it work when stark rivals find themselves collaborating?
Initially, you have to convince people that it's okay to talk to each other. You know the old culture that says, "We're better than them, and we've got a competitive advantage, and we don't want to give away our secrets." When you get down to what we call the pre-competitive stuff—or "pre-Phase Zero," if you will—you pretty much find out we're working on

Don Walkowicz

shared goals and objectives that primarily relate to the environment and safety: the underlying, enabling technologies. We find out that we're pretty much in the same boat. Because of the interaction and dependence on suppliers, universities, and even national labs, you find out that we're all about in the same ballpark. When you get people in the same room comparing notes, you find out that maybe we didn't have so much that they don't have, or at least that they don't know about.

It's synergy that we're getting. We're taking three groups that were doing the same things separately, putting them together and getting more done, better, quicker.

"It's synergy that we're getting. We're taking three groups that were doing the same things separately, putting them together and getting more done, better, quicker."

Agreeing When to Work Together

When we sit down and talk about what we can and can't do cooperatively, there are a number of criteria we look at. Number one, it does have to be pre-competitive or noncompetitive. That's usually pretty obvious and our lawyers help us to insure that our assessment is correct. Then we say that everybody has to already be working on it; it has to be on our prioritized project list at all three companies. It's not like we're going to go away and find out that some company in Florida has some new solar energy technology and we're going to sign-up to work with them and find out how to use it. We already know that we're working on solving the OBD-II* problem for 1998 California emissions, and we're all spinning our wheels on it and evaluating all these different technologies. Like I said, it's already on all of our prioritized project lists, so let's work together on it.

The third thing is that the three VPs agree that we want to cooperate on it. Now sometimes, for business reasons or for legitimate competitive reasons, we don't do that. And you know, in terms of the electric car, the thing that's made it difficult is that it's not just technologies; not everybody has agreed on what the business case is for electric cars. If it were clear and simple—"Yep, we got to do electric cars in order to solve this problem"—then there wouldn't be any question at all. But it's not clear to everybody that electric cars are the way to go. And if we do, what's the best way to get there from here?

*"On-Board Diagnostic-II," an engine emissions system that monitors engine performance and helps to diagnose problems that may cause the engine to run less than optimally. OBD-II is required on all ICE vehicles by the late 1990s.

The National Cooperative Research Act came out in 1984. What role did this play in the formation of USCAR?

Don Walkowicz

The government finally woke up and said, "Gee, our overseas folks are doing this. Maybe we ought to encourage it in the U.S." That opened the door, but it took until 1988, at least, for the U.S. auto industry to come up with its first research and development consortium, which was the automotive composites consortium.

Initially, I don't think everybody jumped up and started looking for things to cooperate on just because an act was passed in 1984. But it took awhile to come to this agreement and understanding so that we could work cooperatively on pre-competitive technologies and still be very competitive in the marketplace. Each time you come up with a new consortium, you have to convince a new and different group of people that that's the case.

Becoming a Stronger Lobbying Force

The formation of USCAR was strictly a case of the Big Three wanting to get together, recognizing that business was changing, the global marketplace was changing, the resource availability was altogether different, and yet global competitive pressures were greater. What can we do to work together? And it was just those three companies that got together and made USCAR happen. The initial focus was not on the government at all.

The initial focus was just on the Big Three and how we get some synergy out of working together. Now the focus has flip-flopped. Now that we're working together, we have to figure out how to take maximum advantage out of what the government has to offer.

The government is nervous about giving an unfair competitive advantage to one manufacturer, yet they are very comfortable in making the U.S. auto industry competitive globally.

What about smaller companies?

Smaller companies are just like they used to be in terms of serving the needs of GM, Ford, or Chrysler, independently. If there were a supplier or a smaller company that was providing technology, services, or products to any one of the Big

> "The government is nervous about giving an unfair competitive advantage to one manufacturer, yet they are very comfortable in making the U.S. auto industry competitive globally."

Don Walkowicz

Three—if that happens to be an area that we're working on cooperatively—they just continue to function, but now it's in an area where all three automakers are working together.

Has USCAR seen any tangible success in terms of products or technologies?

In terms of tangible success in products or technologies, trying to trace what comes out of a research facility into a product—a vehicle—is tough to do. You can do it, but it usually starts as an R&D effort, then becomes an engineering effort, and finally a production process. There has already been one patent that's been issued to the composites consortium for creating polymer composite components for vehicle structures.

The battery consortium is doing a lot to get vendors to live up to their performance requirements, hoping to get, someday, a new battery.

The environmental research consortium has done a lot of work cooperatively with the EPA, in terms of assessing environmental situations and impact. They're working cooperatively with EPA and CARB in order to come up with new procedures and instrumentation, so that when we get to 1998, we'll actually have something to test the cars with to see if they actually do or don't meet the new regulations, because that equipment doesn't exist today.

Most importantly, it's like any research and development: as long as you have the people getting the job done and they're working together, a lot of knowledge is created, which integrates itself immediately into the workplace. The key is recognizing where you have shared goals and objectives. Once you recognize and understand that, I think it's very easy to put the engineers and scientists to work together.

With regard to pure electric vehicles, what might we expect out of USCAR in the next six months?

Hopefully, there will be an announcement about what the three companies will, or will not, do together. I don't know what that's going to be. Certainly as a result of the new partnership, there will be cooperative research and development, including work with the government on electric vehicle technologies as they apply to hybrid-electric vehicles. 🚘

That announcement has not come. But in March 1993, General Motors announced a manufacturing joint venture with Ovonics, one of the lead developers in USABC. In response to GM's action, Chrysler's spokesman, Chris Preuss, responded by asking, "What does this mean to the other USABC participants and our access to Ovonics' nickel metal hydride technology?"

Then, in September 1994, Tim Adams, director of Chrysler's PNGV program (Chrysler's part of Supercars), speaking at the Cobo Conference and Exhibition Center in Detroit, said, "When we complete that research portfolio, it will be imperative that we include suppliers as a 'third partner' in this effort to build a pre-production prototype by 2004.... The U.S. auto companies don't have the full range of expertise required to support this [Supercars] program."

The Strategic Response of an Established Industry

We have heard how the auto industry and the government have agreed that the path to a new, clean mode of personal transportation is to partner with each other to bring about *technological* change in the auto industry. Through the following conversations, we will hear how the auto industry wants technological change, but is not necessarily ready to accept innovative changes in their structure and approach to business. This leaves us to wonder: Even if the Supercars program succeeds in developing new technologies, will the auto industry be willing and able to bring the new technology to market, embracing the organizational changes that will also be required?

To help us answer this question, we now turn to conversations with leaders from the auto industry. The first perspective is that of Jean Mallebay-Vacqueur, from whom we'll hear why Chrysler does not consider the EV product design process to be significantly different from that of Chrysler's existing automobiles. Rather, says Mr. Mallebay-Vacqueur, it is merely a matter of designing a new power train and incorporating this into the existing vehicle platform design process. Perhaps this confidence is evidence of Chrysler's success in melting their superstructures over the last few years. As it happens, Chrysler is leading the American auto industry in its use of suppliers for technology and in bringing new capabilities to the table. Indeed, it has been suggested that Chrysler is on its way toward becoming a *lean enterprise**, but for now we'll continue to classify them as a practitioner of the superstructure strategy, for Mr. Mallebay-Vacqueur's comments do not necessarily represent a new theory of business for the auto industry.

*Womack, James, P., Daniel T. Jones, "From Lean Production to the Lean Enterprise," *Harvard Business Review*, March-April 1994.

JEAN MALLEBAY-VACQUEUR
Coiled and Ready to Strike

When you speak about the zero-emission vehicle, how do you define the vehicle? Because the gasoline vehicle has come a long way. If you define zero-emission as it is defined by California—as zero tailpipe emissions—the only way we know how to do that is with a battery-powered electric vehicle. As soon as we say that, we define the problem as, of course, the battery. It is the biggest problem because of energy density.

In the last century, people have moved away from the lead acid battery at maybe 10 to 18 watt-hours per pound. Today, we have the nickel cadmium or nickel iron batteries at 22 to 25 watt-hours per pound. Even if we take the most advanced batteries we know of, we will only get maybe 80 to 100 watt-hours per pound. But compare that with the energy density of gasoline—at 15,000 watt-hours per pound. If you factor in the low energy efficiency of a gasoline vehicle, maybe you are looking at 5000 watt-hours per pound. Compare that to the energy efficiency of the electric vehicle, which may be 80%, and you are really comparing 5000 watt-hours per pound with 50 watt-hours per pound. How do you deal with this gap?

When you have to compete on the market, the gap is defined by price versus utility. The biggest technical problem of EVs is the battery, and it has implications on the technical side and on the cost side, because it affects range. I think the vehicle cost issue can be met, but if you have a range issue, that's a big challenge. And all these technologies are evolving, maybe evolving forever.

But at Chrysler, we aren't waiting, we're working on a battery. We don't really see how the fundamentals are going to change, but nevertheless, we try to display a can-do attitude.

Research to ZEV to Commercialization

If not for the California 1998 ZEV requirements, we would not do a commercialization effort, but we would have a research effort. We started our research effort before any standard or any rules. The rules came after we were already in our program.

Jean Mallebay-Vacqueur at the time of this interview was general manager, special products engineering, at Chrysler Corporation. This transcript is from an interview held on July 29, 1993.

"I think the vehicle cost issue can be met, but if you have a range issue, that's a big challenge. And all these technologies are evolving, maybe evolving forever."

Jean Mallebay-
Vacqueur

We could almost say that, in a certain manner, the rules have not affected Chrysler because, before the rules existed, the media were not watching very closely, so we have carved our own niche, little by little. But the rules have certainly dragged a lot of people into our little pie. The rules have not made the pie much bigger, if you consider the market for EVs—a free market—which is minuscule. But the rules have dragged in everybody: Ford, GM, and off-shore competitors.

First, we produced the first fully certified electric cars and we brought them to market. So they are very expensive, but they meet all the U.S. regulations. They are competitive because there is nothing else to meet these kinds of regulations. It is like in racing: people can do a lot of different cars, a lot of prototypes, and they can fix them one way or another. When you have to meet all the regulations, it becomes a very different challenge. The electric minivan that we are producing right now meets all of these regulations.

Do EVs offer Chrysler any strategic advantages that are significant?

I don't believe so, because most of the other research that is being made—like lightweight materials or aerodynamics—we are doing anyway. Right now, the EV is more research and engineering, with very little applications, that we know of, to other aspects of our car business. But you never know what you may stumble on.

Because one of the problems is the battery, its energy storage capabilities, and the aspect of charging, lately we have developed a charging system. We have worked with a company on a fast charger that recharges a battery in under 20 minutes. When you do that sort of work, you learn a lot about batteries, and we may have different applications in an electric vehicle for this kind of equipment. So when you research, you never know what you may find and what it may be used for. Sometimes you have no return and sometimes you have a return which was unexpected.

Battery/Propulsion First, then Vehicle Integration

Because of the regulations that are being kicked around, everybody is trying to focus in a timely manner. The way we position ourselves, we really look at the battery and we look at the propulsion system. You have to realize that these two are going together. We don't focus that much on the car, because at Chrysler, we believe that we can engineer a car in two years. There will always be time to integrate the propulsion system within a car when we have designed it. Today, we are defining the propulsion system, which is on the one side the power train and the power electronics; the other side is the battery. All of that has to work together.

Right now, we have a DC system where we use a GE motor and a GE controller and we use batteries which are about 180 volts to start and they cut off at 140 volts. This system is very efficient doing what it is supposed to do and it's air-cooled. It has a lot of advantages. But it has slow acceleration. It has good range, it gives us 80 miles. But the acceleration is not comparable to an ICE vehicle.

We have another program of research with Westinghouse where we have another motor and controller which is AC. Alternating current systems have to have higher voltage, so we moved it up to a 324-volt battery that cuts off at 260 volts. For AC, we basically have a higher voltage battery. The problem is that the kind of chemistry which is good for power is not always good for energy. Look at the lead acid batteries: they are very good for power—that's why they are used for a starter battery—but they are not very good for energy. Now look at nickel batteries: they are good at energy but they are not very good at power.

Therefore, the battery creates an additional uncertainty about technology and investment. The battery issue is not only how to develop the battery, but the business side: what kind of market are you going to target? How much are you going to invest, knowing that you always have this enormous risk that whatever you do is going to be made obsolete the following six months by a new chemistry? So, as a business proposal for the battery supplier, it is an enormous challenge. That is why the government of the United States and the Big Three and the utility industry are working with the battery industry to help them face this challenge.

What If We Can't Make an EV?

If the California ZEV requirements stay, we will do what we can. If they don't, we will do what we want. Let me say that if the battery technology becomes practical, then we may be able to do a car. Then the mandates will stay. If nothing

*Jean Mallebay-
Vacqueur*

happens on the battery technology front, then nobody will be able to make a car, and it will then be for the people who wrote the mandate to step up to their responsibility. I don't believe they don't face reality. I believe they have a problem and they're trying to answer that problem. I'm not complaining about that. It is the cheapest way for them to achieve their goal. They are just dealing with a different problem than ours. Maybe if you were in their shoes you would try to do the same thing. It's just different people trying to achieve different things, and we try to find some kind of common ground. They can't keep the mandate if nobody succeeds at making it happen.

If the only issue is to clean the air in downtown Los Angeles, maybe it would be a cheaper economic proposal to take the old cars off the road. If there is a wider agenda, like defense conversion and so on, obviously taking the polluting cars off the road is not going to solve this kind of question. I don't know what the total agenda of California is, and it is for the Californians to decide what is the right thing to do. They may decide to levy a tax to transfer the cost of this effort to all consumers by getting all the prices of cars in phase—to subsidize the electric vehicle.

There are some interesting things going on to lower cost. One is the Big Three's "Team USA" effort to come up with common systems. I've also seen a proposal from CAL-START to have a "Running Chassis" program. Is this approach possible? Could we have a common EV chassis across the industry?

I have a difficult time understanding how the CALSTART proposal could work. In their minds, the way you differentiate a car is just through body shape and styling. But styling and appearance is only one aspect of differentiation and competition. Another one would be the behavior of the car, the handling of the car. Another one would be the trade-off made between power, range, and a lot of other, different ways to set up the parameters of a car. That is a wide part of competition. If everybody has the same chassis, then everybody is taxed the same for the EV credit rights. So I don't believe the CALSTART proposal of a chassis for everybody is very viable, but I may be wrong. What it may do is demonstrate different components that can then be integrated by other manufacturers, and that was their initial intent. Remember, the marketing side is what got GM into trouble for a while. They had cars that people could not differentiate.

But CALSTART? I'm Not Sure

But speaking of the CALSTART proposal, I do not know if it will work or not. If it becomes a platform to supply electric vehicle components, it will be one strategy; if it is to become a competitor, that is a different kind of strategy. And that is for CALSTART to decide. Do they want to cooperate by offering components or do they want to compete by integrating the components? So far I'm not really sure what they want to do. At a point in time, they will have to face the question of doing cars. Either it is a car that is not asked to meet the U.S. regulations—then you can do one set of things—or it is a car that will meet all U.S. regulations—then you have an enormous barrier to entry, which is to engineer a car.

It's a very expensive process if you have to meet all U.S. regulations. You may then find out you need to have a lot of know-how accumulated, and much more than just technical and capital issues. In my mind, it is much more a matter of know-how and integrating all that needs to be known in order to make a car—from crashworthiness to all the little regulations which may affect the shape of the buttons.

On the supplier side, is there anything different going on with EVs compared to ICE vehicles?

Different from what the industry used to do? Probably. Different from what we do at Chrysler in general and for special projects? No, not specifically. The way we approach this problem with our suppliers for electric vehicles is exactly the same way we used suppliers for the Viper. If you look at cars that we are producing in the mainstream today, or cars that we are engineering today, we have the same philosophy or the same approach of a partnership. We see what they can bring to the party and everybody brings what they know how to do. At Chrysler, we bring the skills to integrate the program and to understand and express in technical terms the customer's requirements. We are an integrator.

The suppliers are doing more engineering for our cars than they may do for cars of our competition, especially if you look at GM which is much more integrated. They buy only

Jean Mallebay-Vacqueur

"At Chrysler, we bring the skills to integrate the program and to understand and express in technical terms the customer's requirements. We are an integrator."

Jean Mallebay-Vacqueur

20% of their components when we buy 80% of our components. This general philosophy of Chrysler reflects on the specific application of electric vehicle and that's why, for the program's electronic propulsion system, we rely on GE and Westinghouse and different battery groups for low and high voltage. We also have suppliers for specific components like air conditioning or power steering. We are teaming up with other suppliers, but it is really not that much different from what we do on the Viper.

We May Be Getting There

I would say that in Detroit there is a better spirit of cooperation today than there used to be. That really started with the 1984 National Research Act, which allowed cooperation on subjects of national interest. People may be frustrated because it took almost ten years to start to see concrete results in the industry. We must realize that it is an industry which is extremely competitive and the culture is, most of the time, the biggest hurdle to overcome.

> "We must realize that it is an industry which is extremely competitive and the culture is, most of the time, the biggest hurdle to overcome."

There are a lot of consortia that have been signed up. The USABC, which is a consortium between the Big Three and electric utilities, is just one of a lot of consortia which have been established under the umbrella of USCAR. Some of the consortia are for composites, or for the way we process data, or for safety...we have a lot of different consortia. I believe whether we have an electric vehicle or not, we are demonstrating the ability to work together because it's a way to increase the competitiveness of America compared to offshore competitors. Whether we have electric vehicles or not will not affect this spirit of cooperation. Either there will be cooperation or there will not, but EVs do not affect this, because there are a lot of subjects for cooperation.

Dummies in Detroit? Not!

There is this idea in different industries—such as the aerospace industry—that they do such advanced research, they are ahead, and that Detroit is actually a bunch of dummies. Maybe they are right, but maybe they are not. Some of these things that happen don't happen because of Detroit, they just happen because of an effect of things we are asked to do.

I will give you an example. If you design a system for the defense industry or the aerospace industry, you know who is going to be the pilot, who is going to operate the system. You know this person will be trained on how to use the system. You also know there will be a lot of maintenance of the system, so you will design it one way. You also know that cost is not an issue, because price is not an issue, because the government and the taxpayer will pay. You really operate at cost-plus. So if you need to have high reliability, you can produce one thousand components and you can pick out the one that works.

But if you are in the auto industry, you are in a battleground of competition where people are never obliged to buy a car. When they buy a car, they are never obliged to buy a new car, and when they buy a new car they are never obliged to buy yours. So when you design a car and you do not know who is going to drive it, you know that the car will not have, most of the time, elementary maintenance. You know the car will be used for almost 100,000 miles. The technical and marketing data, which pressures your cost down, forces you to achieve quality on-line, which means you need to have quality embedded in the process.

You cannot sort-out quality. You need to have the quality directly out of the line. As soon as you say that, you are really playing a different game. Whether the investment is a human asset or an industrial base, the numbers that add up are staggering. On the other hand, the product cost is very low and people believe wrongly that they will create millions of jobs in this business. Even if you imagine that you have one million vehicles per year (which is an extremely far reach), the power train of a car today may have $2000 worth of components. That gives you the cost target for an electric vehicle, should the EV be competitive with the ICE car. So if you have a $2000 cost target for power train including battery, and you have a million vehicles, you have a $2 billion industry. You don't get a $100 billion industry; you have a $2 billion industry, which is small. It's cheap compared to a new aircraft program.

Are EVs creating a new industry, or are they a change in the direction of the existing industry?

It is just part of the normal business. It is not business as usual, but our own business is no longer business as usual.

Jean Mallebay-Vacqueur

"But if you are in the auto industry, you are in a battle ground of competition where people are never obliged to buy a car. When they buy a car, they are never obliged to buy a new car, and when they buy a new car they are never obliged to buy yours. So when you design a car and you do not know who is going to drive it, you know that the car will not have, most of the time, elementary maintenance."

*Jean Mallebay-
Vacqueur*

You could ask me if the Viper is part of the same industry or not. Viper is another car and you need to engineer it the same way. It has as many parts as another car. It takes the same kind of attention and the same kind of drive. If you look at electric vehicles, it will be the same. You will need to have the same competencies and skills to make a good decision, and you will know only after the fact if you are right or wrong.

From the service side, besides the battery, we may expect the maintenance of electric cars will be lower than the maintenance of an ICE vehicle today. But now ICEs are a moving target.

If you look at the way the cars are marketed—if you buy the car and you don't need to see anybody anymore—the car may be marketed in a different way, because you may not need the same kind of continuous relationship with a dealer that you needed in the past when you bought a car. You developed a relationship with a dealer because of all the maintenance you had to do. If you get a car with little maintenance, the personal relationship between the dealer network and the customer may be less important.

So there may be room for new distribution methods?

Yes, maybe. They are being considered. This is not to say there will be new methods, just to say there may. We started with a minivan and we tried to team up with our dealers in the same way that we team up with our customers or our suppliers. Obviously, our cars are sold through our dealer network. Because, even if it is a small number of cars sold, it shows that we try to stick with our friends. It also allows us to test the issues that we may have to face. We could have distributed the car directly, but when you ship a car to a dealer you learn about the requirements needed to take care of the car. It obliges you to map the whole system. When we were faced with this choice—of going separate or going inside the system—we elected to go inside the system, because we believe our system is going to improve every day. Marketing is not the biggest issue; it is going to be something for us to decide later. Right now, our focus is the battery and the integration of the car, the battery, and the propulsion system.

> **"When we were faced with this choice—of going separate or going inside the system—we elected to go inside the system, because we believe our system is going to improve every day."**

Nobody—and No Car—Is Perfect

At the beginning with our approach, we tried to team up with the dealers and with the customers. That is why we went with this system, which allows us to select partners and equipment. We compromised with these people to tell them that the product will not be perfect, because we all know that you do not start with the perfect product. We don't even know what is the perfect product, because we have a lot of different customers and they all have different requirements. A new product is not perfect for everybody. But having given this product to them, we have given them the opportunity to criticize it and give us early design direction for our next generation. Our dealers and customers are providing very good direction. What we have committed to is a "superservice." What I mean by that is that when they call, we are there. Because we have few cars, we react faster than some other people may react. 🚗

Jean Mallebay-Vacqueur

"We compromised with these people to tell them that the product will not be perfect, because we all know that you do not start with the perfect product. We don't even know what is the perfect product, because we have a lot of different customers and they all have different requirements. A new product is not perfect for everybody."

GARY DICKINSON
A Real Question Mark for Automakers

Gary Dickinson is president and CEO of Delco Electronics Corporation. Prior to that, he headed GM's technical research staff where several electric and hybrid-electric concept cars were developed under his watch. This transcript is from an interview held on November 30, 1993.

All three manufacturers have come out with public statements that the electric car is not a good competitor to the gasoline engine and it will be very, very difficult to sell. You're going to have to subsidize it.

Then, around the world, and particularly in this country, there are a lot of manufacturers that are jumping on the bandwagon, maybe for some public affairs, public relations, or image reasons.

Short-term Business, Long-term Prospects

We have activity going on to convert buses, trucks, vans, and passenger cars into electric. And there are small companies cropping up around the world. There is a frenzy around the conversion business, and that may be a good short-term opportunity. We're very active in that at Delco Electronics with the Hughes Powertrain Control Systems operation in Torrance, California. Other units of GM are also in that business in some form. But it's not clear what the long-term prospects are. Once you get the first couple thousand vehicles converted, how many more will be in demand? How much production volume can you really expect from that? Probably not much.

So here we are in a situation where electric vehicles are emotionally interesting and they are fun to drive. There is no question that you can produce an electric vehicle that would be fun to drive. But once you get through the first, cult buyers—the people who buy electric cars because they want to be seen in one, or because they really feel so strongly about the environment that they want to have one in their garage—once you get by that limited market, there is a question about how much investment you can really afford to make. So, at the same time we're trying to respond to a real business interest and opportunity among customers, we're not quite sure how much investment to make in engineering, development, and capital, because we're not certain about the sustainability of this electric car demand at the moment.

We Don't Know What Will Happen with EVs

Gary Dickinson

Electric cars are a fascinating case story, and it is not very clear where the final chapter will lead us. How does this come out? Is it another frenzy like in the early 1900s, when there were electric cars and then they got beat out by the gasoline car? Or is it another frenzy like 1974, when General Motors said we're going to produce one (Ken Baker and the technical staffs were involved in that one), found it to be too expensive, and the range was limited, so you really couldn't imagine a large market for it? And then a new frenzy around our experience with the Impact and what we learned in managing vehicle energy to make it much more practical. Now we can talk about a 120-mile range, but it's still a fairly expensive package of aluminum lightweight construction and 800 pounds of batteries. And still a limited amount of range.

If I've got a gallon of gasoline about one foot in diameter, it can take my Buick Park Avenue 30 miles. But I have to put 800 pounds of high-tech lead acid batteries in this electric car in order to get the same amount of energy. That's very tough competition.

If we consider hybrid cars and their reliance on an electric power train—for example, the "Supercars" initiative announced by the Clinton administration—what are some of the mechanisms that we can use to bring about such a large change in the auto industry, to get three times the miles per gallon of gasoline in cars?

We know how to do that. We did that. The wall of my office (with its large pictures of GM's Impact, the HX-3 hybrid, the Ultralite, and the Sunraycer) is sort of the wall of fame for the technical staffs over the past four years. The Ultralite was designed to get 100 miles per gallon at 55 miles per hour and yet make a practical four-passenger automobile that was fun to drive. We did that. In fact, it's a very sporty car. It's not a slug. It does 0 to 60 miles per hour in eight seconds and has obviously superior range, because you can get 100 miles per gallon on a 55-mile-per-hour cruise. And it has 100 other technical features, but it's made out of carbon fiber composite, aluminum, and magnesium in order to keep the weight down. It's ultralight. While we can achieve the fuel economy targets, we still have a vehicle that isn't practical because of the expense of the materials that went into achieving those targets.

How We've Learned

First we did the Sunraycer, and we learned a lot about managing energy. Then Howard Wilson at Hughes said, "You know, we can make an electric car." "No, Howard, no." "Yeah, yeah, we can think about it and sort of scope this out from a systems perspective." Howard is now retired, but he was the vice president of engineering for Hughes.

So he came with this proposition that we ought to do an electric car. A few of us scoffed at the idea and then sort of got caught up in it. We ended up doing the Impact. Of course, it was so enormously successful that Roger Smith (former CEO of GM) pushed it out in front of the press and said, "We are going to produce this car." In the equivalent of pointing to the center field wall, he said, "I'm going to announce in April our production plans." And he did. So we sort of got caught up in a ground swell. We designed a two-passenger vehicle and we called it the Impact on sort of a whim—it was one of those overnight naming challenges—and found ourselves moving toward a production program.

We said, in this series going from the Sunraycer to the Impact, "What's wrong with this picture? What's the next in the series?" Remember when you do the SAT exams, they say, "Here are three numbers. What's the next one that continues this series of numbers?" Maybe it's cubes, or maybe it's plus-two, or whatever. You have to figure out what the next number is.

Well, we did these two cars and then we said, "What's the next car in the series?" The problem we had with either one of these, particularly the electric vehicle, was range. So we said, "Let's do a hybrid."

We had a project going at the GM Tech Center at the time called the Freedom project, which was quite secret at that time. Essentially, it was a hybrid project promoted by me, but not many others. So we did a research project for doing a hybrid vehicle. The Freedom is kind of a story in itself. But we decided to go public and put a hybrid vehicle together that combined the best of the electric vehicle technologies with an internal combustion engine, which provided on-board power.

"We did these two cars and then we said, 'What's the next car in the series?' The problem we had with either one of these, particularly the electric vehicle, was range. So we said, 'Let's do a hybrid.'"

The hybrid—the HX-3—was done for the Detroit auto show in January 1991. We took our own internal technology, combined what we knew about electric vehicle technologies with a lightweight, low-cost, internal combustion engine, and we put together the HX-3. And we were actually the first ones to ever drive a vehicle in Cobo Hall. We drove out in the electric vehicle and then drove out with the hybrid (the hybrid can operate on electric only.) So we operated it, we drove people around the show on a simulated track, we gave people rides. This vehicle, the hybrid, combined a gasoline engine, which gives you the range you need, but it has two power trains on-board.

Gary Dickinson

Sunraycer, Impact, HX-3...Next?

So that was 1991. Then we said, "What are we going to do for the next series?" What would be the missing element that would follow this series of three vehicles? The Achilles' heel in any one of those vehicles is range. Four of us stood in the center of the design staff studio scoping this out, trying to make a plan for the Detroit Auto Show for 1992. (This was me and the three vice presidents: Chuck Jordan, who was vice president of the design staff at the time and is now retired; Don Runkle, who was vice president of advanced engineering and is now general manager of Saginaw Steering Gear; and Bob Frosh, who was vice president in charge of research and is now retired.) The four of us stood in the center of the studio and said, "Let's go with light weight. Let's go with 'ultralight.'" We made that decision right on the spot. Design staff had already done some mock-ups of a particularly exciting-looking vehicle. We said, "Let's build that," and we set some targets for how we were going to build it. So we did the Ultralite to get the 100-mile-per-gallon car.

You developed the Impact, and CARB passed zero-emission legislation a year later. Then you did the HX-3. Finally, you developed the Ultralite, and the Clinton Administration recently announced the Supercars initiative. Is there any turning back?

No. I think these are excellent research projects. I think the transition from this research level—or advanced engineering level—to production is a longer step than people realize. We were developing the series so that we could continue to work

Gary Dickinson

**"We were develop-
ing the series so
that we could con-
tinue to work on
the technical chal-
lenges that were
represented by this
business."**

on the technical challenges that were represented by this business. Doing one for an auto show is a far cry from doing 100,000 of them in production. That's the thing that the public finds hard to understand. The Ultralite cost more than $1 million to build that one car. We worked with Burt Rutan out in the Mojave Desert. He's from Scale Composites and did the plane that flew around the world on one tank of fuel. He, his brother, and a woman by the name of Jaeger flew that plane around the world. He is really an expert at carbon-fiber composite. The reason we were interested in that at the GM Research Labs is that we had invented a way of growing carbon fibers that might be one-tenth the cost of commercially available material. We were working on that research development at the same time that we were putting this Ultralite together. So we were imagining and beginning to understand the assembly and manufacture of panels made out of carbon fiber as a part of the process of doing the Ultralite. All of this is a long way from the reality of being able to purchase one at a price that is equivalent to a steel-bodied, gasoline-powered car. And that's the reach.

You were very instrumental in helping Don Walkowicz get the USCAR initiative off the ground. Is USCAR one of the mechanisms we can use to make the transition from show cars to production?

Yes. I think those are the kinds of projects that are very natural for USCAR. I was one of the three founding members of USCAR. In fact, the formation of USCAR is kind of an interesting history. First, Bob Eaton, who had the chief technical job at General Motors before me, and then I had breakfast meetings with our counterparts at Ford and Chrysler. The executive vice president of SAE would manage these breakfast meetings. We would talk about things related to the Society of Automotive Engineers—what standards might be required, what kinds of technologies are coming that we should be prepared for as a part of serving the automotive engineering community. These breakfast meetings went on every other month, and went on for a year or year and a half. That was really the foundation for our discussions about having this consortium of the three of us (the Big Three) and we began to develop this whole concept of USCAR.

Gary Dickinson

Don Walkowicz was drawn in at the point at which we were ready to go public, to announce and sign the commissioning documents and to have a press conference on USCAR. Don Walkowicz was brought in as the first executive director of USCAR. He has done a fantastic job for us, because it's gone on to spawn 12-or-so new consortia. One of the first and most significant ones related to electric cars was the battery consortium called "ABC," for Advanced Battery Consortium. Subsequent ones have had to do with lightweight materials.

A lot of the experiences we had in building this series of four cars are the kinds of things being addressed by these consortiums supported by the Big Three, because we need breakthroughs in batteries, low-cost, lightweight materials, and manufacturing techniques for lightweight materials.

It's all going in a very consistent direction. The giant step, though, is to take vehicles like these (pictured on the wall) and produce a vehicle that can operate for 100,000 miles without much maintenance, is priced reasonably, is practical to operate, has the right range, and has a reasonable cost of operation. The gasoline-powered, steel-bodied car is a pretty tough competitor for anything new to knock it out of that box.

Has your perspective changed since coming to Delco Electronics from the GM technical staff?

No, I don't think so. In my own mind, I'm now having to go from the conceptual to having to produce these systems. I guess if my perspective changed at all, it changed in understanding the practical expectations and requirements for producing a vehicle. There's not a clear picture of where electric vehicles are going. In the world of automotive engineering, it's not clear that there will be a huge market. There are some niche products that make sense. But it's not an everyday, everyone-will-have-one product—an "electric car in every garage."

I don't see it as a threat. It's really a challenge and an opportunity. The questions that we have to ask ourselves are: "Can we profit in investing in that kind of a business and in working at it for the next three, four, five years?" "Is there going to be a market at the end of that development process?" As businessmen, we have to invest in engineering, people, and capital in order to position ourselves ready for an electric

> "It's all going in a very consistent direction. The giant step, though, is to take vehicles like these (pictured on the wall) and produce a vehicle that can operate for 100,000 miles without much maintenance, is priced reasonably, is practical to operate, has the right range, and has a reasonable cost of operation. The gasoline-powered, steel-bodied car is a pretty tough competitor for anything new to knock it out of that box."

vehicle market. There is a lot of enthusiasm and we're involved in it, we're active in it. But it isn't clear to me what the ultimate market potential for an electric vehicle is.

The thing we've all talked about, and the thing the ABC consortium is working at, is a breakthrough in batteries. Otherwise, electric vehicles don't look to be good competitors with the gasoline-powered car. The thing that will happen in this country in order to develop those technologies and to bring about evolution—not necessarily revolution— will be by government edict.

Searching for Unobtainium

There is the old story about "unobtainium." It's a metal that all of us are searching for, this "unobtainium." It isn't available, but it does all of these wonderful things. You could say Mercedes and/or Honda or some of those creative people can put together a competitive hybrid or EV, but they have not demonstrated capability beyond what is available right here in the United States. The U.S. is way ahead of the competitors in the world in understanding the requirements for manufacturing an electric vehicle...and it is not practical. I would think Honda would be more worried than we would, because we know where we are with those technologies. We know what has to be done. I think we're at the leading edge in this country on electric vehicles, and they are not yet practical. So there isn't anybody coming up with this electric vehicle that solves all the problems. We have an edge over other countries.

Therefore, when EVs become viable, the U.S. has a strategic advantage?

I think it's convenient to say that, but probably not true. The world is a global market, so as soon as someone creates a breakthrough that makes the EV practical, it's going to be available to everyone. Those vehicles will be sold worldwide. It won't really happen in an overnight miracle. It will happen because of a lot of energy going in, probably supported by government, trying to figure out who has the best technology, and then developing that technology into a more practical form. But it won't happen overnight.

Remember the old stories about the 100-mile-per-gallon carburetor? "Gee, those oil companies are buying those up!" There isn't the 400-mile battery out there.

> "The world is a global market, so as soon as someone creates a breakthrough that makes the EV practical, it's going to be available to everyone. Those vehicles will be sold worldwide."

It's funny, the things we call revolutions. It took the Japanese over 30 years to get where they are with automobiles. It took the personal computer industry over 20 years to get where it is. Yet we call these changes revolutions.

If you start from the Dark Ages or from the Jurassic era, that's revolutionary. Technology is moving pretty quickly, particularly in our business. My God, this electronics business is moving so quickly, we're having to redesign things every two years to stay up with technology and to match the capability and the prices of other technologies. So it's exponential already.

I just don't see the practical electric or hybrid vehicle developing overnight, surprising people as something out of someone's garage. There are a lot of people, very bright people, working on them. And there will be breakthroughs. But it will be many little steps at a time. The picture I have in my mind is that all these developments, all the conversations and networking that will take place among the scientists and engineers will gradually move us closer and closer to having a practical electric vehicle. In the meantime, a gasoline-powered car is a damn nice package. It's very practical.

I got into a conversation with some of our Hughes people early on, about four or five years ago. Hughes, with all of their skills in aerospace and defense systems, says doing an automobile is tougher than putting a man on the moon—and they put a man on the moon—because of all the elements: the lack of training of the people who operate cars, the unknown environment in which it's going to operate, the lack of maintenance, all of those unknowns. In addition, people don't pay you up-front to build an automobile. They pay you after you've got it built. So you have four or five years invested and a lot of man-hours and a lot of tooling, and that's an unknown. And you make it look funny and nobody buys it. Or you make one mistake, and you have to call them all back. So it's a huge hopper of variables that are not controllable and are relatively unknown. So the risk for an automobile manufacturer is much higher than the risk for a defense contractor who gets paid up-front and gets told what the requirements are, and has somebody standing there watching to see that they execute to those requirements. We're trying to bring those cultures back closer together. But there are still a lot of unknowns in the electric vehicle. 🚗

Gary Dickinson

"It will be many little steps at a time. The picture I have in my mind is that all these developments, all the conversations and networking that will take place among the scientists and engineers will gradually move us closer and closer to having a practical electric vehicle. In the meantime, a gasoline-powered car is a damn nice package. It's very practical."

"Hughes, with all of their skills in aerospace and defense systems, says doing an automobile is tougher than putting a man on the moon—and they put a man on the moon."

FRANK SCHWEIBOLD
This Bird Won't Fly

Frank Schweibold is director of finance and strategic planning at General Motors Electric Vehicles.

The production plans for the Impact were announced by Roger Smith in April 1990 on Earth Day, after the car got rave reviews at the auto show in Los Angeles. It was a vision on the part of General Motors to bring an electric vehicle to the marketplace. The team was formed in late 1990 and a program manager was appointed. GM took a strong program manager's approach to the Impact, which was a new concept in managing programs. Ken Baker was the program manager. He had a fully integrated staff, all the way from engineers and planners to sales and marketing and service people.

As far as I know, this is the first time GM ever put that kind of structure underneath one individual. But it made sense, because this vehicle was so unique and had to more-or-less forge its own way in getting an infrastructure in place and creating early market development. So it made sense to do it that way.

"As far as I know, this is the first time GM ever put that kind of structure underneath one individual. But it made sense, because this vehicle was so unique and had to more-or-less forge its own way in getting an infrastructure in place and creating early market development."

Roughly six months after GM's announcement, California chose, as part of the 1990 Clean Air Act program, to mandate electric vehicles for the product portfolio of 1998. At that point, GM was still driven by a vision of doing an electric vehicle early. We had still maintained that we were going to do the production car for the mid-1990s, not the late 1990s. There was still the technological vision, the societal vision, of trying to do an electric car, trying to prove its feasibility. This drove the vision through 1991 and at least a portion of 1992.

I came into the picture in August 1992. At that time, GM was trying to exit Phase 0 of the four-phase planning process. There were still some fairly serious questions that were kicking around at the time. In 1991 and 1992, GM went through the engineering-stage-of-product definition and a lot of work was done to better estimate what it would take to complete the engineering and to capitalize for a production program. When Roger Smith announced the vehicle in April 1990, he announced it as a mid-'90s model. The fortunes of GM during the 1990–92 time frame were difficult. It was a serious time for GM. We were moving and delaying product programs, trimming budgets, and the like. But the commitment to the electric vehicle stayed, despite all of that. The vision remained: to do an electric vehicle.

Then, in 1992, things started to come more into focus about what it would really take to finish the car in terms of engineering expenditures and capital investment. The team here did a really good job bringing the capital requirements down from the earlier estimates. They had reduced the capital requirements forecast by about 50% from the early estimates.

But the engineering job seemed to grow even as the capital investment came down. The product cost also started to rise, partly because of the trade-offs between investment and product cost, but mostly due to the low volume of the car and the early, immature nature of the technology. When we took a look at the whole mix of engineering and capital yet to be spent and what we ended up with—product target cost, the ability to meet target cost, and implications for the price of the vehicle—the business case continued to look more and more tenuous.

Mandate Precludes Incremental Development

There are provisions in the California law for earning early credits. We looked at the mandate to sell 2% of our sales in 1998, 1999, and the year 2000 as electric vehicles. And then you look at a kick-up in the year 2001 that says you have to have 5% of your sales to be electric vehicles in 2001 and 2002, and then you have to go to 10% of your sales in 2003. The Board, Ken Baker, the Management Committee, and a lot of people recognized that the Impact is not the car that is capable of doing that job—probably no single car is capable of meeting 2, 5, and 10. There's going to have to be another car we're going to have to do to meet all the requirements of the mandate. So if you're going to have to do two cars, you'd be well-advised to wait and do one car that has a chance of doing the 2% and 5%, rather than having a car you might have to get through the 2% period, and then you have to do another car that can do 5%, and then who knows what you're going to have to do to reach 10%. In 1992 there was a great deal of uncertainty about whether the mandate would be delayed for technological reasons, but in retrospect, earlier on in 1991 or early 1992 we probably should have looked at

Frank Schweibold

Frank Schweibold

the Impact and asked if it was the car that could ever meet the 2% and 5% provisions of the mandate.

But in 1991 and 1992, GM still wanted to do the vehicle, in part for the technology demonstration it would provide. However, the more we engineered and spent in product-definition dollars, the more we learned that the vehicle was still a long way from being marketable at a popular, affordable price. Finally, the Management Committee and the Board of Directors just had to take a look at the situation and say, "Look, given what we had left to spend on the Impact and what the business case looks like, is this the right thing to be doing, especially when there is a mandate out there in 1998 and 2001 and 2003 that we're going to have to meet?"

In retrospect, it was really the overhanging aspect of the 2%, 5%, and 10% requirements of the mandate that was the enemy of the Impact, interestingly enough. In all honesty, when you look at the product and strategic planning elements of the situation, the mandate is probably what stopped the Impact as much as anything else. The mandate was so severe, it would have required two, if not three vehicles if we had done the Impact. GM just could not afford to do three vehicles during that period. So we said, "Let's stop the Impact production program and consider another program for the later 1990s, when the technology might be more mature and there might be a battery breakthrough, that has more of a chance of being more successful."

There were quite a few scientific marketing studies done. There were a great deal of market surveys and market research. We worked with a group at MIT to do the customer research and the data came back saying that the market at a 2% or 5% level is highly suspect. You had to make some very optimistic (low) assumptions about the price of the vehicle to get an appreciable market. Unfortunately, the more we knew about the cost of the Impact, the more it seemed difficult for it or any early electric vehicle to meet the optimistic price assumptions. You also had to make some optimistic assumptions about battery technology and range before any appreciable market appeared to develop.

> "GM just could not afford to do three vehicles during that period. So we said, 'Let's stop the Impact production program and consider another program for the later 1990s, when the technology might be more mature and there might be a battery breakthrough, that has more of a chance of being more successful.'"

A Mandate to Sell, Not to Buy

But the jury is still out. If EVs have range limitations and prices higher than those of comparable internal combustion

Frank Schweibold

engine vehicles, will 2% of the people in California voluntarily buy an EV? So it's not just a matter of "do we have the right EV to get 2%?" That's one of the flaws in the mandate. The mandate says the manufacturers have to produce and "make available for sale." The problem is that's a production-side mandate, not a demand-side mandate. It won't do anything for air quality if producers make 2% electric vehicles, but nobody buys them. Those of us inside the industry who know what the cost trends are and know what it takes to do one of these vehicles, we know what the battery trends are, about what kind of range you can get for what kind of weight and cost, and we believe the "free expression" market forecast of 2% is highly tenuous.

We're concerned that CARB be fully educated on the subject. We hope they've done as much in-depth customer research as we in the industry have.

At the time of this interview, the electric vehicle is still mandated for 1998. We're doing an incredible amount of scenario playing, of looking at alternatives. We are still very focused on what we can do to try to meet the California 1998 mandate. I don't think the focus has gone completely to the so-called Supercar program. But if you look at it from a financial viewpoint, we're still spending a significant amount of focus on EVs. I'm saying that from the standpoint that there's a mandate pending that says we have to produce a vehicle that will sell 2% of our volume.

Supercar Won't Meet the Mandate

Supercar is a recognition on the part of industry and the Clinton Administration to try to improve CAFE and greenhouse gases. Supercar is a ten-year time horizon. We're talking until 2003, 2004, or 2005 for the industry to develop prototypes. That's vastly different in the work you do, the research you perform, and the approach you take, versus someone who is sitting here saying I have to meet a 2% sales mandate and I have to produce production vehicles for 1998. Supercar is going to require prototypes to be built in the early 2000s. For the seven automobile manufacturers impacted by the mandate, that mandate is still looming out there as a production quota we have to do, whereas Supercar is a research project jointly sponsored by the government.

"For the seven automobile manufacturers impacted by the mandate, that mandate is still looming out there as a production quota we have to do, whereas Supercar is a research project jointly sponsored by the government."

Frank Schweibold

"General Motors cannot afford, on its own account, to spend that kind of money by itself. It used to be that commercial industry could capitalize on spin-offs from the space or military programs."

Supercar, I should say, is a good recognition by the government that the auto industry by itself cannot afford the kind of expenditures required for fuel cells, carbon-fiber composites, flywheels, or anything else that Supercar may turn out to be. General Motors cannot afford, on its own account, to spend that kind of money by itself. It used to be that commercial industry could capitalize on spin-offs from the space or military programs. Advances like the computer chip, which came out of the Apollo program, aren't coming along for the kinds of programs we're talking about.

The electric vehicle is a technology-forcing program. We don't know how to do an electric vehicle that meets the mandate, is at an affordable price, and offers the customer the equivalent range and performance of what they would have with an internal combustion engine car. So in things like the U.S. Advanced Battery Consortium, where we have GM, Ford, and Chrysler, the utility industry, and the Dept. of Energy banding together in what would have typically been a very strange set of bedfellows, you find shared dollars, people, and resources on cooperative research programs aimed solely at batteries, which is the key to the electric vehicle.

We're doing things in a cooperative sense that we used to do in a very competitive sense. You find us doing this in a technology-forcing situation, because there is a recognition on our part that we just can't afford to do it by ourselves. USABC is another example where government assistance is necessary. It's a 50/50 government-industry partnership, where the Department of Energy is funding 50 cents of every dollar of battery research that's going on within the USABC. If government hasn't already driven the new technology to commercial levels through space or military programs, then we need their help in these other ways, like USABC, for technology-forcing programs.

Forcing, As Opposed to Leading, Technology

As I said, the problem is a mandate that is technology-forcing, as opposed to research projects that are trying to be technology-leading. Technology-forcing mandates are command and control: "You will do this, you will create innovation along this time line." Well, that's not the way innovation works.

We can make lead acid batteries. Technologically, we have the electronics that can manage the battery and get its power

Frank Schweibold

to the motor. We can make the motor go around. We believe we can do it with the kind of reliability and dependability that a customer would expect. We know we can stamp the aluminum to make the space frame. We know we can forge the aluminum composite suspension links.

But technological feasibility and commercial feasibility are two totally different things. The team here proved they could engineer a car that would go a 70-mile range in the city, 90 to 100 miles highway, with lead acid batteries. Technological feasibility means that we can make vehicles that will survive on the road, if you're willing to live with the limitations that are inherent in the specifications of that vehicle, and if you're willing to live with the cost. That's when you begin to make the transition from technological feasibility to market feasibility. Will customers buy a vehicle that has a range limitation of 100 miles on the highway? Will they buy a vehicle that has a city-range limitation of 70 miles? Will the buyers be available at the level of 2% that we need? Can you do it commercially? Our answer was, "It looks pretty difficult to do this at a return for our shareholders."

The other question is: Will the customers come if you offer it? That's what the PrEView Drive is all about. We announced in December 1992 that we decided, as a Board of Directors and as a company, not to proceed to high-volume production of the Impact. That's one of the things we decided.

The second thing we decided was to take on one of the industry's more far-flung, most aggressive, most expensive customer and technology research projects ever conceived, now called the "PrEView Drive." (Then it was called the "Proto-Demo" program.) This is to test customer reactions to a car that was technologically feasible. How are they going to use the car? We're going to actually put people in cars. Real retail drivers, potential EV retail customers, personal-use drivers. We're going to build 50 of these cars and put people into them over the next two years.

That production build started in September 1993. We're going to have nearly 1000 drivers over two years test the Impact and tell us what they think about it. Then we will know how the customers will react to the range limitations, to price ranges, to all the things that are new and unconventional about EVs.

> "We can make lead acid batteries. Technologically, we have the electronics that can manage the battery and get its power to the motor. We can make the motor go around. We believe we can do it with the kind of reliability and dependability that a customer would expect. We know we can stamp the aluminum to make the space frame. We know we can forge the aluminum composite suspension links. But technological feasibility and commercial feasibility are two totally different things."

Frank Schweibold

Money for Cooperative Efforts

We aren't leasing these vehicles, but there is some cost-sharing. We have 15 utilities and 12 cities. In each of the cities, we have it set up so there is some amount of the expenses in running the program that can be funded by our utility partners: chargers, facility costs for housing the vehicles, people there to service the vehicle, people there to call up the drivers and ask, "Are you ready for us to bring your vehicle?" There's charger wiring to be done at the homes of the people, and most of the utility money is going into wiring costs, which is a natural role for them. Those are the kinds of expenses the utilities are participating with us on. There is also a plan for some government cost-share that goes along with that. There is also some small amount, several hundred thousand dollars, net expense, to be absorbed by the utilities. It's actually very low for the benefits of the information to be derived.

Comparatively speaking, Chrysler is selling one of their minivans for $125,000 or $130,000. Ford is doing a two-and-one-half year lease on their Ecostars for over $100,000. We're going to put, in each city, ten cars on the road for a period of six months, to be driven by 80 drivers, each one of them a separate driver, so we get a separate data point of customer satisfaction and reaction. We're going to create a focus group of 80 knowledgeable electric vehicle drivers, retail-oriented customers—the people who are going to have to buy electric cars in the future if the 2% is ever going to be achieved—whereas the Ford and Chrysler programs put a commercial vehicle in the hands of professional utility drivers, to be driven back and forth on commercial routes. And we're going to get data back from nearly 1000 potential customers. We're really going to find out what regular retail customers think about electric vehicles.

Real Market Data from Real People

I think there is significant value in the PrEView Drive program. We're going to learn a lot about utility infrastructure in the retail market, whereas the Ford and Chrysler vehicles are going to be charged up back in utility garages. We're going to find out how everyday consumers react to charging up an electric vehicle.

Frank Schweibold

Some of our drivers are going to be unmarried females. Some of our drivers are going to be married folks with teenage drivers. We're going to find out what people really think about electric vehicles, real potential customers with real money that someday will have to part with that cash to buy an electric vehicle. Whatever utilities find out from that is priceless, and what they learn about changing requirements will be very useful. The value of being in this program in Los Angeles or New York or Atlanta, the utilities couldn't buy!

Most people think that electric vehicles are golf carts. When we survey people in a focus group and ask, "Would you buy an electric vehicle?" they don't really know what an electric vehicle can be. So, to an extent, you have to educate the people as to what an electric vehicle is before you can ask them meaningful questions and get meaningful answers. That's what the PrEView Drive program does: give people exposure to the technology, exposure to the vehicle itself, exposure to the advantages and the limitations of the vehicle. We just want to find out how people are going to react to that. We're going to have people drive them for two weeks and for four weeks, different periods of time. Then we're going to ask them, "Based on your drive, now would you buy one of these?"

Money Where Our Mouth Is

The Impact is the car we have. That's the car we decided to build 50 of. These are being built like prototypes. These are expensive. The PrEView Drive program is costing us over $32 million. This expenditure gives you an understanding of GM's commitment to electric vehicles.

That is a lot of money. Nobody else in this industry can afford that and I'm not even sure we can afford it. But if you're going to try to answer the questions about EVs, and answer them with credibility rather than just a gut shot, you've got to do some things and it's this regulation that's forcing us to do them.

Are electric buses and fleet delivery trucks something that General Motors is approaching?

Not as long as we're being held accountable for 2% numbers. Can we build 5000 transit buses? No. Here's another example of the regulations getting promulgated one way and

> "Some of our drivers are going to be unmarried females. Some of our drivers are going to be married folks with teenage drivers. We're going to find out what people really think about electric vehicles, real potential customers with real money that someday will have to part with that cash to buy an electric vehicle."

the niche markets that electric vehicle technology might match are really the other way. I could see electric buses as airport shuttles, when you go to the LAX airport and need to be picked up by Avis to get your rental car. It makes a lot of sense to me that that bus coming to pick you up be an electric bus. One, because it replaces a diesel, and, two, the duty cycle of that bus seems to lend itself very nicely to electrics. It has a lot of waiting time where the diesel engine would otherwise be idling and an electric bus would just be sitting there. These buses have a lot of stops and starts, short range, and an adaptability to either quick charge or quick battery swap. That makes a lot of sense to me.

I think some of the fleet applications make more sense than the way the regulation has been written. I think if your objective was to nurture an infant industry with an infant technology and bring it along into a common sense grow-as-you-go strategy, absolutely, I'd start with airport shuttles and some fleet applications.

We've got to come to some decisions about how we are going to meet that mandate. Jack Smith (CEO of GM) said in January 1994 at the Detroit auto show that we think it's time for the Californians to call time-out and really reassess where they think they are with the mandate, and maybe give some consideration to what's possible. The ultimate battery that everybody is looking for isn't here yet. We've done the best that we know how with lead acid, which is the most affordable battery, and we've worked hard at other battery technologies. USABC is working on technologies, but none of those are ready to be committed to production. We think it's time to call time-out and rethink the mandate.

Is the CALSTART Running Chassis program useful?

I don't believe it's of much value to GM. To their credit, CALSTART is trying to make L.A. the Detroit of electric vehicles. They largely want to take the aerospace folks, who have been displaced by the lack of aerospace and defense business, and some of the aerospace contractors, and turn them into commercial contractors. Well, General Motors has already done that in the case of Hughes. We employed a number of people out in Torrance, California, to do AC inverters and EV chargers.

The mandate is a zero-sum game. The CALSTART Running Chassis program is probably overly optimistic, which is the word I would use, because what manufacturer would use that chassis, if he thought the vehicle would be like the other competitors' under the skin, to meet a mandate in 1998?

It's a competitive game in 1998. The mandate made it that way. It's very naive for the CALSTART and Amerigon people to think that Honda, General Motors, Ford, and Toyota would all use the same running chassis and try to sell against one another to achieve 2%.

General Motors, Ford, and Chrysler met, as an industry, with Dr. Lon Bell (of Amerigon) in February 1993. We said, "Dr. Bell, if you have components for EVs that are part of the Running Chassis program, or are part of the CALSTART consortium, we would like to have you put a garage show together and show us what those people can do." We told Lon Bell we would like to have a garage show, that he can set it up in L.A., he can have it be an EV component fair, and have all of the sponsors of these components—whether they're Lockheed or Hughes or whoever—and we the industry would come out and try to shop the best available. That garage show hasn't happened.

Are there any companies out there you find interesting?

There's an outfit in California called U.S. Electricar. They seem quite interesting from the standpoint of how they've been able to transcend the next step, but the difference is that they have about a half-dozen businessmen. They seem to have an interesting group of executive talent. There is a big difference in their approach. Delco Electronics-Hughes is really U.S. Electricar's major engineering source and supplier. They basically have a technological net under them called DE-Hughes to help with the propulsion system.

The big question is still the battery, though. The Electricar folks, Worden, and all the people doing conversions are still putting in relatively modest-technology, lead acid batteries. The jury is still out on whether that will work. But these converters have the advantage that they don't have to meet a 2% mandate. They can sell any volume they want and try to make a buck out of it. Since they're not forced to sell 2%, they'll probably do some things a lot differently selling hun-

Frank Schweibold

"General Motors, Ford, and Chrysler met, as an industry, with Dr. Lon Bell in February 1993. We said, 'Dr. Bell, if you have components for EVs that are part of the Running Chassis program, or are part of the CALSTART consortium, we would like to have you put a garage show together and show us what those people can do.'"

"These converters have the advantage that they don't have to meet a 2% mandate. They can sell any volume they want and try to make a buck out of it. Since they're not forced to sell 2%, they'll probably do some things a lot differently selling hundreds of vehicles a year, instead of 5000-6000 a year like General Motors has to sell."

Frank Schweibold

dreds of vehicles a year, instead of 5000-6000 a year like General Motors has to sell.

Conversion and Production Are Two Different Things

The market is still in the early genesis stage, where high-value customers like utilities will be willing to pay $40,000-$45,000 for an electric pick-up truck. ARPA is willing to pay that now. The question is: In 1998, could I sell the utilities a $40,000 pick-up truck? It will be difficult, and I probably can't sell 5000 of them at a $40,000 price. There's a big difference between getting a conversion business going and trying to meet a mandate in California that will require some 30,000-35,000 vehicles per year. Nobody has proven that the market is there for 35,000 electric vehicles.

We are seeing quite a departure from the classic competitive posture of the auto industry with things like CALSTART, USCAR, Supercar, the AAMA Fed LEV Proposal, to name a few innovative strategic approaches. How might the ZEV mandates be altering the industry?

The ZEV mandates are forcing cooperation where previously we would have competed. They're also forcing us to look for government funding. We realize that we just can't do this on our own. As private companies, we can't chin this on our own nickel—the stockholder's nickel. It's not fair to ask the stockholder to fund the technology development that has to go on here. The mandate also has us compressing the timing of vehicle programs and racing to get the technology ready when we know there is big risk to do so.

The responsibility for making EVs a success can't rest solely on the automakers. The responsibility has to be on government and utilities, also. If the charging stations and the infrastructure is not there—if the preferred parking and highway lanes for EVs are not there as incentives—then the market may not be there. You can't rely 100% on the auto companies to do that job.

So the mandate has changed our thinking in that we now realize the government has a more substantial role in "incentivizing" the purchase of EVs, and the utilities have a role in developing the infrastructure and helping to develop the market. The government and utilities in California also have a growing recognition of their role. They understand that if

> "The ZEV mandates are forcing cooperation where previously we would have competed."

> "The mandate has changed our thinking in that we now realize the government has a more substantial role in "incentivizing" the purchase of EVs, and the utilities have a role in developing the infrastructure and helping to develop the market."

they don't play their role—no matter what the auto companies do—EVs will not be a success.

The mandate doesn't mandate people to buy, it just mandates the OEMs to produce. We think that's a flaw in the mandate. We think the mandate ought to incentivize people to buy. It ought to mandate to buy. So we have to look to utilities and government to offer incentives like battery leases or purchase incentives if we want any hope of achieving a 2% selling rate.

We Need a Battery

The industry is also in a quandary about achieving 2% without a better battery. We're really focusing on battery a lot more. USABC is our answer. If there isn't a better battery that makes EVs more comparable in cost, range, and performance to an internal combustion engine car, you'll probably not see the 2% or 5% mandates attained.

When Roger Smith announced the Impact, GM thought we were going to be the pioneer in the marketplace, and we could take that risk if we thought there would be a big reward. We thought we could become the Xerox or Frigidaire of the EV industry. But when the mandate came in, it suddenly mandated six more competitors into a small and fragile market, instead of having one person cultivate that market, much the way Apple did with the personal computer, or the way Amana did with the microwave oven. Those markets started small and allowed the technologies to develop, mature, and become commercial.

Dennis Wilkie from Ford said at the Automotive News Congress, earlier this year in Detroit, that the mandate may be kind of like the mother eagle who's pushing the little eaglet out of the nest and asking him to fly before he's ready. The mandate may be forcing the companies to do things that will ultimately be customer dissatisfiers. It may be pushing technology too fast, to where the early customers that buy them may not be very happy. That would be a real shame if it disenabled electric vehicles for the long haul.

In the year and a half I've been involved in this, the issue has clearly moved from clean air to economics and jobs in California. Someone in California has said that if 2% is enough to generate 5000 jobs in California, then they ought to mandate 10% right away, because 10% will be five times as

Frank Schweibold

many jobs! It probably won't work that way. That just isn't practical. I think California may think that electric vehicles are a way for them to jump start an industry that can replace the defense industry. In reality I don't believe the mandate will create the significant number of jobs in California they may hope it will. Most of the jobs will be back in the Midwest, close to the sources of technology.

Right now, if we wanted to put a plant in L.A. to build EVs, I'm not certain we could get a permit. I think the environmental regulations in L.A. would not allow us to restart the Van Nuys assembly plant, for instance. Or there would need to be a major change in philosophy, so that the regulators and environmentalists out in California would approve for us to put even a plant out there that would paint cars.

But I think there are some high-tech industries out there—like DE-Hughes for instance—that are building components. We pointed out to some of the Californians that perhaps they ought to be thinking about jobs in high-technology components that could go into electric vehicles rather than assembly plants for EVs.

"We pointed out to some of the Californians that perhaps they ought to be thinking about jobs in high-technology components that could go into electric vehicles rather than assembly plants for EVs."

The Post-Superstructure Structure

The large automakers are practicing a superstructure strategy to try to bring EVs to market, using the massive industry-government "Supercars" program and the USCAR effort. Both programs propose cost-sharing to reduce overall risk. But, as we've heard, the programs seem to fall short in that they do not promote a fundamental reshaping, or "reinventing," of the industry. For this reason, a strategy of incremental change may not succeed at developing an e-motive industry in the near term—certainly not before the turn of the century. However, there is another strategy being pursued. In the next part we will explore a strategy called *e-structures*. This strategy takes a market approach to electric vehicles, rather than a technology approach as is characteristic of the superstructures strategy.

Part III
E-STRUCTURES:
A Strategy For Innovative Change

> ...In the future, success in the auto industry "may go to companies, both big and small, that learn as fast as computer companies do, that are not afraid of new stuff, and that are accustomed to very market-driven products, most of whose money is made in the first six months and where there are one or two new product generations in a year with extraordinarily short cycle times.... Incrementalism is a bet-your-company choice; but leapfrogging on a risk-managed trajectory, first to ultralights and then to ultralight hybrid-electrics, lets you feel sorry for your former competitors—if and only if you do it first."—*Amory Lovins*

In stark contrast to the automaker's superstructure strategy, others pursuing the e-motive industry are utilizing an enterprise structure, or e-structure, to grow the industry and take advantage of the market opportunities available. This structure represents a theory of business quite different from that being practiced by the larger, more established auto industry, whose strategy is less multidimensional and focused more on the technological factor of their products. The e-structure strategy, on the other hand, has the ability to combine and link the multidimensional "E" forces into a competitive business enterprise.

One form of e-structure, the lean enterprise, is described by Dr. James P. Womack and Daniel T. Jones in their paper "From Lean Production to the Lean Enterprise."* They describe the lean enterprise as a group of individuals, functions, and legally-separate-but-operationally-synchronized companies that creates, sells, and services a family of products. This definition is similar to that of the Japanese *keiretsu* system.

*Womack, James P., Daniel T. Jones, "From Lean Production to Lean Enterprise," *Harvard Business Review,* March–April 1994.

The Keiretsu System as a Model for E-structures

*Porter, Michael E., *The Competitive Advantage of Nations,* Macmillan Press Ltd., London, 1990, pp. 153-154.

The Japanese *keiretsu*s are large, loose groupings of companies with shareholding connections. At the center of each group is a major bank. Companies consult with each other and work well together because of their "special" relationship.* They cooperate on technological development and cooperate in sharing market information. This results in an entire array of business units competing in vertically and horizontally linked industries within a single firm. Because the Japanese firms that began the *keiretsu* system were start-ups instead of acquisitions, exchange of information and skills among these units is remarkably fluid. Indeed, it is the *keiretsu* system which helped to build whole new industries for Japan after World War II.

The principal function of the *keiretsu* structure is to facilitate interchange among related companies. Companies loosely linked in Japanese groups look to each other for guidance and input on new products, new processes, and new businesses. Of central importance to any *keiretsu* is the membership of a trading company. These huge firms, with well-developed worldwide networks, helped many Japanese companies penetrate foreign markets. They also play an important role in marketing to smaller and developing countries and are important sources of information to Japanese companies that lack overseas personnel or that are smaller and less sophisticated in international operations. Therefore, this system is designed to grow new small businesses into larger, globally competitive enterprises.

The *keiretsu* structure is important for it is a proven example of the power of enterprise structures. This system is particularly powerful in helping to build new industries, enter new markets, and introduce new technologies and products. The *keiretsu* worked to build Japan's industrial base after World War II in two fundamental ways: First, the *keiretsu* is extremely efficient as a source of industrial finance, the lifeblood of any new start-up activity. Second, the *keiretsu*, through the sharing of market information among its members, reduces the risk for companies operating in dynamic, multidimensional business environments.

The Japanese *keiretsu* structure is not perfect, however, for it lacks span across the "E" forces. Specifically, one Japanese economist, Miyazaki Yoshikazu, describes the failing of the *keiretsu* to effectively deal with the environmental force:*

> In the past the enterprise had served the interest (albeit a narrow and sectional interest) of the owner or shareholder, and was also to some extent obliged to meet the interests of the consumer. But the corporate structure embodied in the *keiretsu* threatened to create companies that served no interests but their own. The new enterprise group existed neither for the shareholders, nor for employees, nor for consumers, nor for society, but...single-mindedly for the growth and benefit of the company itself. ...[T]he oligpolistic structures that promoted Japan's rapid growth were also precisely the structures that, by promoting the unfettered pursuit of corporate expansion, had created environmental degradation and urban blight.

The *keiretsu* structure is not directly applicable to American or European business environments, either. Japanese companies, with what at first appears to be a public equity structure, are in reality privately held. This arrangement would not be allowed under the investment laws of the United States and a number of European countries—companies would have to explain why only some of their stock was for sale.**

Lean Enterprise

The *keiretsu* structure then, while hugely successful as an enterprise structure, is not necessarily appropriate for building the e-motive industry. We need a structure that spans the "E" forces and a structure that is applicable to the Western world. There is another e-structure, called the *lean enterprise*, which meets the requirements of the e-motive industry.

In their book *The Machine That Changed The World*,[†] Womack and Jones explained how companies can dramatically improve their performance by embracing the "lean production" approach pioneered by Toyota: "By eliminating

*Morris-Suzuki, Tessa, *A History of Japanese Economic Thought*, Routledge, London, 1989, pp. 155-158.

**Womack, James P., Daniel T. Jones, Daniel Roos, *The Machine That Changed The World*, HarperCollins, New York, NY, 1990, p. 195.

†As summarized by James P. Womack and Daniel T. Jones in "From Lean Production to the Lean Enterprise," *Harvard Business Review*, March–April 1994.

unnecessary steps, aligning all steps in an activity in a continuous flow, recombining labor into cross-functional teams dedicated to that activity, and continually striving for improvement, companies can develop, produce, and distribute products with *half or less* of the human effort, space, tools, time, and overall expense. They can also become vastly more flexible and responsive to customer desires."

But as Womack and Jones explain in the "Lean Enterprise" paper, "We've seen numerous examples of amazing improvements in a 'specific activity' in a 'single company.' But these experiences have also made us realize that applying lean techniques to discrete activities is not the end of the road. If individual breakthroughs can be linked up and down the value chain to form a continuous *value stream* that creates, sells, and services a family of products, the performance of the whole can be raised to a dramatically higher level." Womack and Jones describe this new organizational approach as the "lean enterprise." Later in this book, Dr. Womack will demonstrate how lean enterprise thinking can work to help build the e-motive industry.

The Incremental Creation of E-structures

It is difficult to find real-life examples of lean enterprise concepts in practice. Womack and Jones acknowledge this. But they also discuss how large companies such as Chrysler are working to convert their superstructure into a lean enterprise. Chrysler's activities were alluded to in our conversation with Jean Mallebay-Vacqueur when he said, "The way we approach this problem (of trying to bring EV's to market) with our suppliers for electric vehicles is exactly the same way we used suppliers for the Viper. If you look at cars that we are producing in the mainstream today, or cars that we are engineering today, we have the same philosophy of the same approach of a partnership. We see what they can bring to the party and everybody brings what they know how to do. At Chrysler, we bring skills to integrate the program and to understand and express in technical terms the customer's expectations. We are an integrator. The suppliers are doing more engineering for our cars than they may do for cars of our competition, especially if you look at GM which is much more integrated. They buy only 20% of their components (from the outside) when we buy 80% of our components."

As Chrysler is demonstrating, a superstructure can be converted to a lean enterprise. This requires a change to an organizational structure so that it can accommodate lean enterprise practices. Most importantly, as Womack and Jones highlight, is Chrysler's challenge to redefine its supplier relations to those which instill lean practices across the enterprise and to those practices which keep supplier relationships positive, even in times of "pain" such as economic downturns.

Chrysler's *enterprise* needs to improve the way it creates and manages *partnerships*. Today, Chrysler's use of suppliers is more of a *relationship* than a *partnership*. Chrysler tends to avoid equity holdings in its supplier base. Rather, Chrysler prefers to include its suppliers in development activities from Day One, listening eagerly to their suggestions for design improvements and cost reductions, but through an arms-length relationship that asks for a lot, but offers little in the way of future commitments. This supplier structure allows Chrysler to remain focused on its core business, but is arguably weak in supporting its supplier base in times of economic downturn.

Further, Chrysler's enterprise does not show itself committed to the "E" forces that are propelling the formation of an e-motive industry. Chrysler does not, for instance, focus on partnerships with power utilities or local/regional governments that have interests in the energy and economic forces, respectively.

In addition, workers at Chrysler and other automakers are accustomed to a certain routine and way of doing things. Indeed, the written policies and practices at automakers have a long history based on a series of precedents. Changing a superstructure into a lean enterprise comes with many challenges, although such a change should be possible.

Ground-Up E-Structures

It may also be possible to create a lean enterprise with an organizational structure designed from the start to accommodate the special workings of a lean enterprise. In the e-motive industry, we are seeing a strategic style emerge which is focused on becoming an enterprise first, and a lean enterprise in the end.

There are several examples of enterprises emerging in the e-motive industry that are applying an *e-structure* strategy in developing their business.

An e-structure strategy exhibits the following characteristics:

- Exploits business opportunities in large-scale (global), emerging products and markets.
- Unites and re-applies diverse skills based on a commitment to continue long-term, cooperative relationships among a group of individuals, functions, and legally-separate-but-operationally-synchronized companies dedicated to the creation, sale, and service of a family of products.
- Allocates leadership of a function of the enterprise to the member best positioned to lead, be it large or small.
- Integrates the internal creation of the enterprise's products with the external consequences of the product through partnerships that span all elements of the entire system affecting the product (e.g., the "E" forces).

Why an E-structure?

Building an e-motive industry will involve not only complex technological issues, but equally complex organizational and marketing issues. Amory Lovins explained this point well in a conversation I held with him in March 1994:

"To change the existing car companies means you're going from steel to synthetics, stamping to molding, welding to adhesives or simply parts integration, actual to virtual prototyping, mechanicals to electricals, hydraulics to electronics, hardware to software, and mass to information. It's a profoundly different kind of product. For that matter, in particular skills as well, there's a similar transformation—for example, from die making to stereolith. It's such a big set of leapfrogs in so many areas that it's hard to imagine its being successful for most automakers unless they are thoroughly committed to a cultural transformation of unprecedented dimensions. It takes an unconventional style and structure of project management to bring it about.

"I think it will only happen in the companies that pursue it not simply as a fringe activity or as an insurance policy, but as a whole-hearted commitment to the most fundamental kind of reinvention of what a car is, how you make it, how you sell it, and what business the company's in.

"The pace of cultural change in some automakers is certainly impressive and gives me some hope that it may be possible to pull this off, but it's not guaranteed. I therefore suspect that the advantage, to an extent that's hitherto inconceivable in this field, may go to companies, both big and small, that learn as fast as computer companies do, that are not afraid of new stuff, and that are accustomed to very market-driven products, most of whose money is made in the first six months and where there are one or two new product generations in a year with extraordinary short cycle times."

Mr. Lovins is suggesting that the e-motive industry will be led by a new mix of players that rewrite the rules of the auto industry. Certainly, a host of industries will benefit from the emergence of an e-motive industry. Established organizations, ranging from public utilities to rapid transit authorities, from material and component manufacturers to financial services companies, have significant opportunities awaiting them. And indeed, most of the pieces to form an e-motive industry are resident in these industries and ready to be used. However, these industries cannot lead the formation of a new e-motive industry by themselves, since each one represents distinct functional skill sets which were developed incrementally through a superstructure strategy.

The early-stage e-motive companies are not and shall not necessarily become vehicle manufacturers. At the same time, it does not seem the auto industry, with its superstructure status, is in a logical position to kick-start an e-motive industry. Perhaps, as Amory Lovins has said, it will require a fresh start with new skills to create a new industrial model from a set of fragmented pieces. It is through the uniting and application of diverse skill sets that an e-structure derives, using an enterprise strategy that will participate in reshaping the auto industry into an e-motive industry.

An e-structure strategy for the e-motive industry will be based on a grand scale of strategic partnering. Focused on the interactions between organizations, an e-structure strategy facilitates the bonding together of diverse business entities. In theory, by sticking these entities together, innovative new families of products can be successfully produced and sold.

The products of an e-structure are global products that are technologically sophisticated. These are products that each business by itself could not possibly design, manufacture, and market. An e-structure strategy is therefore a strategy aimed at exploiting business opportunities based on large-scale, emerging products and markets.

How Established Companies Can Change

The leader of an e-structure is not necessarily chosen based on size, as is the case in the auto industry's superstructure. Rather, in an e-structure, smaller companies often lead larger companies into new products and markets, bringing new life to established organizations.

An e-structure strategy is designed to capitalize continually on the products of innovation. Most often, it is smaller companies that are best positioned to react to innovations and apply them to commercial products. To support the flow of new products, larger, more established organizations play important roles in, for example, the supply of components, materials, infrastructure, and finance. Smaller companies leading a partnership comprised of larger companies and other small companies into large-scale, emerging products, markets, and competitive practices is another one of the key characteristics of an e-structure strategy.

Form Follows Functional Sets of Skills

Through an e-structure strategy, organizations with differing skill sets find ways to work together, so that the strengths of each organization create even greater worth when assembled into an enterprise to produce a product. This effect is commonly called *synergy*.

An e-structure strategy is also based on long-term partnerships. In principle, once these new working relationships are established, the strategic partners continually develop new ways to work together, grow the enterprise, optimize their *value stream* and produce new innovative products. In doing this, e-structure companies eventually match the perceived value assigned at the start of the partnership. For example, the partners involved in building electric cars may reshape the enterprise to lead it into additional businesses, such as power electronics and motors for elevators, or low-cost structural composites for boat hulls, or energy storage systems for utility load-leveling. In this way the enterprise finds many outlets for its skills. Also, for this reason, an e-structure strategy is sustainable through its ability to reshape itself in reaction to the changing marketplace. E-structures, then, are experts at exploiting new business opportunities.

Rapid Identification and Integration of Emerging Technology

It takes time to reinvent an industry, or to build a new industry from scratch. Many of us recall the frequent hardware and software problems that were characteristic of early personal computer products. Trying to get speedy and informative product support was also difficult. However we, as consumers, understood that it takes time for a new industry and its technologies to mature.

When we speak of a "fundamental reshaping of the auto industry's structure," it is important to recognize that a system of rapid product innovation and introduction, as exhibited in the early computer industry, is not something that can be readily applied to the auto industry. After all, automobiles are infinitely more complex than personal computers, as should logically be the case. Indeed, it would be reckless to propose that automobiles, given the current state of the industry, can be designed and built like personal computer products. If your personal computer fails, your life is not threatened. With automobiles, an unproven design or manufacturing system can result in casualties. At the very least, it can mean expensive product recalls. We must not overlook the uniqueness of the automobile in these regards. Indeed, superstructures do provide a vital role within an e-structure; superstructures represent proven sets of skills that an e-structure can draw upon.

While the computer industry analogy is not perfect, there are important similarities to consider. Today, computer products can be quickly designed and brought to production with the help of powerful computer design and simulation work stations. Electric vehicle makers, because of the high electronic content in electric vehicles and the rapid pace of change in EV technologies, will need product-upgrade techniques similar to the computer industry. Indeed, speed-to-market may become an even more important competitive factor than in the current auto industry.

Unfortunately, the powerful computer tools that would allow vehicles to be built "on the screen" do not exist yet. It still requires the auto industry a minimum of two years to design and bring new products to market. However, more powerful computer design tools are starting to appear. Already U.S. Electricar, a small e-motive industry player that we'll hear from later, is using powerful computer simulation techniques to safety engineer vehicles on computer screens. This allowed the company to pass the Federal Motor Vehicle Safety Standards on the first attempt, without design alterations.

Yet safety engineering is only one small aspect of vehicle design. To bring the vehicle design and manufacturing process close to anything like the computer industry will require a massive, coordinated, global effort in addition to the introduction of powerful new computer tools. It may also require that component suppliers, material suppliers and auto assemblers develop and publish design standards, much like the computer industry has, with its standard packaging for components and operating systems. An e-motive industry will require powerful new computer tools that can dynamically test vehicles "on screen," and then translate the on-screen design to the manufacturing floor, where tooling and manufacturing processes are generated from electronic databases.

The American auto industry and the U.S. government have already confirmed the competitive importance of rapidly identifying, integrating, and manufacturing new technologies. One of the three prime objectives of the "Supercars" program is to develop "advanced manufacturing techniques to make it easier to get new product ideas into the marketplace quickly."

A Job for Global Enterprises

Meeting this objective will not come easily. There are numerous technological and organizational barriers to cross. Add to this the immense, global span of the auto industry and it becomes clear that reinventing the auto industry, or building a new e-motive industry, will require a large-scale, concerted effort. That is to say that the e-motive industry will not evolve out of a regional group of small inventors, as the personal computer industry has. More likely, an e-motive industry will emerge from new, powerful, global enterprises of companies that collectively have the resources to design, produce, and market automobiles that match the safety standards required by law and the extremely high quality and performance expectations of consumers. These enterprises will also develop the organizational skills required to identify and integrate their resources rapidly. This focus on organizational effectiveness is critical to the success of an e-structure.

Managing the "E" Forces

Also important to the success of the e-motive industry is the ability to work with and manage the external consequences of the "product." E-structures therefore define their "product" as part of a larger system and work to manage the external consequences of their product through appropriate partnerships. These partnerships include electric power companies, material recyclers, city and site planners, service providers (finance, repair, auto rental, etc.), governmental agencies, and consumer action groups.

To help us better understand how one type of e-structure, the lean enterprise, works we will now hear from Dr. James P. Womack. Dr. Womack provides a far-reaching vision of how e-structures can promote the building of an e-motive industry.

JAMES WOMACK
The Real EV Challenge—Reinventing an Industry

Dr. James Womack is a partner in the consulting firm The Transitions Group, is co-author of the best-selling book *The Machine That Changed the World*, and is a principal researcher in the MIT Japan Program.

The fundamental EV problem: The current IC-powered motor vehicle is produced in massive volumes by an industry with no incentive to take risks on dramatically new products requiring major investments. This is hardly surprising given the benign operating environment for IC-powered automobiles at this point in history. Current designs meet most user needs; the real cost of fossil fuel energy has fallen to the lowest level in history; and ambient air quality is slowly but steadily improving in even the most polluted urban areas in the developed countries. What's more, intense competition across the world between the American, Japanese, and European automotive giants has driven profits down and caused all firms to carefully re-examine R&D spending. In these circumstances, why innovate?

The automotive giants will respond, however reluctantly, if governments require zero emission vehicles in polluted areas, but these mandates can disappear in an instant as politics and public opinion interact in an era of economic stagnation. And absent direct government orders to make them, it seems fair to say that the established motor vehicle companies will have substantially zero interest in EVs.

Instead, the automakers' natural inclination will be to meet all air quality and energy conservation mandates short of zero emissions through incremental improvements to IC drivetrains and fuel systems (of the type devised to meet the 1994 Clean Air Act regulations) and by means of gradual material substitutions to reduce body and component weight. This approach has low technical risks and maximizes the industry's ability to use its existing capital investment. In short, the traditional motor vehicle industry will resist EVs by regulation and will not be the initiator of a *commercially oriented* EV industry.

This is not to say that a commercial EV industry—one aiming to make an adequate return on investment by offering a product customers prefer and without need for the undependable safety net of government regulation—is an impossibility, using only those technologies already on hand or clearly in sight. It is to say that a commercially viable EV industry

James Womack

will not look like or spring from the existing auto industry. This is for reasons going well beyond the industry's natural conservatism:

• EV designs will offer a performance package different from conventional vehicles. They will be better in some ways (noise and vibration) but probably inferior in others (range and carrying capacity). What's more, the feel of the EV and the routines of daily operation will be different. Therefore, the product will need to be "explained" to the user as something other than a "car" and the initial users will need more support for repairs and reporting performance anomalies than is needed for a conventional car. This will call for a different type of marketing and distribution system.

• EVs will use different body materials and motive power and will be produced initially at lower volumes, compared with conventional automobiles. Thus, the complement of vehicle systems suppliers, the types of fabrication techniques, and the size of production facilities will be different from the conventional auto industry.

• EVs with currently available technologies carry an inherent materials cost-disadvantage, due to their battery systems. And even the most advanced EV designs currently envisioned will need a costly charging infrastructure to permit "refueling" at each long-term parking space. The EV plus its support apparatus will therefore be considerably more costly than a conventional car (even at comparable production scale) if produced, distributed, and serviced using methods which duplicate those of the existing auto industry. New ways will be needed to produce, distribute, and service EVs which will substantially lower capital investment and overall costs.

• Even if EVs are produced, distributed, and maintained in the most efficient ways currently foreseeable, they will still be an expensive product for most households at $10,000 or more per unit. What's more, they will have an unknown and possibly very low resale value due to new technologies that make EVs only a few years old obsolete. In these conditions of uncertainty, even the "enthusiast" buyer will be reluctant to

> "EV designs will offer a performance package different from conventional vehicles. They will be better in some ways (noise and vibration) but probably inferior in others (range and carrying capacity)."

take on the financial risks of ownership, so some means of sharing or eliminating this risk will be needed.

Given these conditions, getting a commercially oriented EV industry off the ground will require considerable innovation of an organizational nature quite aside from the advances in vehicle hardware that seem to have preoccupied most proponents of EVs to this point.

The Solution: A "Lean" EV Industry

Two marketing and organizational innovations are critical to a commercially viable EV industry: The first is to change the nature of the EV from a product for sale (a "car," which inevitably will be compared unfavorably with conventional cars) to a comprehensive service (personal mobility) for which the customer is charged periodically by the amount used. This new service must be different from and better than the old-fashioned "car." The second innovation is to change the nature of the production/service system from mass production to a "lean" enterprise by involving new players to introduce new practices and dramatically reduce costs.

EVs as a Personal Mobility Service

While motoring is still a pleasure for some drivers, even an end in itself, most motorists today simply want to get from Point A to Point B with as little effort as possible. And they wish to obtain and use the means do so with minimum hassle and they want their vehicle to be consistent with their personal values and image. The current motor vehicle performs some of this assignment well—getting from Point A to Point B, and making an image statement suited to many users—but the conventional car creates many frustrations in the process. Negotiating with the car dealer to purchase the vehicle can be a major hassle. Obtaining financing, insurance, and registration is complex and time-consuming. Fueling the vehicle and taking it in for repairs and routine maintenance disrupt daily routines, which for most users require a working vehicle. Many dealers, even in an age of dealer quality ratings, must be pressed hard to fix problems and repeat trips for the same problem still occur. Finally, the vehicle must be disposed of when no longer needed, frequently requiring another haggle with a dealer.

> "While motoring is still a pleasure for some drivers, even an end in itself, most motorists today simply want to get from Point A to Point B with as little effort as possible. And they wish to obtain and use the means do so with minimum hassle and they want their vehicle to be consistent with their personal values and image."

The rapid growth of leasing in recent years demonstrates the appeal of an alternative approach which eliminates some of these problems: Leases typically provide less room for haggling (restricted mainly to the value of the trade-in) and the dealer takes the car back automatically at the end of the lease period at a pre-agreed value. However, most lease arrangements still call for a substantial down payment. The user still faces the frustrations of registering and insuring the vehicle and the need to take it for repairs, inspections, and fueling. Finally, the cost and complexity of operating leasing programs through the conventional dealer system make them an expensive proposition, best suited for luxury car shoppers worried about resale value. The new EV industry must find a way to get the vehicle to the user with less cost and aggravation.

Where We Begin

The place to begin is by creating a new "mobility provider" as an alternative to the conventional dealer system with its expensive showrooms, large repair areas, and massive inventories of vehicles waiting for sale or lease. The "mobility provider" would identify customers, sign them up, order the vehicle from the manufacturer, deliver the vehicle to the user, put the fueling system in place, and take care of all problems encountered in daily use.

The provider would also take care of insurance, registration, financing, and disposal of superannuated vehicles because the vehicles would not be sold or leased to users. Instead, users would pay a monthly fee with fixed and variable elements (the latter most likely based on electricity usage, which would be a proxy for mileage). The mobility provider would convert the EV from a product to be bought and driven away after a one-time negotiating process into a service, consisting of the vehicle plus continuing and comprehensive operational support.

By working carefully with the vehicle manufacturer, it should be possible to perfect EV designs that have extremely long maintenance intervals—perhaps 50,000 miles. Such an interval is feasible because electric motors do not need the routine maintenance of IC engines. It should also be possible for the mobility provider and a new type of EV production system to develop vehicles with a very low frequency of repairs to remedy manufacturing defects. Thus, the mobility

James Womack

"The place to begin is by creating a new 'mobility provider' as an alternative to the conventional dealer system with its expensive showrooms, large repair areas, and massive inventories of vehicles waiting for sale or lease."

provider could offer a major service to the EV user: "You never need to bring the vehicle in and disrupt your daily routine. Instead, we will inspect, fix it, and even replace it at your parking place." Yet this service might entail only a modest cost to the provider. At the same time, low-maintenance vehicles would eliminate the need for large investments in repair facilities of the type now required by conventional dealerships.

By talking carefully with each customer to understand household mobility needs, it should be possible to provide vehicles at the right price and with the right performance. For example, many motorists don't think in terms of the newness of a car but instead in terms of its dependability (the former being a proxy for the latter in the case of conventional cars). Mobility providers might expand their market over time, as the initial vehicles age, by refurbishing high-mileage vehicles to give new-vehicle reliability but at lower cost to the user.

"How Will You Be Using Your EV, Ma'am?"

Similarly, many users have fixed performance requirements for their vehicles, in particular for the second and third vehicles in the household fleet. For example, as long a member of the household continues to work at the same location, the daily commute is quite uniform. Sizing the battery pack and vehicle performance to the precise needs of the user at a given point in time could make many EV applications economic with existing technologies. When needs shift abruptly (due, for example, to a change of job), a new vehicle suited to the new mission could be substituted quickly by the mobility provider. (By contrast, much of the defeatism about EVs in the conventional car industry focuses on the supposed need for every vehicle in the household inventory to have coast-to-coast range, with only brief stops for gas. This is the wrong way to consider the problem on two counts: Only the first vehicle in the household is likely to need such performance, and second and third vehicles lacking performance to meet the needs of a new commuting or other daily-use pattern could be switched easily by the mobility provider.)

The mobility provider could offer each user a single telephone contact point—a real person who is stable over time—to solve all problems in daily use, such as breakdown calls, anomalies in vehicle performance, changed performance

James Womack

requirements, and replacement vehicles in the event of an accident. This approach, perhaps utilizing a telephone installed as standard equipment in each vehicle, could give a sense of support to the user that is simply unavailable with current automotive products.

What's more, this sense of security could be offered without the need for expensive dealership real estate and would have the bonus of being able to capture very nearly a 100% sample of user experience with and reactions to their EVs. By combining market research and service functions while avoiding expensive capital investments, it might be possible to reduce the cost of this service below that required for the current auto sales and service system.

The logical mobility provider is a firm with considerable experience in customer relations and with substantial customer databases already in place. This would permit piggybacking customer billing and support onto existing information processing systems. The two obvious candidates are electric utilities within their service areas and auto rental companies. The utilities have the advantage that they would also supply the fuel and charging infrastructure, while the rental companies have the advantage of a ready source of conventional vehicles to provide users when they need long-distance travel. However, in both the U.S. and Europe, the major car rental companies are mostly owned by the manufacturers of conventional cars (e.g., GM owns National, Chrysler owns Dollar and Thrifty, Ford owns Hertz, and Volkswagen owns EuropeCar). Thus the enthusiasm of the car rental industry for EVs is unclear.

"The logical mobility provider is a firm with considerable experience in customer relations and with substantial customer databases already in place. This would permit piggybacking customer billing and support onto existing information processing systems."

How Might This Work?

Let's suppose for purposes of this discussion that the electric utility is the most logical mobility provider. How might it proceed? Its recruitment mechanism is obvious. It would initially target the two most promising user groups, fleet operators in urban areas (beginning with the parent utility company's own fleet) and higher income suburban households with several vehicles in their fleet and a potential interest in a "green" commuter vehicle that replaces one of their existing vehicles. The most attractive introductory offer would involve no cost to the provider: By switching to EVs with no down payment but instead a monthly fee, both fleet operators

James Womack

and private households could obtain a cash windfall by selling the vehicles to be replaced with EVs.

The mobility provider's organizational structure is easy to specify as well. It will need to be a for-profit, unregulated subsidiary of the electric utility and a firm with a very flat hierarchy. The value created by the service will lie in meeting the precise needs of each potential customer. Therefore, the key employee will be the "mobility representative," with the necessary information resources and authority to place and maintain vehicles and to quickly resolve all problems connected with their use. Other functions within the firm will need to be organized to focus on supporting the mobility representatives.

Because the mobility provider will continue to "own" the EV (although an independent leasing or commercial credit company might hold the actual title), the system is a closed loop: when the vehicle is old or technically obsolete, it can be recycled; when it is no longer needed by a given user, it can be quickly transferred to another. In addition, the provider can think intelligently about life-cycle costing. It may be able to utilize a standard "drive frame" (that is, the basic body structure to which is attached the motive power, energy storage, suspension/steering, and exterior and interior systems) for a very long period, with periodic refurbishment and upgrades and reassignments to users whose needs profile matches a given vehicle's performance profile. (Also, the provider, with its steady base of customers and an ability to plan, can smooth its demand for new EVs, a key requirement for the "lean" production system to be discussed in a moment.)

A final point: The new personal mobility providers might find it useful to link themselves in a horizontal network across geographic areas in order to offer the user a continent-wide service in North America and Europe. The nature of the product will be such that few users will want or be able to drive their EV from one region to another. What they will need instead is a networking service which gets them the mobility they want and need wherever they go. This could include an EV similar to the one they use at home, but it might also include air, rail or a conventional auto to get them there, and some form of local transport—limo, taxi, bus, rail, or conventional rental car—best suited to their mission in the

> "The new personal mobility providers might find it useful to link themselves in a horizontal network across geographic areas in order to offer the user a continent-wide service in North America and Europe. The nature of the product will be such that few users will want or be able to drive their EV from one region to another."

new locality. The mobility provider would not itself operate any of these services. Instead, it would be a new type of travel agent, able to deal with all of a user's mobility needs, both at home and across continents.

By providing a comprehensive travel service to users, the mobility provider might largely eliminate the need for households to retain one or more conventional cars with their practically unlimited range. Thus the extent of the EV market—in particular, the ability to supplant "first vehicles"—might well depend more on the quality of the mobility provider's continent-wide service network than on the operational limits of EVs themselves.

The EV Industry as a Lean Enterprise

Conventional car companies are the result of a century of industrial history. While some (e.g., Toyota) have developed techniques for product development, production operations, and supply-chain management that permit them to be much more efficient than others (e.g., GM or Volkswagen), they are all based on a highly capital-intensive industrial model in which a firm at the top of a mighty pyramid (the "assembler") strives to control firms further down the pyramid ("suppliers"), who often do the bulk of their work within one pyramid. Sales and service systems involve large networks of independent dealers with massive investments and inventories, making most of their living off repairs and replacement parts.

Trying to replicate this industrial system to enter the EV industry would be prohibitively expensive and time-consuming. Therefore, to succeed, the EV industry must employ organizational premises quite different from current industry practices. Specifically, a group of large firms in the materials, electronics, and auto parts industries, each supplying a key vehicle technology and a substantial fraction of the total value in the vehicle, will need to form a long-term collaboration of equals with a group of equally large firms playing the role of mobility providers

For example, an aluminum or structural plastics firm might provide the drive frame; electronics firms might contribute the motive power and storage systems; other plastics firms could develop the exterior skin and interior fittings; a traditional car parts firm could engineer and produce the suspension; and a car rental firm or electric utility could take on

> "Trying to replicate this industrial system to enter the EV industry would be prohibitively expensive and time-consuming. Therefore, to succeed, the EV industry must employ organizational premises quite different from current industry practices."

James Womack

marketing and customer support within each major geographic area.

In a striking reversal of current industry practice, the firm in the middle of the value chain, which would engineer the vehicle as a package of component systems and then install all of the vehicle systems in the body to create the completed EV (the role of the giant "assembler" firms, such as GM and Toyota, in the conventional auto industry), would probably be much smaller than either the component system suppliers or the mobility providers. What's more, because of the unsuitability of the conventional car companies for this task, these "integrator" firms will need to be created jointly by the other participants.

Structure Out, Not Up and Down

"Horizontal arrangements of equals are unnatural in industrial history, yet they are the key to the success of a new EV industry."

Horizontal arrangements of equals are unnatural in industrial history, yet they are the key to the success of a new EV industry for two reasons, unique to this point in time. First, the established component systems and materials suppliers and the mobility providers already possess all of the key technologies needed for successful EVs. The key problem is not fundamental invention but cleverly combining existing or near-ready technologies into the best package. Second, as a result of economic stagnation and the adoption of "lean" production techniques across the industrial landscape, most components and materials firms currently have substantial excess capacity in the form of machinery, people, and plant space. At the same time, the electric utilities have enormous reserves of generating capacity for off-peak charging of EVs. By linking their existing knowledge and finding an outlet for their underutilized production assets, these firms can create a new EV industry, quite separate from the conventional auto industry, with vastly lower initial investment than is available to either conventional car companies or to a new-entrant EV company trying to do the whole job itself.

How might these new, horizontal relationships between perhaps 20 large manufacturing firms and an equal number of large mobility providers, which I will call a "lean enterprise," work in practice? The major firms, one for each category of component system, would need to enter into a long-term agreement to collaborate on the production of EVs. The integrator firm would need to designate a project leader to head the development effort and a production leader to arrange the details of production. These leaders would need to assemble teams whose members have all of the relevant expertise to develop and produce the vehicle. Doing this would not require enormous investments or the creation of a massive organization, because these tasks could be conducted largely with employees detailed from the member firms. What's more, production at the volumes initially needed could probably be contracted to small firms specializing in vehicle assembly, of which there are a number around the world motor vehicle industry.

A Lean Enterprise's Underlying Principles

The greatest challenge in creating the integrator firm is not likely to be technical or even organizational, in the conventional sense. Rather, it will lie in devising a set of principles to regulate the behavior of the component systems suppliers and mobility providers so that the needs of the customer are always placed first, rather than those of one firm or another in the enterprise. In practical terms, this means giving the head of the product development team in the integrator firm the power to reject components supplied by a participating firm if these components are not the best available to create a successful vehicle. (In this case, the rejected firm would become an investor in the enterprise rather than a major supplier.) Similarly, the development team leader would need the authority to conduct detailed cost investigations on each component system, so the other members of the enterprise could be sure that all firms were profiting equally through their association.

The mobility providers would face a similar challenge. To get the enterprise running at the outset, they would need to commit themselves to placing a given quantity of vehicles with users on given dates, even if they had to absorb initial losses to do so. And once the EV design was fully refined and introduced into high volume production, these firms would need to continue to plan their orders carefully and far in advance so the production system could be fully utilized and the flow of production made quite smooth. These measures would be critical to producing and marketing EVs at a cost far below that obtainable by the conventional auto industry, whose firms have massive inventories of finished vehicles as a

James Womack

"The greatest challenge in creating the integrator firm is not likely to be technical or even organizational, in the conventional sense. Rather, it will lie in devising a set of principles to regulate the behavior of the component systems suppliers and mobility providers so that the needs of the customer are always placed first, rather than those of one firm or another in the enterprise."

James Womack

> "It is realistic to imagine that the new EV industry could produce its product with as little as *half* the investment and human effort required to produce the same vehicle by a typical car company and its affiliated suppliers today."

matter of routine and which maintain large amounts of excess capacity during an average year in order to hold on to their market share in periods of strong demand.

If the participants in the new, horizontal value chain worked together in product development and production teams organized in accord with lean principles, much of the backtracking, rework, and waste in the current motor industry could also be eliminated. Indeed, it is realistic to imagine that the new EV industry could produce its product with as little as *half* the investment and human effort required to produce the same vehicle by a typical car company and its affiliated suppliers today. Furthermore, in the process of converting individual facilities to EV work, member firms might be spurred to rethink organization and work practices throughout their businesses.

Lean Enterprise Not a Virtual Corporation

While a number of business analysts have recently been exploring the concept of the "virtual corporation," where firms enter into short-term alliances to exploit a gap in the market, the EV lean enterprise would need to be a very long-term undertaking—indeed, a permanent arrangement for the production life of the basic product. This is for two reasons. Getting a suitable vehicle to market and fully ramping up to produce and service it will take four or more years. Then, driving down production costs and steadily improving the quality of both the physical product and its support services will require very careful joint investigations of the entire value stream by the member firms in the enterprise. It could easily be a decade before the industry has a fully mature product and service, and production of vehicles using the basic technologies adopted could continue for many years afterward. Analogies between the EV industry and the personal computer industry—where firms routinely form short-term alliances to exploit gaps in the market and then disband them quickly once demand subsides — are simply irrelevant to a product and service as complex, technically demanding, and so thoroughly subject to government safety regulations as the EV.

The Prospect

James Womack

There is no guarantee this concept will work; no proof that the conventional auto industry can be reinvented. However, the concept merits careful study by those firms who stand to gain the most from the creation of a successful EV industry, notably the major suppliers of electronic systems, alternative materials, and the electric power companies. The alternative approach, recently employed by CALSTART, of developing a "running chassis" with all of the necessary component systems in the hopes that the conventional auto industry will then jointly adopt it to get past government requirements, is likely to be much less practical. As noted at the outset, the conventional car companies view EVs as a threat rather than an opportunity and will continue to do so. Rather than using a vehicle supplied by a consortium, they would rather develop their own vehicle, probably one with inferior operating characteristics. If the potential winners want an EV industry able to provide new value for the customer and thereby to prosper in the marketplace, with or without a boost from government regulations, they will have to create it themselves.

A final point bears noting. One of the greatest benefits for society from reinventing industry to introduce EVs would be that the conventional automobile firms would be forced to rethink their traditional practices to respond to the challenge. The post-EV auto industry would look very different from the current IC-dominated auto industry, even if EVs accounted for only a modest fraction of vehicles produced and in use. Thus, the success of even one lean enterprise offering EVs could be a watershed event in the history of what is still the world's largest industry.

"One of the greatest benefits for society from reinventing industry to introduce EVs would be that the conventional automobile firms would be forced to rethink their traditional practices to respond to the challenge."

Applying the Theory

Dr. Womack creates an exciting vision of how the auto industry could be reinvented not only to bring a competitive edge to electric vehicles, but to provide society and consumers with a fundamentally new and arguably better mobility system. Dr. Womack suggests that organizational innovation, as much as technological advancement, can bring the vision to reality. Further, and as Mr. Lovins has suggested in Part I, these innovative changes will most likely not come from the existing auto industry. Rather, new entrants working together in an enterprise can lead the way and ultimately motivate the established auto industry to follow suit.

Dr. Womack's vision is interesting. He describes one form of e-structure called the lean enterprise. But are there any examples of companies working along e-structure concepts? In this part, we will describe the activities of companies working along such lines. First, we will let Mr. Bob Stempel set the stage.

BOB STEMPEL
Finding the Fountain of Youth

You and I both know that a battery doesn't contain anywhere near the energy that gasoline does. But how do I go ahead and use what I have more efficiently and apply it better so that all of a sudden I'm pretty competitive? The luxury we have with gasoline is we waste a hell of a lot of it. We don't have to worry about all the efficiency. It's just a new way of thinking and I'm convinced it's going to lead to some wonderful vehicles.

How did you get interested in and involved in the electric vehicle industry?

It goes back quite a few years. In my career with General Motors I've had a number of brushes with electric cars. I've sort of had an interest in them. In 1978 we converted a Chevrolet Chevette to a DC electric drive. I was pretty well convinced that it was a neat car to drive, but, being a mechanical engineer, we had done a mechanical-electric control system and the system just was not efficient. We had a lot of arcing, a lot of energy loss, batteries didn't work very well, and so forth. I thought, well, this is just showing us again the limitations of an electric vehicle.

Then a very interesting event happened in 1987. We were invited to the first solar car race across Australia. We did the Sunraycer. Initially it was one of those proposals where I thought the guys had been out in the sun too long. I said, "Come on, we can't go across Australia on nothing but sun!" But we did—1,950 miles at about 42 miles per hour. The difference was, while we had a battery and electric motor drive and solar cells for the energy source, we had power electronics and computer controls and it made all the difference in the world. We were handling minor amounts of energy very, very efficiently. That's when the light bulb came on and we said, "Hey, solar power is great, but now we know how to handle electric drives without wasting any of the limited power that we have in the battery." So that really convinced me that electric cars were going to come.

We did the 1990 Impact, which was a purpose-built electric vehicle, to see if we could get maximum efficiency—get the rolling resistance down, get the aerodynamics down—and see

Bob Stempel is former CEO and chairman of General Motors Corporation. This transcript is from an interview held in March 1994.

"We did the Sunraycer. Initially it was one of those proposals where I thought the guys had been out in the sun too long. I said, 'Come on, we can't go across Australia on nothing but sun!' But we did—1,950 miles at about 42 miles per hour."

> "The argument has always been, "Well, we don't have a battery, therefore we don't have a car." But any development on the batteries simply accrues to the car, either making it faster, giving it longer range, or whatever."

what kind of range we could get. We did that car using the best lead acid batteries we had available because the argument has always been, "Well, we don't have a battery, therefore we don't have a car." But any development on the batteries simply accrues to the car, either making it faster, giving it longer range, or whatever. I think the car has been eminently successful. In early March, we set a speed record for the flying mile of 183 miles per hour on a closed course. We've now seen the car get ready for its PrEView run with the various constituents. It's proven to be very, very efficient.

The other side of the coin, of course, is we still need batteries. One of the reasons I got involved with Ovonics is I've been following them for some years and it just seemed like we were getting closer and closer. I'm pretty convinced that their battery is a robust design. It's a good, mid-term battery (by the USABC definition of near-, mid-, and future-term battery performance). It's a next step beyond lead acid. So I put forth to the corporation (GM) a proposal on how to productionize the battery so we could get a quantity to bring the cost down, and at the same time get the battery out in sufficient numbers to see if it was indeed a step better than lead acid. With about half the mass, it's got about twice the range of lead acid, so it is a significant improvement. It's certainly not a be-all-end-all, but it looks like it's going to work. We're confident that we can get the production cost to a point where it's affordable for electric cars.

From the Outside Looking In

My current interest is simply being a little bit surprised by the lack of interest among the automakers. Right now I think the U.S. has a market lead on electric vehicles. When I look at the electronic technology coming from Motorola, Texas Instruments, Delco Electronics, I think that's pretty good. I look at motors and controls and clearly the U.S. has just terrific, very high-efficiency drives and very powerful motors in small packages. We certainly have, I think, some very innovative control logic worked out. We're fighting over mandates. We're fighting over things that really are peripheral to the whole discussion. The point is, do you think there is going to be an emerging electric vehicle market, and do you want to be part of it?

So after having left General Motors, I began to worry. I see what's happening in Europe. I see what's happening in Japan. And I think to myself, "Well, we're going to miss another market opportunity because other competitors are going to beat us to the market." So I've been out trying to network with various companies, conversion units and so forth, to see if we can't get some interest that way. But my main thrust is to see if we can't do a ground-up, purpose-built vehicle that would intrigue people. It would be fun to drive and the kind of a product that people might like and want. I think if you can get the enthusiasm around the electric vehicle, we may find we can create a market.

It's not at all difficult today to drive 100 to 120 miles on a charge. I think we'll get up to 175 miles very quickly. We now have computer control rechargers, even for lead acid, that can give you 60% charge in about 15 minutes. The nickel metal hydride battery will take a full charge in about that time. The old saw of not having enough charge to drive to work and back? You can sort of forget that. I think we definitely can do it.

Do you think the role of smaller companies is the leading role?

Yes, I do think the smaller companies are going to lead the way because I don't believe we should be tooling the car in any kind of volume where we are on today's technology. If you take the typical technology curve, we're on the very fast-rising portion of it. In fairness to the automakers, I certainly understand their desire not to lock-up tooling today for three or four years down the road.

I just got back from Phoenix, from the electric car races, and I saw even better technology. Control logic, power electronics, motor design, power transmission: the ideas are coming out of the woodwork at a rapid rate. So you'd really like to do this in small volumes. You'd like to tweak the market and see what the inventors can come up with: Should we be AC or DC? Two motors or one motor, or a motor in each wheel? What is the best arrangement for batteries? There is a whole host of things to be answered. Couple that with hybrid vehicles, like a gas turbine driving a high-speed generator to charge as you go, and some of the work being done with fly-wheels. We ought to be encouraging these derivatives to come forward and really see what kind of vehicle line-up we'll

Bob Stempel

"If you take the typical technology curve, we're on the very fast-rising portion of it. In fairness to the automakers, I certainly understand their desire not to lock-up tooling today for three or four years down the road."

Bob Stempel

have. That's a natural for small manufacturers. Then, as the technology starts to become a little bit mature, we can decide which one or two to pursue in some higher volume production. So, yes, I do see it starting with the small manufacturers.

Is there any danger that a small manufacturer could become large enough to take a bite out of the existing automaker's market?

That's my concern with not having the automakers in from the start. I think they need to think about it from this standpoint: Certainly the industry has wheels, tires, brakes, suspensions, so readily available in quantity. And there's a lot known about that. There are certainly a lot of people who can do a body. If you just simply farm everything out and don't monitor the progress yourself, or don't have an interest in the emerging technology and the technological change that's going on, you run the risk of being a little bit behind the curve. So I would hope the OEMs (original equipment manufacturers) would get involved with the smaller makers, either through partnerships or joint ventures or supplier contracts, and really take an active role in promoting those vehicles.

> **"If you just simply farm everything out and don't monitor the progress yourself, or don't have an interest in the emerging technology and the technological change that's going on, you run the risk of being a little bit behind the curve."**

We're starting to see GM do some of that. There's talk of them using smaller companies as a supplier of electric cars with a GM badge.

I'm certainly urging them to do that. I think it's extremely important and it's a good way, in my mind, for the bigger companies to reduce the risk. I think you can invest in half-a-dozen technologies on a small scale, as opposed to putting all your eggs in one basket. I am pleased that GM agreed to a joint venture on the nickel metal hydride battery production with Ovonics. It's a good chance to productionize it, see what it really does and how cost-effective it can be. I hope we get some arrangements with GM and other OEMs to move these technologies forward.

Technology is Changing the Industry

EVs as "computers on wheels" is not a bad concept, if you think about it. We were driven by mainframe computing. The desktops came along, then the laptops and personal computers, and of course today we're basically on personal computers networked together. We've seen a tremendous

Bob Stempel

change in the technology. So there is some analogy there; we are in a rapidly changing vehicle technology. Yes, it has more to do with computers than with autos. On the other hand, it's still got to be fun to drive. It's still got to meet customer needs. I certainly, personally, don't want to lose one iota of the safety we've gained in automobiles: crashworthiness, our handling and stability. I would like the automobile to continue to advance. So I don't want to regress. I don't want to go back to a "dumb" car. I'd like it to be a very effective, very safe, very efficient vehicle. So there is a role for the automakers there and I think we need to promote that.

By the same token, just like computers did, we've opened up a whole host of new concerns and new reasons to look sharp. I look at some of these electric vehicles and there's 400 volts DC being converted to AC and all kinds of electromagnetic fields. So we've got a whole group of new problems and challenges to understand and take care of. But I certainly think they are all manageable.

Supercars is Not the Be-All-End-All

I think the consortium for the so-called "Supercar" or "clean car" is probably a good idea. President Clinton avoided the industrial policy trap by saying, "Okay, we're going to move away from such a focus on defense, but I don't want to lose the technology of thc laboratories, I don't want to lose their advanced thinking. I want to try and get that into a commercial product." So he took a product, the automobile, which probably has the biggest commercial base, and said, "Let's put a partnership together with the labs and see where we can we go with lightweight materials, lasers, new production schemes, and so on, and see how much is applicable to production to make this a better industry, to make a better car, a more efficient car." I think it is a good way to use the laboratories and to bring lab developments into production. I think that's a great way to transfer technology: grow the technology and see if there are production applications.

I don't think it's a substitute, however, for new model introductions and new technology introductions. The auto companies need to continue to look at alternate fuels—whether it's electric, natural gas, or whatever—in conjunction with the laboratories. It's one thing to have a theory, it's another thing to have a running car. Clearly, I think the "Supercars" pro-

Bob Stempel

"I think the 'Supercars' program can help this activity of alternative fuels and electric vehicles. The thing I don't want it to do is to become a be-all-end-all where that is the only activity the auto companies are working on. I'm encouraging them to support our independent suppliers who are pretty good inventors. I think they should partner or joint venture with smaller companies, entrepreneurs, who may have some very good electric vehicle ideas."

gram can help this activity of alternative fuels and electric vehicles.

The thing I don't want it to do is to become a be-all-end-all where that is the only activity the auto companies are working on. I'm encouraging them to support our independent suppliers who are pretty good inventors. I think, as I've said, they should partner or joint venture with smaller companies, entrepreneurs, who may have some very good electric vehicle ideas.

We've seen the CALSTART consortium, or perhaps I should say Dr. Lon Bell and Amerigon, come out with their "Running Chassis" proposal. How realistic is a program like that?

California has certainly involved an awful lot of folks with it. They're clearly very aggressive in wanting to get the jobs for the state. CALSTART and Project California have put together a tremendous group of folks from all disciplines. Clearly they are off and running and they want to do it. One little thing I see that bothers me, that I think they have a chance to correct and hope they do, is that everybody who's in it is also on the vehicle. What I see are some strange things cropping up: "Because this company is in CALSTART, we've got this device on it, and we've got that device, and we'll use this system," and so on. I'd rather see them go back to a clean sheet approach, where we're really doing what we need to do with the technology to have it be very, very efficient. They're a smart group of people and I think they'll eventually sort it out, but right now, I think they're just a touch compromised by trying to satisfy all their many diverse interests.

Emotive Energy

There are very many young folks out there, 25 to 35 years old, who are doing some great things with circuits, some fantastic things with power electronics. I'm very impressed with their skills and I know we're going to stretch the range even on a very small amount of stored battery energy.

When I went into the automobile business 35 or 40 years ago, I was excited about automobiles because we were in the midst of change. We were really doing things and I was very excited about it. What I sense now is a new excitement among people who are my age when I started in this business.

They're working with something new—it's interesting and it makes sense from an environmental standpoint as an alternative to finite petroleum resources. What I'm finding is youthful excitement and I am convinced that we're going to see some tremendous ideas. That's why I say the technology is exploding. I don't find it at all dull. It's one of those things that, if you're not into it every day, you get obsolete in a week.

Is there a life for EVs without the California ZEV mandates?
The mandate is a funny thing. It was actually one of those days on my calendar. We had announced the Impact and we were starting to go forward with it. Then sometime after that, the California mandates came out. I understand why they did the mandates, but it's unfortunate that they did. I just hope they don't stick, and let me explain what I mean by that.

There's a presumption by the regulators that this is the way to do it: "We need so many electrics, we need so many of this kind of fuel, so many of that kind of fuel." With all due respect, the regulators don't know beans. None of us really know the answer, because we're still learning. I wish they had gone at it with the idea of pulling this technology forward.

It's a little bit akin to when President Kennedy said we're going to go to the moon. Well, we didn't have to go to the moon, but okay, we're going to do it. And what did it do? It pulled technology to make it possible. I think the technology-pull method is a much better way. Maybe not just batteries, maybe a hybrid vehicle. Maybe a natural gas vehicle. Maybe a liquid fuel vehicle. Maybe flywheels.

We know so much more about power systems and how to drive vehicles. We have a much more powerful tool today than we've ever had and that's the computer to do simulation. We have the synergy of combining various technologies. I think the regulators ought to be looking for ways to encourage that synergy, to bring it out of the woodwork, and not just concentrate on batteries and EVs. Maybe it should be batteries and hybrids, or batteries and flywheels. I just hope the mandate does not lock us into a technology that becomes technology-forcing and we decide 20 years later we've latched onto the wrong one.

Bob Stempel

"The mandate is a funny thing. It was actually one of those days on my calendar. We had announced the Impact and we were starting to go forward with it. Then sometime after that, the California mandates came out. I understand why they did the mandates, but it's unfortunate that they did. I just hope they don't stick."

Bob Stempel

A good parallel in my mind is when the emission standards came out for 1975 and we had to go with the catalytic converter. At the eleventh hour they had to back off the standard so we had some flexibility, some breathing room, so we could learn about it. But then as the regulations settled down a bit, we were able to see things like a three-way catalyst. We started to see air-fuel ratio control on conventional gas engines. We started to see feedback controls. Now we're back in the saddle again with good starting engines, good running engines, great fuel economy, very low emissions.

Pulling the technology forward is something we really have to do more of in this country. In a sense, that's what the joint program between the Big Three and the national laboratories can do, if Dr. Mary Good of the Department of Commerce can keep it from becoming a bureaucratic nightmare and can really unleash the creative juices.

Finding the Fountain of Youth

"One of the reasons I decided to leap into the electric car fray is I'm far more excited by a group of people just out of college, or 25 to 35 years old, working with some older guys like myself who are excited about what we might be able to do with an electric vehicle concept or a hybrid concept. To me, that kind of energy is what's going to bring it forward, not a mandate or a regulation."

I've got to tell you very candidly: One of the reasons I decided to leap into the electric car fray is I'm far more excited by a group of people just out of college, or 25 to 35 years old, working with some older guys like myself who are excited about what we might be able to do with an electric vehicle concept or a hybrid concept. To me, that kind of energy is what's going to bring it forward, not a mandate or a regulation.

We shouldn't overlook our real threshold here for vehicle design. I just hope the domestic auto companies don't miss it. We're very good at steel bodies. We're very good at certain structures, and so forth. Electric vehicles and alternative fuel vehicles really like low mass. In a battery vehicle it's absolutely pertinent that you pay attention to the mass equation, because otherwise it will do you in. You can put more batteries in, but the dead weight will defeat you before you go any place.

The Changing Configuration of the Car

It's a little bit like flying an airplane. You have to concern yourself with a payload, but you still need enough power to get it up in the air. That's where we are with vehicle design now. I can see on the horizon some ultralight concepts, some new composite materials combined with steel to aluminum, some vehicles that have great structures but are really super

Bob Stempel

light. Plus, now we have a power train that doesn't need an exhaust system and can be linked up remotely. So all of a sudden, I begin to see that the configuration of the car may change. In my mind, that ought to be very exciting for the auto industry. Style, shape, and form follow function.

I think we're on the threshold of some great things in automotive design. The only problem is that not everybody shares that view and it's going to take a while to get folks there. But I really do think we're going to see some very innovative personal transportation designs come out of this.

In order to do a purpose-built electric vehicle, we're going to have to be able to do it in low volume, we're going to have to do it for a reasonable cost, and modular construction has a role to play there. As opposed to these huge, massive plants with a fixed assembly line, we've got an opportunity for American manufacturing to rise up and really come in with some new innovations on how to produce it with less investment and more rapidly.

Unleashed and on a Mission

The key thing is to move things forward. It may be that I work with people like U.S. Electricar or some of the drive motor people. That work may lead to direct involvement, like it has with Ovonics. But my real motivation is to see if, in this limited time before the mandates supposedly lock us down, we can't bring forward as many pieces of technology as possible to see what we're capable of doing in personal transportation.

It is time for a change in the system. Maybe there are other schemes we can tie in to the idea of "one person per car, any time, any place" that really give us a better, more flexible transportation system and eliminate some of the congestion and the time-consuming, time-wasted commutes.

This past weekend in Phoenix, with some 39 high schools that were running converted electric cars, I didn't talk to one of those kids—they were all 21 or under—that was worried about electric cars. None of them were worried about range, and so on. They were all excited about working on something new and different. So far as they were concerned, that was going to be their future transportation. I thought to myself, there are several hundred customers right out there, right now. I didn't want to tell them electric cars don't work. I was

> "It is time for a change in the system. Maybe there are other schemes we can tie in to the idea of 'one person per car, any time, any place' that really give us a better, more flexible transportation system and eliminate some of the congestion and the time-consuming, time-wasted commutes."

Bob Stempel

"We don't have to reinvent. I think that's where some of the folks that have been in this business a while can make a contribution. Certainly, with maintaining or improving the safety, there are well-known facts. Let's build on that. But then in an area where the technology is brand new, just unleash the young people. Let them go and let's see what we can do."

pretty excited that they were telling me, "Yes, they do and they're fun!"

One of the things I can contribute is my engineering background. And I also think there are some pitfalls in plain vehicle design that we don't have to go through again. We don't have to reinvent. I think that's where some of the folks that have been in this business a while can make a contribution. Certainly, with maintaining or improving the safety, there are well-known facts. Let's build on that. But then in an area where the technology is brand new, which is the drivetrain, power systems, and so forth, just unleash the young people. Let them go and let's see what we can do. 🚗

Toward an E-structure:
Why the ARPA Program Is Important

Certainly, the dramatic changes in organizations required to bring EVs to market are going to result in some pitfalls and setbacks. Rather than take the problems on directly, many companies are attempting to lessen their risk by forming consortia or by seeking government assistance. This is another type of e-structure. The government-industry forum most closely related to the e-structure strategy is the ARPA (Advanced Research Projects Agency) EV program.

ARPA is a government-run program that is funding and attempting to manage several diverse entities in a "cooperative competition" program aimed at commercializing electric vehicle technologies, spinning off benefits to U.S. defense forces. It is a program intended to stimulate invention, application, and, ultimately, sustainable commercialization of EV products.

With the formation of the ARPA Electric and Hybrid Vehicle Technology Program, EVs have been recognized as a national critical technology with application in both military and nonmilitary uses. An EV/Infrastructure demonstration is currently underway. To date, $71.25 million in funding has been made available to develop, integrate, and demonstrate innovative, dual-use technology components that accelerate the introduction of advanced electric and hybrid-electric vehicles for military and commercial applications. Under the federal cost-share program, seven (six at the time Major Cope USMC was interviewed) consortia located throughout the United States are demonstrating a variety of EV/infrastructure support systems.

Certainly the intentions of ARPA are good, as Major Rick Cope USMC, program manager, will discuss in the first interview. However, as with many large government-run programs, the results in practice leave much to be desired. More still, the ARPA program is focused on technology, rather than market approaches, and leaves out the critical organizational elements that are needed for a successful enterprise. In this way, the ARPA program resembles the superstructure strategy. Nevertheless, in the following conversations about the ARPA program, some of the benefits of enterprise structures are apparent.

RICK COPE
Riding High on an Electric Horse

A Military Need for EVs

Since my arrival at ARPA I was assigned the task of designing new future combat vehicles for the year 2000 and beyond. In the process of exploring these new designs, we found that, over time, auxiliary power demand for combat vehicles has been climbing exponentially. As we look to future combat vehicles, we find something interesting happening. One, you can't make them big enough anymore. Most countries can now defeat an M1 tank head-on. You can't make the tank any bigger. They already weigh 75 tons. You can't just keep putting armor on it. You've got to defeat enemy ordnances in a different manner. All these auxiliary loads for things like electromagnetic armor, electrothermal guns, multispectral sensor sweeps, communications, putting robots on board that will go out and look around for you—all those things require extensive electrical power. We found that the electrical power required for operating those systems was in some cases two to three times larger than the power required to move a vehicle across terrain. So we could no longer get electrical power as a by-product of running an engine that moved the vehicle. We had to have a power plant on board the vehicle, and then a smart controller and computer system that allocated the power to the demands that were present at the time. If we did it the right way, there wouldn't be an infrared signature, either. We could turn off the power generation mode and run on stored energy. That was the other advantage. We could run this thing, let's say, on a turbine with energy storage, turn off the turbine, crawl around in silent mode with no infrared signature, no acoustic signature, and when we're running low on power, we'd crawl into a ditch somewhere, since we already had the digitized terrain map in our computer, and fire up the APU (auxiliary power unit) and recharge our energy storage.

We're doing lots of those things. We are proceeding down that path with a number of futuristic combat vehicles. Some of the things we need are very energy-dense electric motors and controllers, electrical generation capability, and storage—for instance, with an electric gun—of about 1.5 megajoules with a discharge time of a half second or less. All this is shrunk into a combat vehicle that is very small in size, can go into the ocean, and survive a rough environment.

Rick Cope

A Way to Get the Technology

We then saw a congressional add for $25 million for electric and hybrid vehicles. I saw it as an opportunity to go about business in a different way. We could continue to proceed in the normal military-industrial complex where we fund the same companies that I've known for years to build us this new hybrid vehicle, or, I thought, here's an opportunity to go out into the commercial world and really push technology along, and take some of that advanced technology and put it back into combat vehicles and drive it around and see where it falls short. Do we just have to paint this motor green? Is that good enough, or do we need to wrap it in thicker copper coils?

A Plug for ARPA

But in either case it's important, because as we look down the road we see the military-industrial base shrinking significantly. For instance, in the M1 tank, we went to Indianapolis, Indiana, and built with Allison Transmission a multi-million dollar tank transmission plant. The only thing that plant can do is make tank transmissions, and it just made its last one and they locked the doors. It can't do anything else. Well, we as a military will no longer be able to afford to do that. And we aren't going to be able to buy thousands of vehicles anymore. We're going to buy 500, or 700, or maybe 1000. But that's about it. The government can't afford to go out anymore and capitalize those plants. We really need to leverage off the commercial technology.

So my hope was to push commercial hybrid and electric vehicle technology down the road so it would become a commercial success. People would be out there building these motors and controllers and all these things I needed. I could take them and do whatever modifications I had to do to them and bring them over to the military world.

Are the military's requirements getting closer to consumer society's requirements?

Consumer society's requirements are coming up. For

Rick Cope

> **We're not going to have the money to capitalize the entire production facility for making the vehicle, unless we really, really have to. We'll get a lot more bang for the buck if we can start with commercial practice and modify it to satisfy military use."**

instance, in the past most of the motors used in the factory have been fixed-speed, DC motors. Now, because they consume so much power—and that's starting to become a concern—people are looking toward variable-speed motors. Well, we need variable-speed motors in combat vehicles, too.

We're not going to have the money to capitalize the entire production facility for making the vehicle, unless we really, really have to. We'll get a lot more bang for the buck if we can start with commercial practice and modify it to satisfy military use.

Dual-Use Technologies and Products

The prime objective of our program is to push commercial technology down the road, build better products, and bring them into military equipment. Then we'll test that military equipment to see what kind of improvements we get out of running that level of hybrid-electric drivetrain. Then we'll see where it falls short and improve upon it. We have a number of pick-up trucks and buses and all kinds of vehicles which we have to buy, maintain, and pay for fueling. We push those commercial vehicles, and continue to push that technology down the road in the commercial sector. Year after year, as we build new things, we bring them over to the military and we test them out and try them. We continue to build new things in the commercial sector—everything from batteries to headlights to composite vehicles—and we bring them over to the military side.

We've got a future military vehicle called the "CAV"—composite armor vehicle—a cavalry vehicle. We're designing the specifications now to make that hybrid-electric. I'm going to ask the commercial guys to build me the components to go into this thing, to build the power train for us.

> **"As we go down the road, I'm looking at the commercial technology coming over to the military side, then using some of the military drivers to refine some of the commercial technologies, so we have good dual-use, back and forth."**

As we go down the road, I'm looking at the commercial technology coming over to the military side, then using some of the military drivers to refine some of the commercial technologies, so we have good dual-use, back and forth.

How is your ARPA program designed to meet these objectives?

All six coalitions are required to do several things. For example, they must demonstrate the utility and efficiency of

Rick Cope

electric and hybrid-electric vehicles for military use. To that end, we're building a total of 300 vehicles in 1993. But we've got vehicles on military bases all over the country, hybrid and electric, pick-up trucks to buses, that are going to be driving around with data acquisition devices on board so we can actually record the usage, the amount of energy used, and be able to determine the differential in pollution, cost, maintenance, and energy used between the standard pick-up truck and the hybrid or electric pick-up truck or bus. So we can actually calculate the savings.

Also, ARPA gives us the opportunity to put some different things in the field. Should we use lead acid batteries or nicad? Should we use permanent magnet motors or inductance motors or DC motors? Lots of things people don't know now. We'll establish a baseline of performance.

To that end, every two weeks, as these vehicles hit the road their performance data will be downloaded to the supercomputer in Hawaii, which is a member of one of our coalitions. They will collate all the data for everybody every two weeks, strip it down to the relevant things we need to know, and ship it back out to all the coalitions, making real practical use of the information highway.

Cooperative Competition

In the coalitions, everyone will know the performance of everyone else's vehicles every two weeks. It's "cooperative competition." It's a key for success. I'm not having the coalitions fight it out among themselves. They are a team. They are a family. It's them building great products against the rest of the global competition.

That goes against human nature.

Yes, it does. Sometimes it's real hard. We've had some significant discussions about this. When we had our first tri-annual coalition meeting in Hawaii, it came together. Every coalition leader, all six of them, stood up and described everything we were doing for everybody else in every other coalition. Then we broke down into specific groups on, for instance, buses. The bus guys all stood up in front of all the rest of the bus guys and described exactly what they were doing and how they were doing it. They found that 99% of what they were doing they had in common. They had com-

> "In the coalitions, everyone will know the performance of everyone else's vehicles every two weeks. It's 'cooperative competition.' It's a key for success. I'm not having the coalitions fight it out among themselves. They are a team. They are a family. It's them building great products against the rest of the global competition."

mon problems and common successes. They were able to share information and make significant progress in the course of a week.

What other mechanisms do you have for sharing?

We have our "coalition meets." They are a requirement in the agreement. When you sign the agreement you agree to share. Failure to do so is a violation of the agreement. Every two weeks, we take all the vehicle performance data and send it via the Internet to the supercomputer that processes the data and sends it back to all the coalitions. We also share that way.

You've talked about one goal for the 1993 budget program. What are the rest?

There are four steps. One is demonstration of electric and hybrid vehicles on a military base. Two is demonstration of their utility and efficiency in a commercial market, real commercial markets where they can sell them and make a buck. We don't want to fund people just for the sake of funding R&D. We want them to be commercially viable entities.

The third objective is technology and all of the technology problems that are out there that keep EVs and hybrids from becoming successful.

Four is crash, fire, safety, rescue training. Those kinds of things that are different with EVs and hybrids. If you have an accident, now you have a lot of battery acid spill, for instance. How do you address that? What do you have to tell a fire department when they roll up to an EV crash? Do they hose it down with water or not?

If taxpayers are funding your program, how do you get around the sensitive issue of funding commercial business? In other words, creating an unfair commercial environment?

The funding is 50-50. These are demonstration vehicles. So we're pushing technology that we're sharing between the coalitions—internal to the United States economy—and with the U.S. government for use. We're building buses that have never been built before, with an electric motor in each rear wheel. I'm taking these electric motors and putting them on a military vehicle. Things they did in integrating the electric motor with a brake drum, with an axle, with the bearings, enable me to put that on a military vehicle. So by doing the commercial vehicles, I learn a lot, plus you learn a lot by actually driving them around, day in and day out, in the cold, the snow, the salt. So I'll get a lot of performance data off of that vehicle that I can use for military purposes. And it helps our companies become more competitive in the national and international markets for vehicles.

We are trying to do something that we're not good at doing as Americans. We're good at inventing things, but we're not good at taking those inventions and turning them into products that are marketable. That's what we're really doing here.

For instance, Solectria is building a ground-up composite vehicle, so we have gotten involved with the Department of Transportation, the National Institute for Highway Safety, who does the crash-testing. We also have involved Lawrence-Livermore Labs. They developed the computer code for crash simulation. In the process of building new computer codes, not only are we coming out with a composite vehicle, but we're coming out with an extensive increase in our overall knowledge of how composites interact and how they crash and how they fail and what the structural tensile strengths of them are, significantly increasing our database of how these materials work. We're doing things that have not been done before.

Why six consortia?

We weren't fixed on a number. It ended up that way. We wanted regional, geographic coalitions that could bring together a number of people in an area into teams to work on these programs. We had full and open competition. We put an announcement in the *Commerce Business Daily*. We received 17 proposals. From there we selected with a committee made up from the Department of Transportation, Department of Energy, myself, the Army, the Marine Corps, the Post Office, and some other people. Through a competitive selection process, we selected the six people that we thought would do the best, based on purely technical capability and on getting the most value for the money spent. We had $25 million for 1993.

All total, there are about 190 companies involved. We've got everything from power companies to major defense com-

Rick Cope

> "We are trying to do something that we're not good at doing as Americans. We're good at inventing things, but we're not good at taking those inventions and turning them into products that are marketable. That's what we're really doing here."

panies—Grumman—to major vehicles companies—Delco Remy—to Westinghouse, General Electric, Ciba-Geigy for composites, down to very small companies that make specific components. We have a small battery-charging company that's a start-up. We've got some vehicle and motor-making companies that are start-ups. So we've got everybody from very small to very large international corporations.

So the plan is this: you want to help build the U.S. economy, because you consider defense to be related to economic strength as well as military strength. Recognizing that, you are attempting to build an enterprise that strengthens our total defense.

That's about it. I'm trying to do things in a different, more effective way, while at the same time making sure that our economy is there to maintain it, to the extent that I can while promoting defense. We end up with a real industrial base that will sustain us. If our industrial base goes away, like it did after World War I, if a new emergency arises there won't be anything left there to build on. History is replete with this happening before.

ARPA Update, December 1994

The efforts of the six coalitions in the last two years have significantly advanced the technology and acceptance of hybrid and electric vehicles in both the military and commercial sectors. We have set a new electric vehicle distance record of 831 miles in 24 hrs using a new battery charging technology that recharges a vehicle in nine minutes. We have two carbon composite flywheels and a new electrochemical capacitor in test. We are bringing silicon carbide to power switching and leading the way to a new standard of zero loss resonant switching. We are also making new technology advances in vehicle manufacturing including all-composite vehicles.

In the next 10-15 years, the number of hybrid and electric vehicles will increase into the multiple millions of vehicles worldwide. Hybrid and electric technology is also sweeping through the military in systems big and small. This technological revolution will dramatically change the shape of the market from manufacturing through sales and service. New industries, companies, and ways of doing business will come and go during this process. It is truly an exciting time. 🚗

LON BELL
Lessons from CALSTART, Recipient of ARPA Funds

Lon Bell

The basic approach of CALSTART is to identify the various entities that are impacted by the creation of an EV industry: customers, manufacturers, labor, energy providers, policy makers, environmental policy makers—and all of the activities that ultimately relate to the creation of such an industry. CALSTART tries to develop processes whereby those entities can work together and satisfy, broadly, the requirements for the creation of such an industry. It's not advocacy, it's a grouping that involves all impacted entities.

Dr. Lon Bell is president of Amerigon and a founding member of CALSTART. This transcript is from an interview held in late 1993.

CALSTART was formed to have a positive impact on California's economy by creating desirable jobs and improving air quality. Thus, part of the strategy is to understand the core competencies and needs within California, and to link capabilities to emerging marketing opportunities within the advanced transportation industry that require innovation, capitalization, or some form of change. Also, CALSTART attempts to develop cooperative efforts that are responsive to government, regional, and customer advanced transportation requirements. For example, the need to convert defense workers' skills and defense facilities to new enterprise and combine with the need to clear our air and tap into sources of funding to create low-emission advanced vehicles.

How have things been going so far?
We have done much so far. The board of directors of CALSTART has brought together those forces that I talked about: financial institutions, government agencies, component suppliers, minority business, small business, large aerospace companies, labor unions, universities, electric utilities advocating electric vehicles, and gas companies advocating natural gas vehicles. All are represented on the board of directors along with regional customers.

Is there a leader in all of this, someone to coordinate all of the various projects that are going on?
CALSTART has a full-time president, chief operating officer—a dozen employees in all. The president, Mike Gage, was previously president of the Los Angeles Department of

Lon Bell

Water and Power. The chief operating officer, Glenn Perry, ran the Los Angeles Air Force Base—thus bringing both a military and an aerospace perspective to CALSTART.

Within the organization are designated program managers, empowered to conduct programs, monitors, and audits to ensure programs are conducted in compliance with state and federal regulations and that appropriate business practices are followed. Nevertheless, the program managers are empowered to form program teams, act as system integrators and coordinators, and structure programs to meet particular objectives agreed to with CALSTART's board.

The Showcase Car Program is an example. It is comprised of companies that are interested in becoming first-tier suppliers to manufacturers of electric and other advanced vehicles. In the case of a bus program, participating companies are building buses and engaging first-tier suppliers. The buses are used by CALSTART participants and others.

What are the barriers or stumbling blocks when trying to break into the auto industry?

There are several barriers. One, aerospace companies must change from supplying a single customer—the government—to dealing with a global customer base. Two, they must transition from low-volume, very high-cost manufacture to high-volume, low-cost manufacture. Three, they must learn the ways of, and be responsive to, the automotive industry. Number three is very hard because auto manufacturers tend to develop deep, long-term working relationships with key vendors. It is a very tight-knit group of vendors and breaking in is difficult.

The reasons success might be achieved, however, are equally important. Many available aerospace technologies are not broadly used in automobiles. Nevertheless, many recent automotive innovations have come from aerospace, and significant fractions of emerging markets have been captured, spawned by the innovations of new aerospace entrants: specifically, Morton International; my former company, Technar; a competitor of ours, Breed Technologies; and another company, Talley Industries. All had aerospace origins. Collectively, those companies dominate the multibillion dollar airbag industry. Ten years ago, they had less than $10 million in airbag sales.

"Many available aerospace technologies are not broadly used in automobiles. Nevertheless, many recent automotive innovations have come from aerospace, and significant fractions of emerging markets have been captured, spawned by the innovations of new aerospace entrants."

What are some of the other technologies that are resident in the aerospace industry but are not yet part of the capabilities of the auto industry?

There are a host of potential entrants: structural design techniques, various types of computer simulation and modeling, aerodynamics, joining and fabrication of lightweight materials such as aluminum, systems substitution such as heat pumps for heating and air conditioning, heads-up displays, fiber optic instrumentation, and so on. For success, the ability to integrate technologies is important, as is developing cost-effective products.

The difficulties in converting and utilizing aerospace technologies are twofold. First, capitalizing and redesigning systems that embody new technologies to achieve low-cost, high-volume manufacture. Second, adapting the aerospace companies' corporate culture so as to effectively service auto companies.

Through your experience with the auto industry, are the skills needed to integrate technology resident in the auto industry today, or are you suggesting that it's better represented through new entrants to the auto industry?

Some of it is resident in the auto industry in their research facilities. But there has been a large disconnect between auto industry research efforts and their process of incorporating the resulting technology into production cars. Existing vendors have had little success in introducing new technologies as well. As a result of the industry downturn in the early 1990s, the vendor base has been restructured to be extremely lean. It's not in robust financial shape. There is little capital available for, say, a supplier of today's air conditioning system to develop and capitalize new cooling technology that uses new technology, manufacturing processes, and capital equipment. That capability, however, exists and is mature in certain aerospace companies, even though the products are of high-cost and low-volume manufacture. What is there is all of the test equipment, technology, knowledge of function, design capability, and quick prototype ability. These are totally capitalized in the aerospace community.

Lon Bell

To summarize, you are saying the cost penalties to EVs are in the cost of change and of retooling, rather than saying that EVs themselves have some longer-term cost problems.

It is my personal estimation that the cost of EVs, if manufactured in high volume—in the same general volumes as conventional vehicles—would be considerably lower in cost than internal combustion engine vehicles by about 10% to 15%. EVs are simpler, there are fewer parts, and the capital cost is substantially lower.

Are they easier to design, also?

"You know a gasoline motor is very complex and getting more so as emission standards become harder to meet. Electric motors are simple, low cost and reliable."

You know a gasoline motor is very complex and getting more so as emission standards become harder to meet. Electric motors are simple, low cost and reliable. The same comments hold for many other parts, except for batteries. Lead acid batteries are cost-effective today, but lack performance. Today, advanced batteries appear to work well, but are too expensive. The long-term, intrinsic cost of several battery types is low. These include bipolar lead acid, zinc air, and possibly nickel metal hydride. So, as competition heats up, we can expect prices to decrease. But on all the other parts, just a one-for-one substitution strongly favors the electric vehicle in almost all cases.

What about the government's role? Is government stimulation required to help cover the cost of this?

Government stimulation is extremely helpful and probably very necessary for the United States to have a leadership role in the global marketplace. Without government stimulation, the process of establishing viable EVs will be greatly slowed.

The government's EV Program of 1976 failed in meeting its objectives. Do you think things have changed to the point now where EVs will be successful?

If the goal of the 1976 program was to commercialize EVs, then I agree that it failed. I think there are several circumstances that have changed to favor EVs now. EVs help solve many problems the world faces. They are very effective in reducing visible pollution. They are very effective in reducing dependence on fossil fuels. In the U.S., they are very effective at creating new proprietary business and manufacturing opportunities, based on core competencies resident in our aerospace industry.

Lon Bell

EVs are not viable in most people's opinion. I have to disagree with this viewpoint. Some feel EVs do not satisfy consumers' demand for car-like transportation. They are not competitive because of the initial cost barriers that we talked about, and because of limited performance. However, with time the temporary high costs will disappear, and some will discover that the advantages offered by EVs—such as home refueling at low cost, quiet operation, no odor or emission, and less frequent and lower-cost maintenance—are more important to them than the positive attributes of ICE vehicles.

The GM Impact has shown that EVs have good acceleration but only a 100-mile range. Is this adequate performance for consumers in Southern California?
It is more than adequate to meet enough consumers' needs to both satisfy our pollution targets and create sufficient demand to allow EVs to be produced in quantities to have economies of scale.

The auto industry is saying, publicly, that they support EVs and it's something that they want to do, but it's fairly obvious that EVs are not in the automakers' best interest. Yet you've alluded to some advantages that automakers can get out of EVs: proprietary components, strategic positioning, etc.
Automotive companies tend to think in three- to four-year cycles, with little linkage between long-term strategic advantage and short-term action. If this pattern changes, auto companies could use the spin-off technology to meet increased CAFE standards at low cost, reduce pollution through efficiency gains, and make lighter-weight, more exciting vehicles.

If we can't rely on the auto industry to lead this EV effort, is there someone else out there who could lead this?
For short-term introduction, it will be led by state and regional mandates. So it will be a mandate-driven market initially, much as airbags, seatbelts, and catalytic converters were. If mandates are not upheld, it will be led by Japanese, German, and French entrants, much as what happened with airbags and the sourcing for economy cars in the past.

> "Automotive companies tend to think in three- to four-year cycles, with little linkage between long-term strategic advantage and short-term action. If this pattern changes, auto companies could use the spin-off technology to meet increased CAFE standards at low cost, reduce pollution through efficiency gains, and make lighter-weight, more exciting vehicles."

Lon Bell

"It's my opinion that consumers will find such vehicles satisfying and useful. So, there is a good prospect that EVs will find significant, viable markets; not 90% of the auto market, but smaller niche markets such as Jeeps and various sports cars have done."

So, as mandates or foreign entrants get more cars in the marketplace, the risk will reduce in the automakers' eyes and will pick up their efforts at the latter stage?

Yes. Once EVs are out there and the automotive companies are in a position where they must sell quantities of the units, for whatever reason, they will do what they did with airbags: turn a negative into a sales tool. It's likely, in my opinion, that some of the automotive companies will opt quickly to promote EVs and develop additional demand so they can create a viable business segment and satisfy an important niche market before it gets crowded. It's also my opinion that consumers will find such vehicles satisfying and useful. So, there is a good prospect that EVs will find significant, viable markets; not 90% of the auto market, but smaller niche markets such as Jeeps and various sports cars have done.

Is it possible for an organization like CALSTART to take a leading role in automobile development and, perhaps, production?

The assembly, distribution, and service of cars is a highly refined art and a very mature business. It is not CALSTART's intent to do that. CALSTART is a nonprofit cooperative that will not manufacture or sell product. CALSTART will help facilitate entities wanting to do that.

Do you think that the industry will see a reshaping of the methods used to design, manufacture and market vehicles?

I think there will be new suppliers heavily engaged in the production of components and subsystems for EVs. And I think the auto industry will restructure to develop cost-effective means of quickly meeting demand for niche vehicles and competitively supplying vehicles in low volumes. 🚗

ARVIND RAJAN
Finding a Niche in an Enterprise

Lon Bell

We have two major lines of business at Solectria. Our vehicle conversion business has two lines of products, the Solectria Force on a GEO Metro platform, and more recently an S-10 conversion, both using our induction drive system. The other part of our business is components. We produce components that go into our vehicles and we also produce others, both auxiliary and drive system components. We sell those to people building specialized racing vehicles, throughout this country and overseas, and also to other manufacturers. Manufacturers are the growing part. We have specialized, auxiliary drive systems for electric buses, for example. Both of those businesses have good potential.

The conversion business we see as a good near-term bridge over the next two or three years. However, we don't see Solectria as a conversion company. That isn't what we were founded on and it's not something we see as the long-term future. We think of technology development as something we are very good at and we see the components business as something we're going to be in the long-term, beyond 1998. We have several R&D projects going on right now, and some component development projects being funded by ARPA which we think will lead to some very good long-term products. We're also doing some specialized R&D work for some of the national labs, as well as for the military. We think that is another strong capability of ours that we think is going to continue in the future. In terms of the other part of our business, vehicles, we are about to begin work on a little-over-a-million project to develop an all-composite, ground-up, electric vehicle, which will be happening over the next 18 months. That's the vehicle we see for the long term for Solectria that we might be producing.

That vehicle will be developed over the next 18 months. It is not a vehicle we plan to produce in low volume. We could produce units of five or ten at a time and sell them for $100,000 each and it would be a great vehicle. But we never intended to be that kind of company. We don't want to be the specialized, high-performance electric vehicle company. We'd like to see EVs in the hands of the public. The challenge is to

Arvind Rajan is vice president of planning and business development for Solectria, a start-up electric vehicle and component company. This transcript is from an interview held on November 4, 1994.

> "The challenge is to see how that vehicle can be brought to production in large volume and low cost. It won't be Solectria doing that by itself, by any means, because it requires substantial capital investment. So we will be exploring by what means we can bring that vehicle to market. Working with a partner of some kind and bringing some companies together to manufacture it."

see how that vehicle can be brought to production in large volume and low cost. It won't be Solectria doing that by itself, by any means, because it requires substantial capital investment. So we will be exploring by what means we can bring that vehicle to market. Working with a partner of some kind and bringing some companies together to manufacture it.

Can small companies compete against major automakers in ground-up design?

We can compete in ground-up design. But it's a different question whether or not we can compete in ground-up manufacturing. There are plenty of companies that make low-volume, ground-up gas vehicles. The real question isn't whether a nonauto company can build ground-up electric vehicles. The question is can a small company build electric vehicles at a low cost. It isn't that the Big Three have composite experience. What they do have is lots of resources. But the base experience with composites doesn't reside in the auto industry. It resides, in part, in the aerospace industry and with the composite manufacturers.

How might a smaller company like Solectria compete in manufacturing against the likes of GM?

It's going to be a challenge. I don't see how a loose consortium of companies is ever going to compete successfully. I'm not a believer in consortium efforts. I think they often don't lead anywhere. You can do R&D efforts in a consortium, but it's tough to bring that together to do manufacturing. I think what you need is one large player working with subcontractors, perhaps. I think that's what might happen. We'll bring several companies together and have one company, that has deeper pockets, in the lead. Our belief is that we don't have to be in competition with the Big Three. It would be great to work with a larger vehicle manufacturer. As long as you can maintain some kind of decision-making control. 🚗

Toward a Lean Enterprise

We reviewed the strategy of the ARPA Electric Vehicle program and, through the words of Dr. Bell and Mr. Rajan, heard how the philosophy of such a program, while good at facilitating the growth and application of technology, is not focused on bringing electric vehicles to the commercial market. Perhaps more importantly, the ARPA program is not designed to reinvent the existing auto industry or in any other way create a lean enterprise. The ARPA program is focused on technology, not organizational engineering.

Now we will consider the e-structure strategy as is exists in the free market, rather than as controlled through a government program. Through an enterprise structure, competitive, profit-making enterprises are being built. This extends beyond the scope of government-run programs, which are not permitted to create competitive advantages for selected companies (at least in the United States).

The Automakers' Response to E-structures

Henry Kelly suggested in Part II that the auto industry is like a huge supertanker that turns and maneuvers slowly and steadily. Indeed, the auto industry is a massive industry, an "elephant" of an industry with elephant-sized players. These analogies reflect the industry's structure, which resists change, as well as the industry's size. However, if you don't turn the wheel, the tanker will never come about. There are signs of a "turning wheel" in the auto business. Perhaps it is a shift of the magnitude recently experienced in the computer industry as it moved from a centralized, mainframe format to a distributed, personal format.

The automakers are aware of something lurking in the shadows. We are now seeing automakers facilitate the growth of small, aggressive companies which are building and marketing electric vehicles and components. Initially, these small companies will sell credits to the larger automakers to help them meet vehicle mandated volumes. This will also provide the large automakers with a buffer of time, allowing automakers to offer EV products some time after the California mandates take effect. This time is needed to prepare the marketplace for these new products, and to develop and produce an EV suitable for mass consumer markets.

Smaller companies are also working with the automakers to develop new technologies and market approaches for EVs. These smaller companies are in effect "greasing the skids" for the more established automakers. With this strategy, automakers hope to waltz into a new market once its size merits the automakers' attention and the technology has proven itself.

Appearing Foolish

With this activity it may appear as though the auto industry is not committed to a cultural transformation or reinventing of the industry. Rather, the automakers' response to electric vehicles appears to be inaction, or perhaps action applied as a resistance to change. This response to the call for EVs reminds us of what happened in the computer industry as new entrants like Apple and Microsoft capitalized on a new product market while IBM and other mainframe makers waited.

Inaction on the part of the auto industry creates opportunities in the marketplace. Accordingly, new companies that find the electric vehicle business appealing are joining in the dance in an attempt to capitalize on new product opportunities before the larger automakers have a chance to react.

The automakers might seem foolish. But the silence from the established automakers may only be a facade and a sign, ironically, of true leadership. The automakers have formed new strategic alliances that will serve to pull them into a new EV product line. Most notably, in addition to Chrysler's well publicized use of suppliers for technology, Ford is using U.S. Electricar to help them apply new technologies, build EVs, and explore new market opportunities. Perhaps these alliances are the makings of a new strategic style for the large automakers. Certainly, the EV challenge is serving to reshape the larger auto industry.

Automakers are allying themselves with leading-edge electric vehicle makers to help build a buffer to change. But, at the same time, these small companies are allying with dozens of other companies, both big and small. This is now resulting in a formidable enterprise based on e-structure strategies. U.S. Electricar is proving to be one of the most visible examples of how to build an e-motive industry through e-structure strategies. To explore the workings of an e-structure company, we will now discuss this company in more detail.

The E-structure in Action

U.S. Electricar's approach is based on e-structure principles. To illustrate this point, let's re-examine the principles of an e-structure and apply them to some of the history, projects, and partnerships of U.S. Electricar's enterprise:

E-structure Principle #1: Exploits business opportunities in large-scale (global), emerging products and markets.

U.S. Electricar's president and CEO, Ted Morgan, is not a "car guy." He learned his business skills as a sales manager for Xerox Corporation. Later, after leaving Xerox, Mr. Morgan started Office Club, which went on to reshape the nature of competition in the office supplies business. After a merger with Office Depot, the company gained a net value of almost $4 billion. Mr. Morgan knows the power of arriving first in emerging markets with new, innovative products and services. He also knows the power of strategic alliances.

Being first to market is a key component of U.S. Electricar's strategic approach. Rethinking the market-entry activities is a core part of the company's success.

The company has internalized the goal of bringing fully safety-certified vehicles to market quickly. Certifying vehicles for on-road use has been a barrier to entry for many automotive companies, both big and small. U.S. Electricar, however, breaks through this barrier by, in part, investing in leading experts and equipment capable of computer-simulating crash events. In 1993 and 1994, the company passed the FMVSS tests on the first attempt with an electric pick-up truck (based on a Chevrolet S-10) and with a sedan (based on a GEO Prizm), thanks to the systematic use of powerful computer simulation tools. The company is now working to be the first vehicle integrator to utilize "virtual prototyping," the process of going from computer design to production-ready products.

The company has also focused on a strategy that positions it as technology integrators, able to consistently bring the "best" technologies to market in a timely fashion. By creating strategic-technology partnerships and preferred-supply relationships, the company is able to gain some of the best technologies at the lowest cost and quickly apply the technologies to vehicles. In this regard, the company's first tactic was to align itself with Hughes Power Control Systems (part of the

General Motors family of companies), a leading producer of advanced electric drivetrain systems. As a result, the company is able to put electric power on the road at a time when other companies are trying to simply put drivetrain systems into production, much less into a working, salable vehicle.

Next, the company positioned itself to commercialize the most competitive near-term batteries. By working early with Hawker, an advanced lead acid battery maker, and then with other energy storage companies, U.S. Electricar promises to offer greater than 50% improvements in range and 100% improvements in battery life (compared to traditional lead acid battery designs), again, at a time when other electric vehicle makers are still trying to put their first vehicles on the road.

U.S. Electricar also recognizes that the automobile industry is a global industry and that focusing on one market or one region is too short-sighted. Rather, the company has entered into a host of international activities, aligning itself with some of the best and biggest international companies. These range from vehicle manufacturing and R&D in Malaysia and Singapore, to distribution agreements with Itochu (one of the world's largest trading companies—à la *keiretsu*). Other agreements have been made with Troy Design and Manufacturing (a large automotive engineering firm in Detroit), and CASA (one of Mexico's largest bus producers). Now the company is actively pursuing partnerships with large, multinational aluminum, plastics and composite material companies which will help them bring ultralight vehicles to market.

Also, in line with e-structure principles, the company has partnered with small companies, including composite experts (Advance USA and Consulier Automotive) and several smaller firms active in ARPA research projects. All of these strategic partnering activities are creating an enterprise aimed at exploiting business opportunities based on large-scale, emerging products and markets.

E-structure Principle #2: Unites and re-applies diverse skills based on a commitment to continue long-term, cooperative relationships among a group of individuals, functions, and legally-separate-but-operationally-synchronized companies dedicated to the creation, sale, and service of a family of products.

U.S. Electricar is aggressively acquiring or partnering with, on a long-term basis, the core capabilities required to form and compete in an e-motive industry. This is an activity that few companies that have pursued EVs in the past have undertaken.

Traditionally, EV people have risen from the grass roots. In the past, this group has tended to include persons with a somewhat rebellious nature. Rather than seeking help from other companies with key enabling technologies and skills, these grass-roots groups traditionally took it upon themselves to create their own, all-encompassing company to develop and market EVs, as exemplified by the CitiCar which was produced by Bob Beaumont in the 1970s and was a miserable failure. This sort of "go-it-alone" strategy is also being exhibited by the auto industry's superstructure strategy. In the case of Bob Beaumont's CitiCar, the failing of this strategy may have helped to set the e-motive industry back 20 years. (People still today, largely because of the high-profile of Mr. Beaumont's CitiCar, see electric vehicles as dangerous, glorified golf carts.) This was the doing of one company, working essentially out of a garage, without help from the partners that were needed to ensure a successful product. Yet, people bought it by the thousands because it was inexpensive and considered it progressive because it was electric.

U.S. Electricar and other companies pursuing an e-structure strategy, on the other hand, recognize the power of strategic alliances, and are making them central parts of their plan for success. U.S. Electricar has also pinpointed those technologies where proprietary designs and processes create competitive advantage and therefore lie outside the somewhat "softer" strategic alliances. It is this sophisticated composite of hard and soft alliances that is leading the company to success.

And What About Strategic Partnerships?

Partnering, especially in the form of joint ventures, tends to be an appropriate method for developing the e-motive industry. Conversely, for a mature industry like the existing auto industry, joint ventures and other partnerships are viewed as short-term methods that may bring important qualities to their business, but at the same time bring the established industry a threat: the creation of a competitor and the duplication of existing resources.

Established industries in established markets, like the auto industry, have a difficult time gaining and holding a competitive advantage. For the most part the auto industry exhibits a level playing field. The product technology is, for the most part, mature and the profit levels are too low for these industries to ward off imitation and new competitors (e.g., Saturn's "innovative," no-hassles sales approach was quickly imitated by its competition). Therefore, the established company's basis for competition is usually price, rather than innovation. Strategic partnerships are usually avoided or, at best, short-lived.

However, in the e-motive industry, the technology is moving at such a pace that joint ventures and other forms of partnerships may create more opportunity than threat. This is because EV technology, especially at this early stage of the industry, has a short life span, much like that of consumer electronics products. Due to this technology evolution, the e-motive industry is taking on more of the structure of the computer industry than of the traditional auto industry.

Recognizing this trend, U.S. Electricar is entering into broad, long-term strategic relationships that execute activities through a series of shorter-term, product program agreements. For example, in Malaysia, the company has entered into a long-term strategic alliance with Proton, the first national car maker of Malaysia, and United Motor Works, a company with a broad product line including the second national car of Malaysia. The partners have charted out a broad range of products to explore, including on-road vehicles, off-road vehicles, advanced materials, and advanced electronics. A series of shorter-term business plans are being created to capitalize on each of these product areas over the long-term.

U.S. Electricar's partnering strategy allows its enterprise to operate innovatively within a broad base of strategic partners. This enterprise can continually re-apply the diverse skills that reside in the partners, based on a belief in long-term, cooperative relationships among a group of individuals, functions, and legally-separate-but-operationally-synchronized companies. Fundamentally, the enterprise is designed to create, sell, and service a family of products, rather than just a few specific products. This mix of long- and short-term objectives is a key characteristic of an e-structure strategy.

E-structure Principle #3: Allocates leadership of a function of the enterprise to the member best positioned to lead, be it large or small.

There are many companies that have much to gain from the birth of an e-motive industry (and many companies that have much to lose). Power utilities will increase sales and improve capital asset utilization. Advanced material suppliers will gain over steel suppliers. Electronics and semiconductor manufacturers will increase sales and grow new product bases. Battery manufacturers will increase sales. And so on. Yet, with all of this opportunity available, there are few, if any, large automobile companies that are willing to lead the birth of the e-motive industry.

Likewise, material, battery, and utility companies are not willing, or necessarily able, to lead the e-motive industry. This creates an opportunity for a new kind of leader. U.S. Electricar has now taken the leadership position in its e-structure and is pulling diverse resources together to commercialize electric vehicle technologies. Larger companies, like GM-Hughes Electronics (parent of Hughes Power Control Systems), Itochu, Proton, UMW and electric utilities, are likely cooperators of U.S. Electricar's efforts. For the larger companies, U.S Electricar serves as an ignitor of new markets and a "beta" tester for new products.

E-structure Principle #4: Integrates the internal creation of the enterprise's products with the external consequences of the product through partnerships that span all elements of the entire system affecting the product (i.e., the "E" forces).

The automobile comes with many consequences. It is a vast user of raw materials, energy, space, and people. While U.S. Electricar recognizes itself as a leader in the e-motive industry, it also recognizes that EVs need to be more than good vehicles if they are to succeed. It is the "E" forces (environment, energy, economy, and education) that are motivating the birth of an e-motive industry. These are forces that are shaped by the impact of the automobile on the economic and environmental systems. Maintaining alignment with these forces will be an important part of the strategy for success. Certainly government plays a central part in the establishment of environmental and energy policy. Local and regional governments, together with their business communities, play a central part in the development of new businesses and economic policies. Colleges and universities are the storehouse of academic knowledge and opinion. Finally, while it is true that the world is constantly changing, certain standards can be established which impact the road on which change travels. The "E" forces can therefore be somewhat managed by identifying the shapers of the forces and working with them. This is what U.S. Electricar is attempting to do.

The model that U.S. Electricar uses to expand its production base relies on regional satellite production facilities, and a *franchising* of its technology and practices around the world. As an example, in August 1994, U.S. Electricar formed a partnership which leverages the "E" forces. This partnership with Niagara Mohawk, a large Northeast U.S. power utility, was supported by the then-governor of New York, Mario Cuomo. Under the agreement, U.S. Electricar will establish a regional production facility in New York, bringing new jobs and economic development to the region. This venture will also work to help the region meet its air quality goals by supplying and promoting the use of electric vehicles in the region. Finally, the production facility, which aims to place 3500 EVs on the road in the next few years, will serve as an outlet for the company's products and those of its partnership in the enterprise. U.S. Electricar used this partnering model with Hawaii Electric Company and with the city of Los Angeles as part of the "Rebuild L.A." program, and is working to form similar production partnerships throughout the United States.

Internationally, U.S. Electricar works closely with national governments to foster the creation of an e-motive industry in their region. When U.S. Electricar entered Malaysia, it did so by first approaching the prime minister of Malaysia and his key staff members. Today, U.S. Electricar has a joint venture with the two largest automakers in Malaysia, but equally important, electric vehicles are now in the national spotlight of Malaysia. This will help to create the proper infrastructure, market incentives, and research and business development atmosphere for the growth of an e-motive industry in that country.

Organizational Challenges of an E-structure

Working within an e-structure does not come without its challenges, most of which are related to the unique structure of this business organization. There are three basic challenges now facing U.S. Electricar: (1) managing an overabundance of business opportunities, (2) effective resource planning, and (3) managing relationships with enterprise members.

The e-structure, by its very nature, promotes the creation of new business opportunities. In some cases of overabundance, determining the best strategic opportunities can become a burdensome activity which stretches the enterprise's resources.

U.S. Electricar started by "up-fitting" on-road passenger vehicles to electric. The company then acquired Nordskog, a manufacturer of electric utility vehicles and buses. This brought the company a full portfolio of electric products that it could offer its customer. As the company grew and formed new partnerships, enlarging its enterprise, a flood of new opportunities came in. First, on the international front, the company's enterprise brought new vehicle development opportunities. This led to the formation of a joint venture in Malaysia.

Then members of the enterprise identified outlets for the company's industrial vehicle products throughout Asia—over nine potential partnerships with large companies were identified in the span of just two months. Later, a Taiwanese partner recognized that U.S. Electricar's enterprise had the technologies and capabilities to develop and market a new product in Asia, electric scooters.

Automakers recognized the value of U.S. Electricar's enterprise and began discussions related to designing and "up-fitting" vehicles for the automakers' own "badge." This led, first, to a formal relationship with Ford Motor Company. At the same time, battery suppliers and power inverter suppliers wanted U.S. Electricar to use its strong relationships with power utilities to help market utility load-leveling devices.

As U.S. Electricar's enterprise grows, inventors, businesspeople, and "blue chip" companies from the four corners of the world are recognizing an outlet for their ideas and products. The company is flooded with opportunities, many of which show strong potential. At the same time, U.S. Electricar is passing new opportunities on to others in the enterprise. All these opportunities, if not handled appropriately, can stretch resources.

An e-structure is designed to exploit business opportunities in large-scale (global), emerging products and markets. The emerging nature of the business creates special challenges for the enterprise. To remain effective, an e-structure company must first develop sophisticated ways to filter opportunities, choosing only those that have the best chance for success and which leverage the company's existing resources or grow critical new resources. Second, the company must find methods to effectively manage its resources.

Managing resources in a growing business which is largely unpredictable is difficult. With each new technology, capability, and partnership comes a new set of opportunities. The emergence of most of these opportunities cannot necessarily be predicted. Also, since these opportunities are focused on emerging products and markets, they generally require a high degree of product or business development before they return a profit. It usually requires quite some time before the opportunities become "cash cows" (to use a dated phrase).

However, e-structure companies, by holding a leading position in emerging markets, are offered one good way to help with resource stretch. E-structure companies are often positioned to receive funds and resources up front, before they are expected to turn a profit and often before they even expend valuable resources. One way to generate this "start-up" capital is to transfer "know-how" and partnership alliances to others and be paid a fee at the onset. Also, e-structure companies represent a future value in an emerging market. Therefore, they can often enter into joint-venture relationships having been allotted considerable "in-kind" value. This means that e-structure companies enter new profit-making ventures having to spend little up-front capital, but are well positioned to share heavily in the later profits. This helps to finance new ventures as they come along. Lastly, e-structure companies, through a growing family of products, find that more mature products can help finance new opportunities.

The third challenge for an e-structure company is managing relationships within the enterprise. As the enterprise grows, it takes a great deal of discipline to both (1) keep the enterprise lean, and (2) keep enterprise members from stepping on each other's toes. Keeping the enterprise lean requires that clear rules for behavior be set in place between enterprise members. This requires clearly defined legal agreements, members being educated on the customer requirements and expectations for cost and performance, and time to allow the enterprise members to develop processes for working together.

Enterprise members must also be kept abreast of their value-adding role within the enterprise and must have their performance clearly and fairly measured. An "audit" process and system for reciprocal analysis of performance is developed to handle this activity. These processes help to instill trust among members. This trust is critical to the performance of the enterprise. It has yet to be seen whether U.S. Electricar can adopt these critical features and maintain a lean enterprise.

An e-structure usually results in a complex web of manufacturing and distribution rights. Discipline is required within the enterprise to keep members from infringing on the rights of other members, whether it be by accident or deliberation. U.S. Electricar has attempted to reduce the possibility of this happening by regionalizing its partnerships. However, challenges still remain.

To better understand some of the workings of an e-structure strategy, we will now turn to two leaders from U.S. Electricar, Bob Garzee and Ted Morgan. First we will hear from Mr. Bob Garzee. His roots are in Silicon Valley. He was an IBM area manager, then a computer consultant that marketed packaged systems for business. This is where he came to believe in the power of "synergy," the idea that groups working together could produce more value than individual companies not working together. In 1991, Mr. Garzee was hired as a consultant to Nordskog Electric Vehicles (an electric industrial vehicle company purchased by U.S. Electricar) where he helped launch new products. Then in 1992, Mr. Garzee joined the design team for CALSTART and helped formulate the structure of CALSTART. CALSTART, by its consortium structure, is fundamentally designed to take advantage of the power of strategic alliances. (However, as Dr. Bell demonstrated earlier, it lacks vital links to the marketplace.) Now Mr. Garzee works for U.S. Electricar.

Mr. Garzee's EV philosophy is centered on the need to pull together, synergistically, five basic functions, or corporate examples, to exploit the opportunities available in the marketplace for electric vehicles:

1. A leading edge public utility
2. A specialized defense industry, "dual-use" partner
3. An experienced EV manufacturer
4. Multiple, contributing component suppliers
5. A technology-testing opportunity

This philosophy is based on Mr. Garzee's own experience in forming two electric vehicle consortia. One consortium, situated at Sacramento's McClellan Air Force Base, focuses on composite technology; the other, in Silicon Valley at FMC Corporation, focuses on electronics.

BOB GARZEE
Thoughts on Strategic Partnering

Bob Garzee is president of Synergy, now a wholly owned subsidiary of U.S. Electricar, and a vice president of U.S. Electricar. This material was taken from an interview with Mr. Garzee in June 1993.

Electric utilities have a good reason for becoming involved in EVs and making them successful. Utilities themselves want to use electric vehicles because they want to show people it can be done. Utility companies can convince other people that EVs are good, useful products. Therefore, our utility partner becomes a good means of identifying fleet customers for buses and cars. If you look at the nature of utilities, they would probably do an awful lot to educate fleet owners and people in the areas they service about why electric vehicles make sense. It's part of their mission.

As a utility, if you purchase different types of electric vehicles, you can promote the electric vehicle industry in your region. You have then taken what I consider the first two of the three major steps that a utility can implement and what an EV manufacturer needs to get the product to the consumer or, in this case, to the fleets: awareness, demonstration, and applicability.

Is that why your company, Synergy, worked with utilities?

One of the reasons I went to SMUD (Sacramento Municipal Utility District) is because they are, in my opinion, one of the leading utilities in understanding how to build electric automobiles. They truly have depth in their organization and know how to do that. We both believed that some of the companies should be working together—Nordskog Electric Vehicles, Synergy, Ciba Composites, and a Swiss company called Horlacher. If you combine those talents, you could put together a consortium that would be very effective. But they felt it would be easier if you could put all of these companies under one name, working together. For location, McClellan Air Force Base was a good choice, for it is the Air Force's composite material center.

But how could you ever work commercially with an Air Force base? Because of its focus on composite materials, and because it wanted to be a "dual-use" facility. We looked at the different components and we looked around for other partners. I picked Solar-Electric Engineering (now U.S. Electricar) as another company that had tremendous experience in retrofitting electric vehicles. We decided if we could bring these people together, we would have a truly fine group of resources.

On the electronics side, which is centered in Silicon Valley, we felt that buses were very viable and a solid application for electric vehicle technology today. Nordskog was building those already. We felt we needed a more sophisticated manufacturing approach if we were going to do the business effectively in the long term. FMC had expressed an interest in becoming part of the consortium to build electric buses in Silicon Valley. They would bring their ability to use aluminum. They were one of the largest aluminum users and had a world of understanding that could be used to build aluminum frames for buses, using their labs and test capabilities with other EV manufacturers and building buses which we would originally test in their facilities and then move into airports, where we all saw a tremendous opportunity for electric buses.

FMC uses electric drive systems in military personnel carriers of some 40,000 pounds. If you are going to be building buses, you need torque and regenerative braking capability, and what better testing ground than an armored tank out in the desert?

PG&E (Pacific Gas and Electric Utility of California) was supportive of all of this. In June 1993, they formed a consortium that was the city of San Jose–FMC–Nordskog–Synergy–Inductran consortium. What I had done after four and a half years was to bring together (1) the utilities, (2) the dual-use partners, (3) the experienced EV manufacturers, (4) the multiple component suppliers, and (5) the technology-testing opportunity for buses and for automobiles.

What does a company like Synergy do when, perhaps ten years from now, major automobile manufacturers offer EVs to fleets and consumers? How do you compete then?

That's when you have to ask: Does the formula of working with utilities, dual-use partners, and all these five elements, do they make sense in both markets, the consumer market and the fleet market?

In June 1993, I took what I had put together through these various partners and made it more formal. I went to Ted Morgan, who was president of Solar-Electric Engineering. I showed him what I put together from the auto and the bus standpoint. He felt it made sense, because he was also focused on a fleet market. That's why we merged our companies. Solar-Electric became part of the consortium relationships, thus bringing another knowledgeable and experienced EV manufacturer in to join the other companies on a formal basis. Then Nordskog Electric Vehicles became part of Solar-Electric. And Consulier, which specializes in composites, is part of Solar-Electric. So what's happening is that the Synergy consortium is strengthened even further with a company whose mission statement is to focus on fleets.

What will we do ten years down the road? I think fleet users will look at the Big Three for products, when they're available. But what you have to understand is that the Big Three, if they follow their pattern, like to produce vehicles that sell 300,000 to 600,000 units. There are many, many niche markets out there that are not ever going to be that high in volume. We can focus on station cars, neighborhood EVs, utility trucks, shuttlebuses—products that typically do not sell 300,000 or 400,000 units, but are very strong niche markets. Even if Detroit builds other commuter vehicles that are comparable to the product of today, I see tremendous niche markets in other products available for someone who really does it correctly.

I don't really see it as a head-on competition. If all of our strategies were to go after the consumer market, then I think those would be head-on against Detroit. But I don't really see that as what we are all about.

One of the things that people overlook is that there are probably 100,000 electric vehicles that have been built in California, sold, and are in use today. Some people say, "Well, those are industrial types and we shouldn't really look at those." But these people are buying industrial EVs not because they want to solve the pollution problem, but because it's the best way to solve a business problem.

Many people will tell you that the electric shuttle bus makes all kinds of sense. If you look at the task of moving people around in town as a second car, then an EV makes all kinds of sense. The real question is: Will it be effective as a replacement for the car that's on the road today? But if, for some reason, Detroit decides that's not a good thing and they back out, I don't see the utilities saying that EVs don't make any sense.

Bob Garzee

"Even if Detroit builds other commuter vehicles that are comparable to the product of today, I see tremendous niche markets in other products available for someone who really does it correctly."

Bob Garzee

"EVs are a perfect, let's say, 'appliance' for the utility company, if people driving EVs re-energize them at night when those power plants are currently sleeping."

EVs are a perfect, let's say, "appliance" for the utility company, if people driving EVs re-energize them at night when those power plants are currently sleeping. In almost all the applications I've mentioned, they should be charging at night, or they should have switch-out battery systems which can be charged at night and then switched out during the daytime. EVs become another revenue base from which the utility can draw.

On the other hand, Chevron probably thinks the internal combustion engine automobile industry is good. We can say the same thing about utilities and electric vehicles. So I think the Detroit influence is important, but I don't think it's the whole industry. Whatever happens in Detroit, I certainly don't think that's going to cause the EV industry to go down. There are an awful lot of uses for EVs that are darn good today. Now and two years from now.

In the final few months before Synergy came into U.S. Electricar, what was the force that drove you to that alliance?

Fleet focus, capitalization, and component choices. I believed that fleet markets are truly where I should spend my time, and Ted Morgan and Solar-Electric felt that way, too. The second issue was capitalization. In my opinion, Ted is the premier executive in knowing how to raise funding. There is very little knowledge in the electric vehicle industry on how to do that. Capital is a real barrier for a lot of EV companies. But Ted has a tremendous background raising capital in other industries. If you're going to bring these companies together in strategic alliances and you're going to work on multiple product lines, you have to have capital to make that happen. Ted saw what I brought together, which he liked, and I saw what he brought together, and we felt that made a very strong fit.

"I think customers should have choices. I don't think customers should have just one type of component that they have to rely on."

I think customers should have choices. I don't think customers should have just one type of component that they have to rely on. If you're building buses, you really need a heavy-duty drive system. If you're building cars, you want a different drive system—lighter duty and less expensive. With buses, you probably want to use aluminum frames for construction. If you're building a car, you probably want to build it completely out of composites.

How does a smaller company build a vehicle that has the quality and reliability that markets expect today?

Look at how many cars Solar-Electric has already built, outfitting vehicles to EV—I think it's over 200. That's enough to know what works and what doesn't. With a company like Nordskog, who's built over 50,000 electric vehicles, you also get pretty good experience with what works and what doesn't. Then you take the other companies with similar experience and put it all together under one company—you have quite a brain trust and experience base from which electric vehicles can be built. It's not real lonely when you've gone out and brought all those companies together.

When you pull companies together, you cause other companies to want to come together with you as a supplier, a tester of the technology, or as a partner. It's not as lonely as you might think for a small company if you've gone out and pulled all these companies together, even though we're much smaller than most automobile manufacturers. But automakers have to be concerned with making less volume. That's a challenge that will cause the industry to relook at the way they build vehicles.

Will your fleet vehicles be comparable in cost to Detroit vehicles?

As in any new product, there will be a higher cost in the beginning. It's the same as with computers or calculators. EVs will cost about 15-20% higher than their ICE counterpart, but it doesn't take long to make up that percentage once in operation. My lessons are from Silicon Valley. But I think it's very transferable. 🚗

Bob Garzee

"When you pull companies together, you cause other companies to want to come together with you as a supplier, a tester of the technology, or as a partner. It's not as lonely as you might think for a small company if you've gone out and pulled all these companies together, even though we're much smaller than most automobile manufacturers. But automakers have to be concerned with making less volume. That's a challenge that will cause the industry to relook at the way they build vehicles."

Bob Garzee

Ted Morgan is president and CEO of U.S. Electricar. This transcript is from an interview held in December 1993.

TED MORGAN
Growth Through Strategic Alliances

What I've been involved in for the last 11 or 12 years has been capital financing, principally for start-up companies, most of which I have created myself. So I have a good background in what institutional investors look for in financing entrepreneurial companies. Some of those same rules apply here. The interesting difference here is raising money privately; I've really not had access to that previously.

All of the investment work that I have done is institutional. And the interesting aspect of the private individual financing is the fact that a lot of people have invested in this company based on environmental issues and not for return-on-investment purposes. So it's primarily been an investment of love, or concern, or philosophy, or principle, but not for economic return. That's been an interesting switch for me. I've not been involved in a company that's been able to raise money on that basis.

The focus is definitely beginning to shift now, because the company has such significant strategic plans that it's going to require really substantial capitalization. So we are now moving to the institutional market. There I think the company will come under much greater scrutiny in terms of its strategies, operating plans, performance, and that sort of thing. With institutional markets, I'm referring to more traditional investment banking-type financing, where typically you have various types of pension funds or large portfolio managers investing alongside investment banking firms.

How did you get involved in U.S. Electricar?

I left an earlier commercial retail project, a medical-dental distribution project. My home is in Sonoma County in Santa Rosa. Most of the businesses that I've started have been in the [San Francisco] Bay area. So it's required having an apartment in the Bay area and coming home on the weekends, which is not the greatest situation for family life. So this time around, I decided to look at developing a business here in Sonoma County. When I returned—this was March 1991—I basically became a consultant and assisted companies in restructuring, hiring management, and finding financing. So I acted as the interim CEO for a number of companies.

An investment banking firm that I worked with previously, a company called Cruttenden and Company in Newport Beach, had received an unsolicited private placement memorandum from Solar-Electric Engineering, which was the predecessor company to U.S. Electricar. Cruttenden asked if I would, as part of a due diligence process, take a look at the company. Coincidentally, it was just a few blocks from my office. So I actually walked over and took a look at it and was pretty appalled.

It didn't look like something that I wanted to get involved in. It was a very convoluted business. There was a retail store selling environmental product. There were electric cars inside of a storefront operation downtown. It was just a chaotic environment.

Solar-Electric Engineering came up through the grass roots, didn't it?

Boy, I'll tell you, it was still there when I went in! It sure didn't look very promising, and I so advised the investment banking firm. But the board of directors of the company persisted in discussions with me. After I really got into it and started looking at all of the regulatory mandates and so on, there was a glimmer of something there that I hadn't seen previously. So I agreed to consult for the company, help the company raise money, act as its interim CFO, that sort of thing. That started in June 1992. I was able to raise a million dollars for the company, which I thought was remarkable based upon its financials. But we were able to convince an investment banking firm of the potential for the company. Then I began acquiring management and it just slowly built up its own momentum.

Finding a Spot in an Enterprise

If all of the ancillary alliances were divested—the catalog company, the retail store, the building of solar houses, and whatever else they were involved in—and professional management was brought in, if a real clear focus could be developed for the company, I thought there was some potential. The fact that it was a small public company also was attractive from the viewpoint of being able to raise money.

> "It didn't look like something that I wanted to get involved in. It was a very convoluted business. There was a retail store selling environmental product. There were electric cars inside of a storefront operation downtown. It was just a chaotic environment."

> "After I really got into it and started looking at all of the regulatory mandates and so on, there was a glimmer of something there that I hadn't seen previously."

*By the time this book is printed, the company should have raised close to $100 million.

Based on all of that, I was offered the CEO position permanently in November 1992 by the board and I accepted. At that point, I really began assembling a very strong management team and put a full-court press on raising capital. Over the last year or so, we've been able to raise about $10 million in capital* for the company and recruit a management team that really has the ability to execute our strategy. We've divested ourselves of everything other than the vehicle business. We've cleaned up the company. It's no reflection on the founders, but it was very poorly managed and financially in disarray. We were able to clean all of that up and position ourselves so we became very attractive to the investment community.

Then we began focusing on strategic relationships, the most important of which really came via General Motors. The cancellation of the Impact program left Hughes Power Systems without a customer. We happened to be at the right place at the right time to enter into a relationship with Hughes and acquire the rights to the drive system for up-fitting vehicles. Once that announcement was made, it had a dramatic impact on the stock price and raised a considerable amount of interest in the company. I would say that was one of the major turning points for the company. Also, just the fact that General Motors and the other two major carmakers decided to withdraw from the business suddenly left a major vacuum in terms of where public utilities and others could actually buy electric vehicles. They were all counting on General Motors being their major supplier for electric vehicles. When General Motors pulled out they felt stranded and they began scrambling to find other opportunities, companies that could provide electric vehicles. We, Solectria, and Solarcar were about the only three meaningful companies in the U.S. doing that.

What attracts management to your company?

It had a lot to do with the fact that I had done this before. I had one big home run with the Office Club, later called the Office Depot. People like Mike Chobotov and others looked at that kind of success in a relatively short period of time and felt that I had, perhaps, the ability to do that again. They wanted to associate with someone who had that background.

Of course, the industry itself is quite appealing in that it's a new industry and one that is truly a pioneering effort. That certainly appealed to people as well. The fact that they could have ownership, equity participation, and really be able to take something from infancy to a substantial company was quite appealing to some of these guys.

Credibility

The key to success is to have, up front, a very coherent strategy that is simple, easy to communicate, and one that can be verified and validated. It's got to stand up to the test of due diligence. One thing that I believe in very strongly is market research. With the Office Club, we did an extensive amount of consumer research before we launched that business. Here I think the same applies. A tremendous amount of due diligence went on before I made a decision to jump in here. That's the first key piece. It's got to stand up to close scrutiny. It can't be just the wild-eyed pronouncements of an environmentalist. It's got to really have substance and meaning.

The second piece is you've got to bring in the very best talent that you can find. Because in reality, in my opinion, 90% of it is execution, 10% of it is concept. At the Office Club, early on, we brought in the best management that we could get our hands on and we fully staffed. So it wasn't just an issue of staffing the CEO and CFO and one or two others. We fully staffed all the way down to the buyer level in the organization, in anticipation of our growth. There is a lot of criticism to that approach sometimes, because you incur very significant expenses up front. But the reality is, if you don't have that team formed up front, it becomes a major distraction if you have to go out and find a team once you're actually an operating company. So I believe strongly in building that team first. That's exactly what we did here.

The third thing is to develop a very realistic business plan. The plan itself has to withstand the scrutiny of very sophisticated investors who have had lots of disappointments in investments that they've made. If you look at the venture capital community, they traditionally only look at one winner out of every ten investments. So they're very keen as to what works and what doesn't work. When you're dealing with very sophisticated investors, blue-sky projections and pronouncements that can't be validated just don't fly. So we took a lot of

Ted Morgan

"The key to success is to have, up front, a very coherent strategy that is simple, easy to communicate, and one that can be verified and validated. It's got to stand up to the test of due diligence. One thing that I believe in very strongly is market research."

Ted Morgan

"We just stopped
building cars, peri-
od, and went in
and did the engi-
neering that need-
ed to be done. We
did all of the
analysis, all of
the safety
consideration
review, all of that
before we decided
to begin building
vehicles again. "

time making sure we drafted a very realistic and achievable
business plan.

Finally, in my opinion, you're very, very careful not to go to
market before you're ready to go to market. In the case of the
Office Club, we spent a year before we actually opened the
retail store. Here we basically spent a year and a half before
we actually built a car. There were cars built under the management of the old company that were, in my opinion, not
representative of the kind of product that we want in the
marketplace. So we just stopped building cars, period, and
went in and did the engineering that needed to be done. We
did all of the analysis, all of the safety consideration review,
all of that before we decided to begin building vehicles again.
So, "don't introduce the concept or the product before its
time" is a fourth key to success. We've been very careful
about that.

It all boils down to one thing and that is credibility, being
taken seriously in the market. The only way you can do that
is to really have the infrastructure, the philosophy, the strategy, the business planning, and the management team behind
it to execute it. Otherwise, you're not going to be taken seriously in the market, or if you're lucky enough to raise money,
you're very likely to fail and you won't be able to raise another nickel. That's the downside. If there is a downside to a
public company, that's probably one of the biggest. If you
make pronouncements and then don't deliver and your stock
goes to pot, it's going to be virtually impossible to raise
money. So we're very, very careful about that.

*Bob Garzee talks about "synergy" and the idea of pulling
many groups that fit well together into one enterprise.
Does this vision match the way you see your business
growing?*

Probably not. We're a little philosophically opposed in that
area. I think it's a bit idealistic as it relates to the real business
environment. I think we will certainly take advantage of strategic opportunities like SMUD or, potentially, FMC or others.
But I have a hard time visualizing an entity that is truly just a
strategic partnering entity without economic returns. So we
have a little difference of opinion on that. We're moving
towards more of a structure that I think is really going to provide return on investment for things that we do.

Do you see yourselves as value-adding system integrators?

That, for sure, is the key role that we play. Ultimately, as time goes along, through licensing of technology or internal development of technology, we hope to control at least certain key components that will be necessary to evolve a cost-effective or high-performance hybrid or electric vehicle. So we're also opportunists from the viewpoint of acquiring technology.

We're not favorably disposed to do in-house development of technology. So our principal focus is the acquisition of technologies. We're interested in licensing technology, integrating various technologies in a proprietary way that can be either patented or protected. For example, we just submitted a patent on the battery container integration that we do with our vehicles. We'll be submitting other patents on other integration techniques that we use. Through a combination of licensing, acquisition of technology, and patenting of integration techniques, we intend to develop a proprietary position.

How do Nordskog and Consulier fit into what you've just described, in terms of technology?

In the case of Nordskog, we're looking at a fully verticalized product line, and being able to offer to the same fleet operation or buyer—whether commercial or public entities—the ability to fulfill all their electric vehicle requirements. So the guy that buys the on-road vehicles in a large operation also typically buys industrial vehicles and may have a role in making decisions regarding shuttle buses.

The intent is to not be a single product company, but to fill every transportation need that a fleet operator might have, as it relates to an electric vehicle application. That was the primary objective in the acquisition of Nordskog. It gave us 46 new vehicles, which could be offered to our fleet users, and also the bus program, which we believe is a very significant business opportunity.

Separate, but Operationally Synchronized

What we've attempted to do is continue to operate each of these business entities as separate operating divisions. So they're separate profit centers. They're subsidiary corporations. In the case of Nordskog, it's really a stand-alone business entity with its own staffing from engineering through

Ted Morgan

"The intent is to not be a single product company, but to fill every transportation need that a fleet operator might have, as it relates to an electric vehicle application."

sales, general management, production, and so forth. So it is a profit center.

Our fleet vehicle division will also be a stand-alone profit center. The composite vehicle business is really an R&D project at this time. But we think within the next 24 to 36 months, there will be viable commercial products that come out of that group, as well. So that also is being structured as a stand-alone operating division.

How does this relate to the work you did with Office Club? Are you growing in a similar fashion?

The carryover there is really in restructuring distribution. What we're doing here is, for the most part, eliminating the use of dealers or distributors in getting products to the end users. That's number one. Number two, the other carryover example would be that in the business of Office Club the idea was to develop a store model that could be replicated many, many times around the country. The key was to shake down the store model to really understand the economics—how it worked, what kind of margins it would deliver at various levels of volume—and once that was done, to be able to very quickly boiler plate that, based on demographics, around the country. The carryover example here is with the satellite production facilities that we have developed, such as, for example, the Los Angeles production facility.

"We believe that the entrée to the business is really initially going to be in the up-fitting or conversion of on-road vehicles. Our intent is to shake down the model of an up-fitting satellite production operation, such as we have in L.A., and then be able to replicate that around the country."

We believe that the entrée to the business is really initially going to be in the up-fitting or conversion of on-road vehicles. Our intent is to shake down the model of an up-fitting satellite production operation, such as we have in L.A., and then be able to replicate that around the country. We have very, very strong interest with various public utilities which have commercial divisions around the country that are looking at the electric vehicle business as their diversification strategy. We are in negotiations with a number of these large public utilities to open satellite facilities in other parts of the country to up-fit or retro-fit ICE vehicles to electric. So that would be the other carryover example.

How are you measuring the success of your business in the short and long terms?

In the short term, it's the ability to raise capital. That's the measure of success. The only measure of success. In the long term, success will obviously depend on how receptive the key target customers are to the strategy that we've employed, which will be a combination of tools, including full turn-key product leasing. You'll be able to lease a fleet of vehicles and have maintenance, warranty, training, and service.

For example, the station car consortia idea is to have various rapid transit districts around the country provide electric vehicles as a convenience for their riders to use. When a rider gets to a destination to make a business call, he'll be able to use, on a rental basis, an electric vehicle to make the sales call, or whatever, and return to the station. We're working with the Bay Area Rapid Transit (BART) district on the first of the turn-key programs which will use our GEO Prizm product as the base product. They are a transit district. They don't want to get into the management of rental fleets or automotive fleets. So we will take on that responsibility as part of the lease package. The lease package will be an amortization of the product itself, but it will also contain a fee for the services that are provided to support the vehicles.

Office Club became the $3 billion business now called Office Depot. Is this a good model for the way U.S. Electricar should grow and evolve?

Yes, I think so. We went into a market that everyone believed could not be sold. Basically, the way stationery products—office products—were distributed before we entered the market was through commercial stationers. There was a perception that businesses would buy office supplies only through direct sales representatives and delivery. The market research that we developed indicated something different. We went after a market segment that wasn't well served—the market segment of one to fifteen employees.

We did our homework and demonstrated that, indeed, there was a sizable market there. In fact, as it's turned out, we've actually done a tremendous amount of business with Fortune 1000 companies as well, because of the pricing issue. It was very, very difficult initially to round up the funding for that project, because there was a mindset that products could only be distributed one way and that customers would only accept products that were delivered a certain way.

Ted Morgan

Leading by Example

We demonstrated that, in fact, consumers would change their buying patterns if there was an incentive to do so. The incentive that we offered was tremendous discount in price. So people were willing to put up with some inconvenience if the price was right.

I think the same is true here. At $120,000 for an electric vehicle, it's kind of tough to convince fleet users to make the transition to electric vehicles. But, in quantity, if you could begin to sell S-10 electric pick-up trucks for $20,000 or less, in my opinion every electric utility company in the country will have a very sizable fleet of S-10 electric pick-up trucks.

The opportunity exists. I think the barrier right now is really the barrier of pricing, not performance. I think the Big Three have a different opinion. They view it as a combination of pricing and performance, but I don't think performance is really the gating item here. I think it's really pricing.

How do you go about exploring and proving your concept through market research? Or does the concept emerge after market research is complete?

Actually, we develop the concept first and then engage market research to validate the concept and then make changes in the concept, based on the research. For example, in the case of Office Club, I think we spent close to half a million dollars in market research. Based upon what we learned, we slightly altered our concept. Here, largely because of capital constraints, we've not engaged in the same level of market research, but we've done a tremendous amount of industry research. Based upon the industry research, we think there is a substantial market—somewhere between three and five billion dollars—for electric or electric-hybrid vehicle sales to fleet operators. The issue that we're dealing with right now is primarily getting the price down to the point that it's going to be acceptable to the fleet manager.

You rarely mention the word "consumer" when you speak of market research. Is that based on the realization that these products, or perhaps this industry, is not ready for consumers?

That's part of it. I think the other part of it is I simply don't believe that we want to be a consumer vehicle company. The

> "The opportunity exists. I think the barrier right now is really the barrier of pricing, not performance. I think the Big Three have a different opinion. They view it as a combination of pricing and performance, but I don't think performance is really the gating item here. I think it's really pricing."

position I've taken is that we're just simply not going to enter into the consumer market...at all. Not now, nor in the future. Our intent is to really focus on our niche market and leave the consumer market to others who feel they've got the capital, tools, and distribution to accommodate it, which we do not have and don't intend to build.

Our customers are really the rapid transit districts. They will essentially be the customer for the vehicle. We have no problems selling vehicles to public utilities, who will then resell the vehicles to consumers. No problem there at all. But our customer really must be the fleet operator, or the large corporate entity, and not the individual consumer. There are all sorts of liability issues. Certainly, to get to consumers, you have to use dealers. The automobile business is already notoriously bad for low margins. If we have to use dealers, our margins will go to pot. We've got to try and protect our margins here.

Do you think all the mechanisms are out there to let you do your business successfully?

I think so. I think we're still tweaking the technology, but I think there's enough right now to build a several-hundred-million-dollars-a-year business by 1997. I think that's a very achievable goal.

The impression I get with this whole industry segment is that everybody is attempting to paint grandiose pictures of what's going on here, and it's very, very confusing. You've got to weave your way through it. The reality is that the business-to-business transaction is the only transaction right now in the electric vehicle arena. That's the area I've had the most experience in, and that's the area we're most aggressively pursuing. We'll leave the others to their dreams of building hundreds of thousands of electric vehicles. It may or may not happen. But I think the market we're going after is a very real market and very substantial for a small company. I think we really have a chance to dominate at least a small segment of it. 🚗

Ted Morgan

"I think we're still tweaking the technology, but I think there's enough right now to build a several-hundred-million-dollars-a-year business by 1997. I think that's a very achievable goal."

Some Final Points

The world seems to be moving toward a new form of transportation and a new form of transportation industry. For the purpose of simplicity, we have called this new industry the "e-motive" industry. It is an industry that is emerging from the systematic influence of the four "E's": environment, energy, economy, and education. It is suggested that an enterprise structure is the organizational model which can build an e-motive industry by combining the power of these "E" forces.

We have heard how those firms who stand to gain the most from the creation of a successful e-motive industry, notably the major suppliers of electronic systems, alternative materials, and the electric power companies, are embracing the concept of e-structures and allowing others to lead them to new life. Yet, there is no guarantee that electric vehicles will succeed and an e-motive industry will be built.

Still, the alternative approaches seem less likely to succeed. The auto industry's superstructure strategy, with its avoidance of change, looks to be a long road as far as EVs are concerned. The ARPA EV Program, while somewhat promising in its military-commercial partnership concept, is also proving to be more research driven than commercial products-oriented.

It appears that if the potential winners want an e-motive industry to prosper in the marketplace, with or without a boost from government regulations, they will have to create it themselves. "Create it" means more than designing and building a product. Indeed, as Thomas Edison and countless others have proved, we cannot invent our way into an e-motive industry. Rather, a concerted effort to work within a larger system of forces is required. We must look beyond technology approaches and adopt new organizational approaches.

The Critical Step: From E-Structure to Lean Enterprise

This will come with numerous challenges. While e-structure companies attempt to design and market products, they are also burdened with the tasks of building a whole new industrial form and market mechanisms to support new products. These are challenges that will certainly come with some setbacks and failures. We have reviewed the progress of one e-structure company, U.S. Electricar, for it is a visible sign of a new kind of strategic industrial model. However, to date U.S. Electricar has built and sold only a few hundred on-road electric vehicles and this young entrepreneurial company has yet to show a profit. U.S. Electricar may or may not succeed.

Still, the convergence of powerful environmental, educational, economic, and energy forces are filling the sails of a new e-motive industry. This industry is coming and with it, the auto and its industry will become a more balanced force in our world.

Building Lifestyles?

Bringing more efficient modes of personal transportation to market is only the start of our journey. As Don Chen* expressed to me, "I feel that if you look at the broad range of transportation issues that we are going to have to confront over the next few decades, it's apparent that electric cars won't save us. That's because the fundamental cause of our transportation problems isn't cars, but rather the fact that we keep driving them farther and farther every year. Since the Corporate Average Fuel Efficiency (CAFE) standards were passed 20 years ago, we've learned an important lesson—even though the efficiency of our cars has doubled, we also drive twice as far. So not only are we still plagued by oil consumption problems, but we're also faced with worsening levels of congestion, urban sprawl, and immobility and abandonment among people who don't drive. Replacing today's cars with electric vehicles will probably yield modest potential air quality benefits, but in pursuing that goal we may overlook the root problem—our over reliance on driving as a form of transportation, as the determinant of land use planning and design, and as a way of life.

"It's not difficult to see why so many people are advocating clean car technologies. We know, for example, that the technical barriers to building affordable electric vehicles are rapidly being overcome; for efficient cars the technology has long been available. We've also learned from CAFE that, to a large extent, mandating technical improvements works. And of course, technological change is often a lot easier to implement than social change. But as important and relatively simple as it will be to improve vehicle technologies, the real challenge will be to begin thinking about our transportation sys-

*Don Chen is a former senior research associate at Rocky Mountain Institute. Prior to that, Mr. Chen worked for the World Resources Institute and co-authored *The Going Rate: What It Really Costs to Drive* with James J. MacKenzie and Rodger C. Dower. (World Resource Institute, 1992).

tem as a true system with many components—not just cars and highways. This will be an uphill battle, because for decades policy makers have made transportation projects virtually synonymous with paving more and more roads to accommodate more and more traffic. And they're just beginning to realize that Americans can no longer afford to subsidize motor vehicles while also absorbing all of the social costs associated with driving. In turn, many are also realizing that there are plenty of cost-effective ways to provide access to people that are compatible with existing communities. Some of these are old measures, like public transit, walking, and biking, and some are new, like electronic access services. But transforming our transportation system from one that is vehicle dominated to one that is integrated and multimodal is going to require profound institutional and cultural change."

E-structures offer us some hope that the larger societal desires for friendly cities can be created, for the e-structure provides room for various interests to invest in the future of the enterprise. If e-structures become efficient at not only generating income but also *value* for a wider society, then enterprises of this sort might help us move closer to the more far-reaching goals of "transportation for communities instead of commuting" that Don Chen speaks of, for they will become mechanisms for lifestyle development as much as they are for industrial development.

As Theodore Roosevelt said:*

> *Far better it is to dare mighty things, to win glorious triumphs, even though checkered by failure, than to take rank with those poor spirits who neither enjoy much nor suffer much, because they hide in the gray twilight that knows not victory nor defeat.*

Appendix

Scott Cronk

Scott A. Cronk is the director of business development for U.S. Electricar, Inc., of Santa Rosa, California. In this position, Mr. Cronk leads U.S. Electricar's strategic partnering activities.

Mr. Cronk has more than 12 years of experience in the transportation industries. From April 1991 until April 1994, when he joined U.S. Electricar, Inc., Mr. Cronk worked at the corporate headquarters of Delco Electronics Corporation, a subsidiary of GM Hughes Electronics. There Mr. Cronk was a lead member of the company's international business development and planning team. While in that position, Mr. Cronk worked to reshape the basic structures of Delco Electronic's international organization, then helped to create a global, lean manufacturing operation which is now recognized as among the most efficient and cost-effective automotive electronics operations in the world.

Prior to that, from August 1988 through March 1991, Mr. Cronk managed an avionics product line in northern Europe for Delco Systems Operations, a division of General Motors. At that time he was one of the youngest international service personnel in the history of General Motors Corporation.

Based in London, England, Mr. Cronk traveled extensively throughout Europe, working with more than nine commercial airlines and government defense organizations. His responsibilities covered all areas of customer and product support and extended to the role of quality assurance Manager for the service center in London.

Mr. Cronk holds a master's of business administration degree in international business from the City University of London Business School. While studying there, Mr. Cronk's lifelong interests in electric vehicles and experience in the transportation industries culminated in a research thesis discussing the emerging EV industry.

Mr. Cronk began working for General Motors at an early age. Starting in 1982, GM sponsored Mr. Cronk's engineering studies at General Motors Institute (now called GMI Engineering & Management Institute) located in Flint, Michigan. Mr. Cronk interned at Delco Electronic's facility in Milwaukee, Wisconsin, and graduated from GMI in 1987 with a bachelor of science degree in electrical engineering.

Maryann N. Keller
Managing Director
Furman Selz Incorporated

Maryann N. Keller is a managing Director and automotive analyst with the brokerage firm of Furman Selz Inc. Since 1972 Ms. Keller has been continuously engaged in the study of the automotive industry. She has been a guest speaker at the Financial Analysts Federation Conferences, the Automotive News World Congresses, Financial Times Conferences in Europe, the International Metalworkers Federation and the Financial Post Conferences in Canada. In addition, Ms. Keller is a frequent speaker before industry and dealer organizations.

She is a six time guest on the nationally televised program Wall Street Week. Ms. Keller has frequently appeared on other television programs in the United States and overseas as a commentator on conditions in the automotive industry. Ms. Keller has appeared before the Senate and House Banking Committees of the United States Congress as an expert witness on a variety of auto-related topics. Ms. Keller was a participant both four-year studies of the automobile industry conducted by MIT. Ms. Keller served as a member of the Committee on Advanced Vehicle and Highway Technologies, for Transportation Research Board of the National Academy of Sciences, of Automobiles and Light Trucks and the Committee on Fuel Economy.

Ms. Keller writes monthly on various automotive topics for *Automotive Industries* and *The Japan Economic Journal*. Ms. Keller's book on General Motors in the 1980s, <u>Rude Awakening</u>, was published in August 1989 by William Morrow & Co. <u>Rude Awakening</u> was awarded the Eccles Prize by Columbia University for excellence in economic writing in 1990. In October 1993 her second book, <u>Collision: General Motors, Toyota and Volkswagen and the Race to Own the 21st Century</u>, was published by Doubleday.

Ms. Keller is a member of the Board of Directors and President of the Society of Automotive Analysts.

Amory B. Lovins
Co-founder, Vice President,
Director of Research, and CFO,
Rocky Mountain Institute

Amory B. Lovins cofounded Rocky Mountain Institute in 1982 with his wife and colleague L. Hunter Lovins (BA, BA, JD, LHD, *h.c.*). RMI is an independent nonprofit resource policy center in Old Snowmass, Colorado, whose mission is to foster the efficient and sustainable use of resources as a path to global security. Mrs. Lovins is the Institute's President; Mr. Lovins is its Vice President, Director of Research, and CFO. Originally a consultant experimental physicist, educated at Harvard and Oxford, he has received an Oxford MA (by virtue of being a don), six honorary doctorates, a MacArthur Fellowship, the Nissan and Onassis Prizes, and (shared with Mrs. Lovins) the Mitchell and Right Livelihood ("alternative Nobel") Prizes; held a variety of visiting academic chairs; briefed nine heads of state; published twenty books and several hundred technical and popular papers; lectured and broadcast extensively; served on the Department of Energy's senior advisory board; and consulted for scores of utilities, industries, and governments worldwide. He is founder of and Principal Technical Consultant to E SOURCE, which serves hundreds of electric utilities, industries, governments, design firms, developers, and other organizations as the premier source of technical information on advanced electric efficiency. The *Wallstreet Journal's* Centennial Issue named him among 28 people in the world most likely to change the course of business in the 1990s.

Paul B. MacCready
Chairman, AeroVironment Inc.

Dr. Paul MacCready, with an academic background in physics and aeronautics, has become meteorologist, inventor, world champion glider pilot, and explorer of new horizons in conserving energy and the environment and the teaching of thinking skills.

He received a B.S. in physics from Yale in 1947, an M.S. in physics from Caltech in 1948, and a Ph.D. in aeronautics from Caltech in 1952.

In 1977, his Gossamer Condor won the $95,000 award offered by British industrialist Henry Kremer for the first sustained, controlled human-powered flight. Two years later, its successor, the Gossamer Albatross, won aviation's largest prize, the $213,000 Kremer Award for a human-powered flight from England to France. Subsequently, he has led teams at AeroVironment Inc. that have created many additional pioneering vehicles. In 1981, his DuPont-sponsored Solar Challenger carried a pilot 163 miles from Paris to England at 11,000 feet, powered solely by sunbeams. Another of his human-powered airplanes, the Bionic Bat, won two Kremer speed prizes in 1984. Under the sponsorship of the National Air and Space Museum and Johnson Wax, his team developed a radio-controlled, wing-flapping, flying replica of a giant pterodactyl—a creature from 70 million years ago with a 36-foot wing span. The replica is the key "actor" in a wide screen IMAX film, On the Wing, which connects biological flight aircraft. In 1987, his group, working in conjunction with General Motors, built the GM Sunraycer, which won the solar car race across Australia (50% faster than the second-place vehicle). Next, the same team developed the GM-Impact, a battery-powered car with remarkable performance. This was introduced to the public in early 1990 and, shortly thereafter, GM announced that the car will be mass produced.

The Gossamer Condor now hangs in the Smithsonian Institution's National Air and Space Museum in Washington, D.C., beside the Wright Brothers' 1903 Flyer and Lindbergh's Spirit of St. Louis. It is one of five vehicles developed by MacCready's teams that have been acquired by the Smithsonian. His activities have been featured internationally in museum exhibits, TV documentaries, books and magazines. He lectures widely for industry and educational institutions, emphasizing creativity.

He is international president of the International Human Powered Vehicle Association. His many awards and honors include memberships in the National Academy of Engineering and the American Academy of Arts and Sciences, numerous honorary degrees, and the following:

- **The 1982 Lindbergh Award** for his "significant contributions toward creating a better balance between technology and the environment."

- **The Engineer of the Century Gold Medal** presented in 1980 by the American Society of Mechanical Engineers.
- **The Collier Trophy**, awarded annually for the greatest achievement in aeronautics or astronautics, presented in 1979 for his design and construction of the Gossamer Albatross.

Dr. MacCready lives in Pasadena, California, with his wife, Judy. He founded AeroVironment Inc., a company providing air quality and hazardous waste services and consulting, development of alternative energy sources, design and manufacture of products for atmospheric monitoring, and creation of efficient vehicles for land, sea, and air. He is on the Board of Directors of two public companies, National Education Corporation and the MacNeal-Schwendler Company.

Tom Cackette
Chief Deputy Executive Officer, California Air Resources Board

Tom Cackette is the Chief Deputy Executive Officer of the California Air Resources Board, where his principal responsibility is directing his state's efforts to reduce motor vehicle pollution. Tom has been working to reduce air pollution for 20 years, beginning as a regulation writer for the USEPA. He later directed USEPA's efforts to gain state adoption of vehicle inspection and maintenance programs. Currently he is overseeing implementation of California's Low Emission and Zero Emission Vehicle program. Tom holds Bachelor and Master's degrees in Engineering.

John R. Dabels
Vice President, Sales, Marketing and Government Relations, U.S. Electricar

John Dabels is the Vice President of Sales, Marketing and Government Relations at U.S. Electricar. Prior to joining the Company in May 1994, Mr. Dabels served as the principal in the consulting firm Dabels & Associates, a firm focusing on the development and introduction of new products, particularly in the EV industry. Mr. Dabels served as the

Director of Market Development for the General Motor's Electric Vehicle Program ("Impact") from October 1990 to March 1993, where his duties included marketing, sales and service, public relations and government relations. He also served as Director of Marketing for Buick Division of General Motors from 1979 to 1990. Mr. Dabels holds a B.S. degree in finance from Drake University, an M.S. degree from the Massachusetts Institute of Technology, and an M.L.S. degree in American Culture from the University of Michigan. Mr. Dabels teaches new product development and personal selling at the university level.

Dr. Mary Good
Undersecretary of Commerce -
U.S. Department of Commerce

Mary L. Good was nominated by President Clinton and approved by the Senate to be Undersecretary for Technology at the U.S. Department of Commerce's Technology Administration. The Technology Administration is comprised of the National Institute of Standards and Technology, the National Technical Information Service, and the Office of Technology Policy. The Technology Administration is the focal point in the Federal government for working in partnership with U.S. industry to improve its productivity, technology and innovation in order to compete more effectively in global markets. In addition to her role as Undersecretary for Technology, Dr. Good chairs the National Science and Technology Council's Civilian Industrial Technology Committee, and coordinates the Clinton Administration's Partnership for a New Generation Vehicle ("Clean Car") effort.

Dr. Good was senior vice-president of technology at AlliedSignal, Inc., where she was responsible for the centralized research and technology organizations, with facilities in Morristown, NJ; Buffalo, NY; and Des Plaines, IL. This position followed assignments as President of AlliedSignal's Engineered Materials Research Center, Director of the UOP Research Center, and President of the Signal Research Center. Dr. Good's accomplishments in industrial research management are the achievements of a second career; she moved to an industrial position after more than 25 years of teaching and research in the Louisiana State University system. Before joining AlliedSignal, she was professor of chemistry at the University of New Orleans and professor of materials science at Louisiana State University, where she achieved the University's highest professional rank, Boyd Professor.

Dr. Good was appointed to the National Science Board by President Carter in 1980 and again by President Reagan in 1986. She was the Chairman of the Board from 1988 until 1991, when she received an appointment from President Bush to become a member of the President's Council of Advisors on Science and Technology.

Henry Kelly
Assistant Director for Technology, White House Office of Science and Technology Policy (OSTP)

The OSTP provides policy direction and coordination for all federal applied research and development programs and programs designed to ensure that technology is efficiently placed in the hands of organizations that can put it to effective use. It coordinates technology programs with other federal organizations charged with using fiscal, regulatory, and other programs that can create a climate favorable to innovation and the adoption of innovations.

Prior to coming to OSTP, Kelly directed a number of projects at the Congressional Office of Technology Assessment on topics including energy, the environment, and economic policy. Studies considered ways that technical change and other factors could lead to major transformations in U.S. education and training, construction, manufacturing, and other sectors. He has also worked on strategic arms limitation at the Arms Control and Disarmament Agency, was Assistant Director of the Solar Energy Research Institute (now the National Renewable Energy Laboratory), and served as a special assistant to the Deputy Under Secretary for Policy Planning and Analysis and to the Assistant Secretary for Energy Conservation and renewable energy at the U.S. Department of Energy.

Kelly has a Ph.D. in Physics from Harvard University and is a fellow of the American Physical Society. He is the author of numerous books and publications.

Don Walkowicz
Executive Director, USCAR

Don Walkowicz is executive director of the United States Council for Automotive Research (USCAR), an organization formed by Chrysler, Ford and General Motors to strengthen the technology base of the domestic automotive industry through pre-competitive cooperative research and development.

USCAR currently monitors joint research projects and consortia in such diverse areas as environmental science, occupant safety, automotive composites, advanced battery development, vehicle recycling, and high-speed serial-data communications.

Mr. Walkowicz had been manager of technology and business planning for the General Motors Technical Staffs Group since 1989. A native of Detroit, he has a bachelor's degree in mechanical engineering from General Motors Engineering and Management Institute (GMI) and a master's degree in advanced management from Michigan State University.

Mr. Walkowicz joined General Motors in engineering as a cooperative student in 1960. After his graduation in 1965, he held a variety of positions in engineering, cost analysis, product program coordination, administration and technology planning.

In 1971, he was promoted to senior staff coordinator of administrative services for GM's Engineering Staff. Three years later, he was appointed engineer-in-charge of administrative services and in 1981, he became a staff engineer for GM's Advanced Engineering Staff. Mr. Walkowicz served as manager of the technology planning process for GM's Technical Staffs Group from 1987 until 1989, when he was named manager of technology and business planning. He joined USCAR in June of 1992.

Mr. Walkowicz is a charter member of the International Association for the Management of Technology and is also a member of the Society of Automotive Engineers and the Engineering Society of Detroit.

Jean Mallebay-Vacqueur
General Manager - Special Products Engineering,
Chrysler Corporation

Jean Mallebay-Vacqueur joined Chrysler Corporation as General Manager - Special Projects Engineering in May 1989. He is responsible for engineering small volume vehicles including the Chrysler TE Van (electric vehicle) and the Dodge Viper. He also provides technical support to international operations.

His work and technical background include:

- General Manager - New Business Development, Renault International, June 1988.
- Engineering Operations General Manager, Renault, January 1985.
- Body & Paint Plant Manager, Flins Factory, Renault, December 1983.
- Automated Body Shops Supervisor, Douai Factory, Renault, June 1982.
- Production Control Supervisor, Douai Factory, Renault, May 1981.
- CAAE post graduate, Pantheon Sorbonne Law University, Paris, France, 1978.
- MBA, INSEAD, Fontainebleau, France, 1978.
- MS, Engineering, Ecole Speciale Mecanique & Electricite, Paris, France, 1974.
- BS, Engineering, Ecole Speciale Mecanique & Electricite, Paris, France, 1973.
- Mathematics, Pothier Orleans University, Orleans, France, 1970.
- Elementary Mathematics, Lycee Classique, Bouake, Ivory Coast, 1969.

He was born on April 3, 1953, in Paris, France. He now lives in Bloomfield Hills, Michigan.

Gary Dickinson
President and Chief Executive Officer, Delco Electronics Corporation
Executive Vice President, GM Hughes Electronics Corporation

Gary W. Dickinson is president and chief executive officer of Delco Electronics Corporation, and executive vice president of its parent organization, GM Hughes Electronics, the General Motors subsidiary composed of Hughes Aircraft Company and Delco Electronics. He also serves on the board of directors of GMHE and its executive committee.

Dickinson was appointed to his present positions in 1993, after serving from 1988 to 1992 as vice president and group executive in charge of the GM technical staffs, managing the GM Research Laboratories, design staff and advanced engineering staff, including all GM proving grounds.

Dickinson joined GM in 1960 working on the development of early automotive emissions control systems and later establishing GM's emissions laboratory in El Segundo, California. He was a founding member of the environmental activities staff, and served for a time in Washington, D.C., working with Federal agencies on emission control activities. In 1976, he became GM's first congressional fellow with the National Industrial Conference Board, working as a staff member for Senator Robert Dole (R-Kansas) on the Senate Budget Committee.

Dickinson subsequently served as manager of advanced design for Buick Motor Division, assistant chief engineer for Buick and director of engineering for AC Spark Plug Division. In 1984, he was named program manager for development of the new mid-sized GM models, and a year later was elected a GM vice president and promoted to group director of engineering for the Chevrolet-Pontiac-GM of Canada Group.

Born May 12, 1938, in Montclair, New Jersey, Dickinson received his bachelor of science degree in mechanical engineering from Duke University, where he is currently a member of the Dean's Council of the School of Engineering. He is a member of the board of the Intelligent Vehicle Highway Society of America and the Indiana Chamber of Commerce. He also serves on the advisory council for the National

Society of Professional Engineers and is co-chairman of the Society of Automotive Engineers' Emerging Technologies Advisory Board.

Frank Schweibold
Director, Finance and Strategic Planning
General Motors Electric Vehicles Program (GMEV)

Frank L. Schweibold was appointed Director of Finance and Strategic Planning for General Motors Electric Vehicles Program on August 1, 1992.

A native of Dayton, Ohio, Mr. Schweibold joined GM in 1965 as a cooperative engineering student attending the General Motors Institute (GMI) in Flint, Michigan. He graduated from GMI in 1970 with a bachelor of mechanical engineering degree and began his GM career as a Production Engineer with the Inland Division in Dayton, Ohio. In 1973, Mr. Schweibold received his master's degree in business administration from Harvard Business School, majoring in finance. He rejoined Inland as a member of the division's Comptroller's staff.

A year later, Mr. Schweibold transferred to GM's Treasurer's Office in the New York Headquarters building. He held various positions in New York and, in 1977, was promoted to Assistant Director of the Treasurer's Office Administration Section in the GM Detroit Central Office. In 1979, he moved to the Corporate Comptroller's Staff, serving as Director of several staff sections. In 1982, Mr. Schweibold transferred to the newly formed GM Worldwide Truck & Bus Group in Pontiac, Michigan, where he served as Group Assistant Comptroller.

In 1984, Mr. Schweibold was appointed Comptroller of GM de Mexico, the corporation's wholly owned car and truck subsidiary headquartered in Mexico City. He was promoted to Director of Finance of the subsidiary later that same year. In 1988, he returned to the U.S. and was named Comptroller of Pontiac Motor Division headquartered in Pontiac, Michigan. Later that same year, Mr. Schweibold returned to the GM Truck & Bus Group and was promoted to the position of Director, Medium Duty Truck Operations, where he headed the Group's Medium Truck Business unit. In August 1992, he joined the GM Electric Vehicles Program.

James P. Womack
Principal Research Scientist - Japan Program, Massachusetts Institute of Technology; Member - The Transitions Group; Author

James P. Womack has been associated with MIT since 1975. He has been involved in a series of comparative studies of world manufacturing practices.

From 1985 through 1990, Dr. Womack was Research Director of MIT's International Motor Vehicle Program, a fifteen-country study of the motor vehicle industry. He was the lead author of the book summarizing the Program's findings, The Machine That Changed The World (Harper-Collins, 1991). It has sold more than 300,000 copies in eleven languages.

Dr. Womack is currently writing a new book (working title: Lean Enterprise) to be published by Simon and Schuster in 1995. This volume will expand the ideas presented in The Machine That Changed The World and apply them to a wide range of industries producing services as well as goods. Some of the ideas in Lean Enterprise are presented in the March/April 1994 issue of the Harvard Business Review in the lead article, "From Lean Production to the Lean Enterprise."

Dr. Womack joined the Transitions Group in 1991. He advises companies making the difficult transition to lean production and lean enterprise.

Robert Stempel

Robert C. Stempel retired as Chairman and Chief Executive Officer of General Motors Corporation in November 1992. He was named Chairman and CEO in August 1990. Prior to serving as Chairman, he had been President and Chief Operating Officer of General Motors since September 1, 1987.

Mr. Stempel was born July 15, 1933, in Trenton, New Jersey. He graduated from Bloomfield High School in New Jersey in 1951. He received a bachelor of science degree in mechanical engineering from Worchester Polytechnic Institute in Massachusetts in 1955. He was granted a master's degree in business administration by Michigan State University in 1970.

After graduation from college, he began his engineering career in Bridgeport, Connecticut, with the Wire and Cable Division of General Electric Corporation. In January 1956, Mr. Stempel began his active service with the U.S. Army as a Lieutenant in the Corps of Engineers at the Engineering School, Fort Belvoir, Virginia. He completed active duty and received an honorable discharge as a First Lieutenant in January 1958.

After joining GM's Oldsmobile Division as a Senior Detailer in the Chassis Design Department in January 1958, Mr. Stempel held various positions with Oldsmobile including Senior Designer, Transmission Design Engineer, Motor Engineer, and Assistant Chief Engineer.

Mr. Stempel was appointed Special Assistant to the President of General Motors in 1973. He joined the Engineering Department of the Chevrolet Division in 1974, first as Chief Engineer - Engine & Components, then as Director of Engineering.

On November 6, 1978, Mr. Stempel was appointed General Manager of the Pontiac Motor Division and elected a Vice President of General Motors. In September 1980, he was appointed Managing Director of Adam Opel AG in Germany, with responsibility for European-sourced passenger-car operations. Two years later he returned to the U.S. and was named General Manager of Chevrolet.

In January 1984, he was appointed Vice President and Group Executive in charge of the Buick-Oldsmobile-Cadillac Group. In February 1986, he was elected an Executive Vice President in charge of the Worldwide Truck & Bus Group and the Overseas Group. He also became a member of the Board of Directors. He served on the Board until his retirement in November 1992.

Mr. Stempel is a member of the National Academy of Engineering. He is also a member of the Society of Automotive Engineers, the American Society of Mechanical Engineers, and the Engineering Society of Detroit.

Mr. Stempel is a business and technical consultant to the Ovonic Battery Company, a subsidiary of Energy Conversion Devices, Inc., in Troy, Michigan, and an engineering and technical consultant to General Motors on electric vehicles and batteries. Mr. Stempel is also active in numerous community, educational and charitable groups.

Major Richard C. Cope USMC

*Program Manager, Hybrid and Electric Vehicles,
Advanced Research Projects Agency, Department
of Defense*

Major Cope was selected for this position in the summer of 1992. From 1990 to 1992 Major Cope served with the U.S. Central Command, Tampa, FL, initially as the USMC special operations officer during the Gulf War, and was then selected to become the executive officer to the Deputy Commander in Chief, U.S. Central Command. From 1987 to 1990 he was assigned to the Research Development and Acquisition Command as a program manager for surface to air weapons. While there he developed and instituted a number of significant new technologies that dramatically increased the combat capability of Marine Corps surface to air weapons. Prior to this he served in a number of Marine Corps combat commands both here and abroad and participated in military deployments from Korea to Norway.

Dr. Lon E. Bell

President and Chief Executive Officer, Amerigon, Inc.

Dr. Bell formed Technar Incorporated in 1967 and served as its president until 1986 at which time he sold majority interest to TRW, and the remaining interest in 1991. He then formed Amerigon Incorporated, a developer of advanced automotive technologies for conventional and electric vehicles, in April 1991. In June of 1993, Amerigon completed a successful initial public offering.

Dr. Bell holds over 30 U.S. and foreign patents. As president of TRW Technar, he received Toyota's Award for Technology and Development Excellence (the only non-Japanese company to do so), as well as numerous quality and technology awards from BMW, Chrysler, Ford, Toyota, and Volkswagen.

Dr. Bell is one of the founding members of CALSTART, a California non-profit consortium developing advanced transportation technologies, and currently serves on its Executive Committee.

Arvind Rajan
Vice President - Planning & Business Development, Solectria Corporation

Arvind Rajan is on the management team of Solectria Corporation, an internationally recognized manufacturer of advanced electric vehicles and components. Since 1992, Mr. Rajan has spearheaded Solectria's growth from approximately $350,000 in annual revenues and three employees, to over $3 million in revenues and 40 employees in 1994. Prior to joining Solectria, Mr. Rajan was an associate at the Boston Consulting Group where he developed corporate strategy for Fortune 500 companies in the fields of forest products, natural gas, publishing, distribution, food processing and utility industries. Mr. Rajan has served on a presidential task force charged with developing an alternative fuels strategy for the federal government, and has coordinated litigation research projects for the Hoover Institute. Mr. Rajan holds a bachelor's degree in economics from Stanford University, where he graduated with distinction.

Robert P. Garzee
Vice President, U.S. Electricar, and President, Synergy EV Group

Mr. Garzee joined U.S. Electricar when the company acquired Synergy, Inc., in 1993. Mr. Garzee brought to the company relationships with Sacramento Municipal Utility District (SMUD), the city of San Jose, California, FMC, Pacific Gas & Electric, and Nordskog. He served as a member of the CALSTART design team and created Nordskog's electric vehicle shuttle and bus programs. Mr. Garzee established a $1,500,000 EV backlog with supportive Air Quality Management District (AQMD) legislation and developed electric utility companies with "neighborhood" EV development programs. From 1978 to 1990 he was CEO of Wilsey Distribution, Inc., a $70 million subsidiary of Wilsey Bennett, Inc., and prior to that spent 12 years at IBM, including eight as a marketing manager in Silicon Valley. Mr. Garzee holds a B.S. degree in business administration and an MBA from California State University.

Ted D. Morgan
President & Chief Executive Officer, U.S. Electricar

As President and Chief Executive Officer of U.S. Electricar since November 1992, Mr. Morgan has led the development and implementation of the company's business strategy. Mr. Morgan was instrumental in the launching of several other start-up companies over the last ten years and has had extensive experience in managing and financing growth ventures, developing niche marketing strategies and creating alternative distribution channels. Prior to assuming his current position, Mr. Morgan co-founded and was the Executive Vice President of The Office Club, a retail office products super-store chain which evolved into a $3 billion NYSE company through a merger with Office Depot in 1991. He has also spent 14 years in various sales and marketing management positions with the Xerox Corporation. Mr. Morgan holds a B.S. degree from California State University in business administration/production management and attended the MBA program at Golden State University.

Donald Chen

Donald D.T. Chen holds bachelor's and master's degrees from Yale University. He has worked as a senior research associate at Rocky Mountain Institute, a researcher at the World Resources Institute, where he co-authored The Going Rate: What It Really Costs to Drive. He has also worked with the Taiwan Environmental Protection Administration and Natural Resources Defense Council.

Index